The Chernobyl Effect

Protest, Culture and Society

General editors:
Kathrin Fahlenbrach, Institute for Media and Communication, University of Hamburg
Martin Klimke, New York University Abu Dhabi
Joachim Scharloth, Waseda University

Protest movements have been recognized as significant contributors to processes of political participation and transformations of culture and value systems, as well as to the development of both a national and transnational civil society. This series brings together the various innovative approaches to phenomena of social change, protest, and dissent which have emerged in recent years, from an interdisciplinary perspective. It contextualizes social protest and cultures of dissent in larger political processes and socio-cultural transformations by examining the influence of historical trajectories and the response of various segments of society, and political and legal institutions on a national and international level. In doing so, the series offers a more comprehensive and multi-dimensional view of historical and cultural change in the twentieth and twenty-first centuries.

Recent volumes:

Volume 32
The Chenobyl Effect: Antinuclear Protests and the Molding of Polish Democracy, 1986–1990
Kacper Szulecki, Janusz Waluszko, and Tomasz Borewicz

Volume 31
Rethinking Social Movements after '68: Selves and Solidarities in West Germany and Beyond
Belinda Davis, Friederike Brühöfener, and Stephen Milder

Volume 30
The Walls of Santiago: Social Revolution and Political Aesthetics in Contemporary Chile
Terri-Gordon-Zolov and Eric Zolov

Volume 29
The Aesthetics of Rule and Resistance: Analyzing Political Street Art in Latin America
Lisa Bogerts

Volume 28
Political Graffiti in Critical Times: The Aesthetics of Street Politics
Edited by Ricardo Campos, Andrea Pavoni, and Yiannis Zaimakis

Volume 27
Protest, Youth and Precariousness: The Unfinished Fight against Austerity in Portugal
Edited by Renato Miguel Carmo and José Alberto Vasconcelos Simões

Volume 26
Party Responses to Social Movements: Challenges and Opportunities
Daniela R. Piccio

Volume 25
The Politics of Authenticity: Countercultures and Radical Movements across the Iron Curtain, 1968–1989
Edited by Joachim C. Häberlen, Mark Keck-Szajbel, and Kate Mahoney

Volume 24
Taking on Technocracy: Nuclear Power in Germany, 1945 to the Present
Dolores L. Augustine

Volume 23
The Virago Story: Assessing the Impact of a Feminist Publishing Phenomenon
Catherine Riley

Volume 22
The Women's Liberation Movement: Impacts and Outcomes
Edited by Kristina Schulz

Volume 21
Hairy Hippies and Bloody Butchers: The Greenpeace Anti-Whaling Campaign in Norway
Juliane Riese

Volume 20
A Fragmented Landscape: Abortion Governance and Protest Logics in Europe
Edited by Silvia De Zordo, Joanna Mishtal, and Lorena Anton

For a full volume listing, please see the series page on our website: http://berghahnbooks.com/series/protest-culture-and-society

The Chernobyl Effect

Antinuclear Protests and the Molding of Polish Democracy, 1986–1990

Kacper Szulecki, Janusz Waluszko,
and Tomasz Borewicz†

berghahn
NEW YORK • OXFORD
www.berghahnbooks.com

Published in 2022 by
Berghahn Books
www.berghahnbooks.com

Originally published in Polish as *Bez atomu w naszym domu. Protesty antyatomowe w Polsce po 1985 roku*

Library of Congress Cataloging-in-Publication Data

Names: Szulecki, Kacper, author. | Waluszko, Janusz, author. | Borewicz, Tomasz, 1963–2015, author.
Title: The Chernobyl Effect: Antinuclear Protests and the Molding of Polish Democracy, 1986–1990 / Kacper Szulecki, Janusz Waluszko, and Tomasz Borewicz
Description: [New York]: Berghahn Books, 2022. | Series: Protest, Culture & Society; volume 32 | Includes bibliographical references and index.
Identifiers: LCCN 2022019400 (print) | LCCN 2022019401 (ebook) | ISBN 9781800736191 (hardback) | ISBN 9781800736207 (ebook)
Subjects: LCSH: Antinuclear movement—Poland. | Nuclear energy—Political aspects—Poland. | Chernobyl Nuclear Accident, Chornobyl′, Ukraine, 1986—Political aspects.
Classification: LCC HD9698.P72 S98 2022 (print) | LCC HD9698.P72 (ebook) | DDC 621.48/3509438—dc23/eng/20220511
LC record available at https://lccn.loc.gov/2022019400
LC ebook record available at https://lccn.loc.gov/2022019401

British Library Cataloguing in Publication Data

A catalogue record for this book is available from the British Library

ISBN 978-1-80073-619-1 hardback
ISBN 978-1-80073-620-7 ebook

https://doi.org/10.3167/9781800736191

Contents

Figures

Acknowledgments

This book would not be published, and certainly not in its present form, if it were not for the invaluable assistance of many people and institutions. We would like to thank all the interviewees for their time, their recollections, and for the additional materials they provided. Special thanks go to those who helped us gather the unique photographic material that illustrates this book: Wojciech Jaroń, Marcin Poletyło, Mirosław Wrąbel, and Ireneusz Ziółkowski, as well as the team of the independent photographic agency NAF Dementi and the employees of the Pamięć i Przyszłość archive in Wrocław. Much of the work on the book—above all the interviews conducted by Tomasz and their transcription—was made possible thanks to the support of the University of Oslo and the Heinrich Böll Foundation in Warsaw. We thank Wiktor Sadłowski for transcribing the interviews and Wojciech Góralczyk for providing the initial translation of the Polish version of the book into English. Special thanks go to Katarzyna Ugryn for subtle pushes, and to Radosław Gawlik for taking care of the project when it seemed like it would grind to a halt and for putting us in touch with Katarzyna Kluczka, who used her legal expertise pro bono to help us clarify all the permissions and rights issues. Funding from the Include research center for socially just energy transitions at the University of Oslo covered the copy editing, and we thank James Longbotham as well as Elizabeth Martinezz for their efforts. During the rewriting process—turning a very descriptive and "raw" Polish monograph into a more theoretical work for an international audience—we benefited from the comments provided by the participants at the 2020 ASEEES Convention and the May 2020 Oslo School of Environmental Humanities seminar. Their reactions to the story we presented helped us in refocusing some of the sections and probed us to ask completely new questions, which the final version of this monograph tries to answer. Helpful feedback was also provided by two anonymous reviewers, as well as by Julia Szulecka and Piotr Trzaskowski, who critically read the entire manuscript. We thank Padraic Kenney for providing a new foreword (we hope he sees this monograph as something of a postscript to his own work) and Dolores Augustine, Kate Brown, and Jeffrey Goldfarb for their endorsements and words of encouragement. We are very grateful to Anna Grønvold for taking care of Tomek's legacy. We would also like to thank our editors, Amanda Horn, Sulaiman Ahmad, Mykelin Higham, and Chris Chappell for their patience. Patience is also something Kacper wants to thank Gustaw, Hugo, and Aleksander for.

Foreword

Political Isotopes

Padraic Kenney

When the Chernobyl reactor exploded in late April of 1986 and a cloud of radioactivity spread across north-central Europe from Soviet Ukraine toward the Baltic, it precipitated not only dangerous isotopes but profound social and political fallout. The political isotopes fell on fertile ground especially in Poland, where protest had already become a powerful force. The "Chernobyl effect," the subject of this book, thus moved in multiple paths across the continent.

The verb *precipitate* seems particularly apt in the history that Kacper Szulecki, Janusz Waluszko, and Tomasz Borewicz, as well as the many activists they interviewed, have to tell. The term, as applied in chemistry and other disciplines, presumes that something is already present and ready to be made manifest—like vapor suspended in the atmosphere that appears as moisture in response to changes in temperature. Thus, a generation of activists in Poland, already engaged in environmental, pacifist, anarchist, anti-communist, and other projects, rapidly focused their attention on the dangers of nuclear power, responding to a dramatic change in the air.

It is remarkable to consider, for example, that perhaps the very first post-Chernobyl protests in the world took place in Warsaw and Wrocław, Poland, just a few days after the explosion in the Soviet Union. Despite the difficulty of obtaining clear information about just what had happened, Polish activists were well prepared to articulate the radioactive threat. In fact, they quickly became trusted sources of news and advice for those who encountered their street actions. People desperately needed to know about the danger, and only these few brave individuals, holding signs or banners in public places, could break through the information blockade the communist regime attempted to maintain.

Protests concerning nuclear power have continued in Poland ever since, a rare example of activism spanning the communist and postcommunist eras. For this reason alone, the antinuclear movement in Poland is worthy of broader attention. Its significance extends beyond this feature, however. First of all, there is no doubt that the movement contributed to the fall of communism in Poland, and thus in the entire region. The regime of General Wojciech Jaruzelski did not have to fall in 1989; one could easily imagine it lumbering on, supported by widespread social apathy and perhaps some kind of economic reform. Chernobyl itself could have actually solidified Jaruzelski's hold on power if he had been able to portray his government as the protector of Polish sovereignty against uncertainties across the border. Antinuclear activists instead laid bare the regime's incompetence and demonstrated the value of social mobilization. The actions described in this book include some powerful examples of the communist regime backing away from its plans in the face of popular dissent; such successes inspired trust in the ability of anti-communist activists to provide an alternative.

Equally importantly, the antinuclear movement is but one example—albeit among the most persistent—of the Polish tradition of political protest. No society anywhere in the world staged more consistent opposition to communist power, and few countries have seen such extensive protest in the last thirty years. Polish commentators frequently complain about growing apathy in society, yet outside observers see in Poland little to complain about in comparison to their own societies. Social scientists have for decades been offering various explanations for why Poles are so frequently rebellious, no matter the form of government. One way to understand this phenomenon is through close study of a protest movement—precisely what Szulecki, Waluszko, and Borewicz provide.

It's good to live in a country whose people take to the streets, even when protesters get in one's way. Direct action is surely as much a part of democracy as is voting. Poland's democracy, much under attack in the years since the Law and Justice Party took power in 2015, perseveres in large part thanks to those who step off the sidewalk, banner held aloft, to express their dissent. In the nearly forty-year history of antinuclear protest in Poland, we can see how protest emerges and why it matters.

Bloomington, Indiana, January 2022

Padraic Kenney is a professor of history and International Studies at Indiana University, Bloomington. He is the author of several monographs including *A Carnival of Revolution: Central Europe 1989* (Princeton University Press, 2002) and *Dance in Chains: Political Imprisonment in the Modern World* (Oxford University Press, 2017).

Introduction

Everyone has heard of Chernobyl, most of us have heard of Fukushima, probably only a few have heard of Three Mile Island. But who has heard of Żarnowiec? Even students of environmental and antinuclear movements, familiar with iconic names like Wyhl, Fessenheim, or Aldermaston, will probably be at a loss. Yet the protests against the construction of a nuclear power station near the village of Żarnowiec had a significant impact on Poland's history and are the only example of a successful campaign against nuclear power in the Eastern Bloc.

Someone might be outraged that we are putting here side by side the three biggest nuclear disasters in history and a power plant on the Baltic coast in Poland that was never built. But in a sense, Żarnowiec was also a disaster: a catastrophic waste of money and resources, a waste of time and energy of hundreds of people, those who were involved in its construction as well as those who worked to stop it.

Unlike declared nuclear power enthusiasts, we will not mourn Żarnowiec as an irreparable loss and a missed opportunity for Poland to join the nuclear club. For us, Żarnowiec is rather a warning—against reckless planning, the hubris of those in power, and the capture of the energy sector by a unanimous technocratic lobby. It is an illustration of the weakness of communist governance and the fragility of Polish democracy. It is a story about the failure to get along and the unfortunate consequences of secrecy, of limiting political participation, and of ignoring dialogue.

But our book has yet another purpose. It is also a story of the determination, sacrifice, and—we are not afraid to use this word—courage of dozens of people who considered it their duty to stop what they saw as a bad political decision, a risky investment in unnecessary infrastructure. Two of the coauthors were active participants in those events. Unfortunately, one did not live to see this monograph's publication.

This book, therefore, is a memorial to the dedication of many people, but in a special way it is a memorial to Tomasz Borewicz né Burek, known during his years of dissent under the nickname "Belfer." Tomasz was an inspiration to many—throughout his adult life, but especially when it seemed that antinuclear protests in Poland had no chance to succeed. Perhaps without him the story would have turned out differently, perhaps the construction of "Żarnobyl" would have been brought to completion. Certainly, without him this book would not have been written, and thus the history of Poland's antinuclear project would remain untold.

This book was many years in the making—not least because one of the authors passed away while the text was being written. It is worth thinking of the book as part of a larger story. The process of writing the history of the antinuclear protests began when two of us—Tomasz and Janusz—met so that the latter could conduct a lengthy interview with the former, on the topic of antinuclear protests (Waluszko 2011a, 2011b). The next step was Janusz's 2012 thesis, published in 2013 by the Institute of National Remembrance (Waluszko 2013). That study focused on Żarnowiec, the Gdańsk area, and the independent movements (one of the currents of democratic and anti-communist opposition, as we will later explain). Kacper joined the writing team in 2014, having conducted research on dissent, environmental protests, and Polish antinuclear mobilization (Szulecki 2011, 2013; Szulecka and Szulecki 2013; Szulecki, Borewicz, and Waluszko 2015). We set out to take the third step: to write a monograph bringing together all antinuclear protest in Poland, one where documents and secret police files would be supplemented by testimonies of all the actors involved. The first draft was completed in 2014, and Tomasz still had time to start working on the revisions suggested by a group of academic reviewers as well as helpful friends. After Tomasz died in late 2015, the project lost much of its momentum. In 2018 and early 2019 the manuscript underwent a massive overhaul, and the result was published by the European Solidarity Center in Gdańsk in April 2019 (Borewicz, Szulecki, and Waluszko 2019). The present book is our fourth step. We quickly realized that the significance of the story we want to tell goes beyond regional and national contexts, and that there is an important gap to be filled in the history of European environmental and antinuclear protests. For these reasons, the book had to be rewritten again, parts of it from scratch, while new chapters were added to put the main story in its proper context. This work is reflected in the current order of authorship. But that is not the end of the journey. Tomasz dreamed of creating an archive of the Polish environmental movement, collecting relevant accounts, memories, photos, flyers, stencils, and documents. This is a task for the coming years, though the work on the earlier steps of our project has already allowed us to gather a significant corpus of materials.

Aimed at an international audience, the present book seeks to add Poland to the existing literature on the origins, mobilization, and triumph or decline of antinuclear protest movements. This is a considerable body of research, dating back to the early 1980s, when the first accounts and analyses of Western antinuclear protests were written (e.g., Chafer 1985; Touraine 1983). Germany has attracted most of the scholarly attention over the following three decades, largely due to the visible political significance of its environmental and antinuclear movement, reflected in the emergence and growth of the Greens (Joppke 1991; Radkau 2009; Augustine 2018; Mayer and Ely 1998; Milder 2019). Only recently has the transnational turn in contemporary history resulted in analyses that speak of *an* antinuclear movement with national organization but operating across borders (Tompkins 2016; Milder 2019), or that seek to provide an overview of antinuclear protests across Europe and even globally (Arndt 2016).

This large body of literature, as well as the broader scholarship on environmental protests and social movements, provides answers to important questions that, in the Polish context, were hitherto not even posed. The most general of these is: What were the drivers of antinuclear protest? However, in the context of Communist Poland, where the first antinuclear mobilization occurred only in the mid-1980s, one should also ask: Why did the antinuclear movement emerge then, and why so late? What was the antinuclear movement's relationship to the older opposition, the Solidarity trade union, and to the post-Solidarity government? Finally, how did the transition—from a communist autocracy to a capitalist parliamentary democracy—impact the antinuclear protest movement, and how was that movement grafted onto the changing political landscape? In the remainder of this introduction, we briefly explain our argument, the approach we adopted to tackle these questions, and the chapter-by-chapter structure of the book.

The Argument

> Utopian aspirations per se are not dangerous. . . . Where the utopian vision goes wrong is when it is held by ruling elites with no commitment to democracy or civil rights and who are therefore likely to use unbridled state power for its achievement. Where it goes brutally wrong is when the society subjected to such utopian experiments lacks the capacity to mount a determined resistance.
>
> —James C. Scott, *Seeing Like a State*

In 1982, shortly after the military takeover in Communist Poland, the decision was taken to construct the country's first nuclear power plant by the Żarnowiec Lake near Gdańsk. The administrative work and early construction efforts went unchallenged by society at large. However, after 1985 new movements emerged within the broader democratic opposition, and environmental protection became an issue that mobilized surprisingly many Poles. When in 1986 an unprecedented accident occurred in the Chernobyl atomic station in Soviet Ukraine, a wave of antinuclear protests swept across Poland, and in the second half of the 1980s domestic nuclear energy projects began to galvanize protest, both in big cities and small towns. But nuclear dreams outlived communism, and while the Polish United Workers' Party (Polska Zjednoczona Partia Robotnicza—PZPR) agreed to semidemocratic elections and a peaceful handover of power in 1989, the construction at Żarnowiec continued. The antinuclear movement became increasingly alienated. Finally, in 1990, after a prolonged battle that saw desperate hunger strikes, violent clashes, grassroots mobilization, and expert debates on the economics of nuclear energy, the construction site was shut down and domestic nuclear plans shelved for almost two decades.

Why was the antinuclear campaign in Poland the only successful one in the Eastern Bloc? Where did the antinuclear movement emerge, and to what extent can we speak of a "Chernobyl effect" on societal mobilization

Figure 0.1. Map of Poland before 1991, showing planned and constructed nuclear facilities, waste disposal sites, and cities where the most important protests occurred. Authors' own elaboration.

and bottom-up protest? This monograph casts the story of antinuclear mobilization in Poland against the broader background of the political processes that occurred there in the second half of the 20th century, and it situates this mobilization in the context of political dissent and growing environmental awareness. We often speak of the environmental or the antinuclear movements, which we do not see as formalized organizations or networks, but as *social movements*. They are, like all social movements, examples of a "distinct social process, consisting of the mechanisms through which actors engaged in collective action are involved in conflictual relations with clearly identified opponents; are linked by dense informal networks; share a distinct collective identity" (Della Porta and Diani 2006, 20).

We devote the most space to Żarnowiec because the protests against the construction of this nuclear power plant lasted the longest and had the most dramatic course. In addition, their ending—only in the autumn of 1990, long after the 1989 Round Table Agreement and the June 1989 semi-free elections, and after the swearing in (and even the resignation) of Tadeusz Mazowiecki's noncommunist government—is an issue that eludes the dominant historiography of transition in Central and Eastern Europe.

Our book shows the fluidity of the political situation under the conditions of transformation—and also the continuity between the 1980s and the 1990s, surprising for many present-day observers. This is not, in any way, a prelude to a conspiracy theory or revisionist history characteristic of the anti-communist Right. The protagonists of the events described here were active in the 1980s and entered the new reality of the 1990s—the reality created by the negotiated transition—marked by all their previous experiences, conflicts, ideas, and hopes. In this sense, the dominant way to analyze the 1980s and 1990s—where the former is left to historians, and the latter is (still) seen as part of an extended "present" and thus the domain of social scientists—is inadequate. Historians of communism very often purposefully refrain from seeing the object of their study as the root of present-day cleavages and conflicts, while political science and sociology students—"transitologists"—who have analyzed the post-1989 evolution of political systems and societies have a stake in emphasizing change over continuity, and are often unaware of the long-lasting effects of the sociopolitical phenomena they describe. Furthermore, unlike most historians of opposition in Poland, we see the movements that we analyze as national incarnations of social phenomena that are transnational in nature.

For that reason, and thanks to the uniqueness of the Żarnowiec protests as a bridge between the 1980s and 1990s, we can look at the environmental and antinuclear movements in Poland as elements of the much broader late-modern and (post)industrial processes of social, cultural, economic, and political change. The struggles of the 1980s have their roots in earlier events, and thus require us to look back at least to the 1960s. The conclusion additionally highlights the significance of the events that took place over thirty years ago for today's politics.

We also try to deal with some popular misconceptions. First, while antinuclear protests in Poland occurred some five to fifteen years after they took place in Western countries, this should not be interpreted as a sign of backwardness. In the first chapters of the book, we explain the different orientations and preoccupations of Polish activists. We also emphasize their roots in the particular experience of the Polish 1968, which at the same time made them part of a transnational generation and set them apart from Western counterparts.

Second, we strongly object to the simplistic notion that antinuclear protests were driven solely by emotions, particularly fear, and as such were at their core irrational. The roots of antinuclear movements are manifold, but fear, or the question of nuclear safety, is neither the sole nor even the most important driver. In the literature on antinuclear protests, there are many conflicting concepts regarding what drives antinuclear mobilization: fear and reactor safety (Radkau 2009), local NIMBYism (Tompkins 2016, 29), environmentalist and postmaterialist values (Inglehart 1994), and resistance to technocracy and democratic revival (Augustine 2018). Historians of Poland could also add anti-communist more than anti-systemic motivations.

Especially in the final chapters of the book we show the political struggle for recognition, participation, and democratization that occurred around the nuclear issues, as well as the way expert knowledge and scientific arguments were employed by both sides of the controversy, which indicates that rather than a clash of irrationalism with enlightened knowledge, the Żarnowiec issue was a political conflict cutting across many divides. This problem touches upon broader questions: Why do people dissent in the first place? Is it because of relative deprivation? Is it an expression of rational self-interest? Or is it perhaps the effect of resource mobilization? The latter implies that as political dissatisfaction and conflict exist in all societies, the formation of social movements depends on the creation of organizations to mobilize this potential (Dalton and Kuechler 1994, 9). The title of our book—"The Chernobyl Effect"—should already imply that we see in the Chernobyl catastrophe an important catalytic event, which helped to mobilize and channel resources that would otherwise have remained untapped. But saying this is not the same as saying that Poles opposed nuclear power after Chernobyl because they were afraid of accidents, and that the mere improvement of safety standards would translate to social acceptance of the technology.

Third, we challenge the history of Poland's democratic transition as it is most often told—through the eyes of political elites and with political elites as the sole important actors. This is not only a Polish fallacy but rather the result of disciplinary divisions. Whereas social movement scholars are interested in protests, dissent, and bottom-up processes that lead to political transitions, other scholars produce narratives centered on elite actors. With regard to the three phases of regime transition and democratization—liberalization, transition, and consolidation—most of the current writing on Poland sees space for civil society actors and social movements only in the first phase, occurring before 1989. Transition is said to be an elite endeavor, while consolidation remains something unproblematic in hindsight. We see our contribution in looking at the role of independent activists and social movements across these three phases.

As Sidney Tarrow, one of the most important theoreticians of social movements, notes: "Most scholars of democratization have either ignored movements altogether or regarded them with suspicion as dangers to democracy, while most students of social movements have focused on fully mature democratic systems and ignored the transition cycles that place the question of democratization on the agenda" (Tarrow 1995, 221–2). The reason for this skepticism might lie in protest itself—and in its unconventional positioning in the repertoire of political engagement. Defined, counterintuitively perhaps, as "nonroutinized ways of affecting political, social, and cultural processes" (Della Porta and Diani 2006, 165), protest and direct action in modern democracies are accepted forms of political engagement and no longer seen as deviancy. However, for authoritarian regimes they constitute forms of open dissent, which can hardly be tolerated. Is it possible that established elites, who occupy the same conflictual situation but on the opposite side, share this view of protest as something dangerous that has to be tamed?

Protests, especially strikes, often constitute precipitating events that start liberalization, spreading the perception among the authoritarian elites that there is no choice other than opening the regime if they want to avoid a civil war or a violent takeover of power by democratic or revolutionary actors (Della Porta 2013, 133; 2014, 12; Bermeo 1997). Donatella Della Porta, the world's leading expert on democratization and social movements, observes that in the normative and empirical literature the importance of civil society and social movement organizations in the construction of democracy is increasingly emphasized, while democratization literature has focused on elites (Della Porta 2013, 125–26). The already mentioned tradition of "transitology," although replacing the focus on macrostructures with a focus on agency, has emphasized elite leadership and elite strategic choices. What is more, transitology "tended to consider movements and protest actors as manipulated by elites and focusing on very instrumentally defined purposes" (Della Porta 2013, 130). In the Polish case, this is illustrated by the attention the Solidarity trade union (established in 1980) receives as an example of the incredible potential of civil society mobilization and self-organization, while accounts of the transition of 1989 are most often limited to elite negotiations between prominent dissidents, the Communist Party leadership, and the Catholic Church (Codogni 2009; Skórzyński 2014). In contrast, our analysis does not suggest that elites do not matter but rather emphasizes that the dynamics of social movements are not reducible to elite manipulation. The protest that is analyzed in this book has been sustained not just despite but against elite steering of the transition.

We know from studies of social movements across the globe that, in the transition to democracy, movements have often participated in large coalitions asking for democratic rights as well as social justice. This is crucial in building support against authoritarian regimes. So it happens that the more radical protesters help the moderates, giving them legitimacy to negotiate. This is often forgotten in Polish accounts of the transition written from the perspective of the Solidarity elite, which at times cast the protest movements that remained active throughout 1989 and 1990 as villains, on par with the illiberal, hardheaded party apparatchiks. Again, such vilification is not a purely national trait.

Furthermore, what we see in the history of the environmental and antinuclear movement in Poland is an illustration of pushback from the remnants of a social movement and its adherents' contestation of a new hegemony and mode of democratization before it gained the upper hand. This brings us to the last misconception we try to challenge: that the Polish transition to a particular form of parliamentary liberal democracy was swift and unproblematic, and that "there was no alternative"—as if the final outcome was clear when the process started. This is similar to the problem that we see in so-called modernization theory, which is good at explaining the survival of established democracies but "tend[s] to ignore the role of social actors in crafting democracy," leaving the timing and tempo of democratization processes unexplained (Della Porta 2013, 126).

Yet social movements are also active during consolidations, a step that is generally considered to start with the first free elections and with the implementation of a minimum quality of substantive democracy. As Della Porta notes, "Social movements active during liberalization and transition rarely totally disband; on the contrary, democratization often facilitates the development of social movement organizations" (Della Porta 2013, 133–34). What is more, the networks connecting movements play an important role in mobilizing against persistent exclusionary patterns. Keeping elites under constant pressure can help in consolidation. Movements' alternative practices and values help to sustain and expand democracy (Della Porta 2013, 134). Last but not least, in the commotion of transition away from bureaucratic and authoritarian communism towards a liberal regime with a capitalist economy, where market forces are not yet regulated by democratic rules and practices, new social movements often oppose both business and labor in conflicts around environmental and antinuclear issues. This is related to the visible opposition of populist (in the more traditional sense) and participatory values to the bureaucratization of interest groups (Dalton and Kuechler 1994, 11). The last chapters of our book contribute to the still very limited research on the input of social movements in postcommunist democracy consolidation and the molding of the exact shape Poland's democracy would eventually take.

The Approach

Since this is the first monograph on the Polish antinuclear protest movement, our book necessarily follows a roughly chronological approach and describes a long series of protest events. However, it is not a chronicle but an analytical narrative. Using the terms coined by Charles Tilly, and later developed by Sidney Tarrow and Donatella Della Porta, the book combines some of the elements of an *event history* and *eventful history* (Tarrow 1996; 2012, 116) but is perhaps best understood as an attempt at writing what Tilly termed *events-in-history*, combining an account of protest episodes, performances, and repertoires (Tarrow 2012, 124–26). We seek to reconstruct protests during episodes of democratization, investigating protests' origins, characteristics, and short-term effects. To achieve this, we analyze the frames, repertoires of action, transnational influences, social and political opportunities, and organizational characteristics of social movements (Della Porta 2014, 20–22), as well as the characteristics of the authoritarian regime that is the backdrop of the protest movements' activity.

In this monograph we use a variety of sources. In the notes, readers will find references to archival materials (from local archives in Gdańsk as well as national sources), to records of parliamentary sessions where nuclear power and protests were discussed, to secret police files gathered by the Institute of National Remembrance (IPN), and to official and second-circulation (samizdat) journalism, leaflets, and even films. We were also able to compare the written and oral sources with photographic documentation of the events described, and some of the original photos of protests are also reproduced in this book.

That said, the most important method given the subject matter is oral history. The recollections of the participants in the events make up a significant part of this book—and this is just a sampling of the many hours of interviews conducted mainly by Tomasz Borewicz. If an interview quotation is not accompanied by a citation, this indicates that it was conducted by Tomasz. Unfortunately, before his death he did not pass on a record of when and where the interviews were conducted, though we are in possession of full verbatim transcripts and most of the recordings. Any additional interviews conducted by the other two authors, as well as quotes from interviews published elsewhere, are accompanied by a reference in an endnote.

Basing the book so heavily on oral history affects the style. We tried to edit the participants' recollections in such a way as to preserve the perspective of each of the interviewees and the "spoken" style of narration, but we also strove not to tire the reader and to combine quotations with descriptions and our own comments into a coherent whole. For that reason, we often merge different accounts into one description of an event, particularly if we do not have written sources to draw on.

To tell their story, we invited not only representatives of groups that protested against nuclear power. You will also find voices of supporters of nuclear power, managers from Żarnowiec, ecological experts, and members of parliament. Opponents and supporters of atomic power meet on these pages a bit like veterans of a long-forgotten war, because although they looked at each other from opposite trenches, for many of them the fate of the Żarnowiec Nuclear Power Plant was in some sense a turning point in their lives.

We are trying to present the arguments of all sides here and, through a critique of sources, to arrive at as objective a description of events as possible. Our point of reference, however, remains first and foremost the street. Our departure point is the "politics of small things" in Jeffrey Goldfarb's well-known formulation, starting from a random meeting in the queue in front of a shop, at the kitchen table, at a party, on the bus (Goldfarb 2007). The story of the streets has also remained untold because those who played the most important role in street protests did not have such easy access to the media as other participants in the events. For this reason alone, we take their point of view as the main one. Many of the interpretations are made through their eyes, and the level of detail in the description of direct actions, protests, pickets, demonstrations, hunger strikes, and finally riots is greater than in the description of the progress of construction, the legislative process, and the backstage discussions of politicians.

The Book's Structure

Our book combines a mostly chronological account with a structure based on specific issues and research problems. This means that while the main story advances from chapter to chapter, there are also retrospective parts, which usually bring some additional contextualization. Each chapter is an element of the broader story but also a narrative in itself. Although the years 1989–1990 are the climax of the Żarnowiec protests, we begin our story much earlier. In chapter 1, we explain why the first antinuclear protests in Poland occurred as late as 1985, and why, despite a dynamic civil society that challenged the communist system and spawned the ten-million-strong Solidarity trade union, the evolution of social movements in Poland differed from Western societies. We do this by returning all the way back to the different experiences of 1968, which saw student protests on both sides of the Iron Curtain. The political processes triggered by 1968, however, diverged throughout the 1970s.

Having sketched the context of dissent and opposition to communism, we then trace the gradual emergence of an environmental movement in the early 1980s and its evolution towards political environmentalism around 1985, when the first Polish "new social movement" entered the stage. By the early 1980s, Poland was experiencing an environmental crisis that began to affect all aspects of life, creating an overlap between nature protection and public health. In chapter 2, we explain the mindset that ruled the nature-culture relationship, a communist environmentality, which was important for the way the country's nuclear energy projects were designed and also constituted the background against which political environmentalism would develop and rebel. Finally, we tell the story of the first antinuclear (weapons) protest in Mrzeżyno on the Baltic coast, a symptom of the Polish activists tuning into the West European frequencies in terms of values, goals, and agendas for the first time since the 1960s.

Chapter 3 concentrates on the Chernobyl catastrophe and its immediate aftermath. The withholding of information on the radiation danger, as well as the uncoordinated and chaotic reactions of the Communist authorities, fueled the first mass protests against nuclear power across Poland. We reconstruct the protest wave chronologically, starting with a spontaneous protest in Warsaw, and then moving on to qualitatively new events that took place in Wrocław and Kraków, signaling the emergence of a new kind of dissent—not only in its focus on nuclear power but, more importantly, in the fresh and engaging protest repertoire that would become the trademark of the new movements, particularly environmental, in the second half of the 1980s. We finish the chapter by bringing together the elements of a "Chernobyl effect" and highlighting the unique convergence of factors that accounted for the visible change in environmental protest.

In chapter 4, we show how the antinuclear protest that was sparked by the Chernobyl disaster spilled over to the domestic nuclear sector. First, the history of Poland's nuclear energy plans is outlined, taking the reader back to the 1950s and 1960s, before introducing the Żarnowiec Nuclear Power Plant (NPP) project, which became an object of the first protests shortly after the 1986 accident in Soviet Ukraine. However, the first spectacular and successful protest campaign around nuclear energy was related to a used fuel depot in the old bunkers of Międzyrzecz. We recount this story in detail, highlighting local, regional, and national mobilization patterns; the way activists were able to pool resources using a variety of preexisting structures; and how they managed to achieve unprecedented levels of protest intensity in a small and relatively remote town, far from the main centers of anti-communist opposition.

The story of domestic nuclear facility contestation is continued in chapter 5, which looks at the local campaigns against the planned Kopań and Warta nuclear power plants. These two campaigns were quite different, one expert based, the other relying to a much greater extent on street demonstrations. Taken together, they illustrate the diversity of the Polish environmental movement. Both campaigns also ended during the period of transition from communism and show the ways in which environmental protest was intertwined with the ongoing regime shift. The police violence against the environmentalists and independent activists in the streets of Poznań in early 1989 was puzzling in many respects but provided an important prelude to the finale of the Żarnowiec campaign, as well as to the difficult history of the posttransition environmental movement as a whole (which we briefly discuss towards the end of the chapter).

From chapter 6, we focus entirely on the anti-Żarnowiec campaign and on the democracy transition process that Poland experienced in 1989 and 1990. First, we explain how the new political situation impacted the environmental and antinuclear movement, both in terms of changing opportunity structures and in the way individual activists responded to new political realities. Beginning in early 1989, the anti-Żarnowiec campaign accelerated, first in the form of regular Friday protests in Gdańsk, which saw the mobilization of a new generation of activists, while those who were active before 1989 gradually left the stage. From Gdańsk, the dwindling core group of protesters moved to Warsaw to be closer to the newly established post-Solidarity government and the halls of power, but this attempt was exhaustive and largely futile. In parallel to the events in the streets, we also show how those members of the environmental movement who chose a formal political path—as Solidarity representatives and, later, as members of parliament—tried to influence the political debate "from within."

However, faced with the apparent unwillingness of the new government to enter into a dialogue with the protesters, as well as a media injunction against covering the antinuclear demands, the anti-Żarnowiec campaigners could only escalate their campaign with more and more desperate means. Chapter 7 describes four acts of desperation: the physical blockade of the cargo terminal in Gdynia, where elements of the Żarnowiec reactor were transported; an initial limited hunger strike; a subsequent indefinite hunger strike; and finally, the violence that occurred when the terminal blockade was broken.

Although the desperate protests, combined with expert activities and struggles in parliament, brought the Żarnowiec NPP construction to a halt, this was not a formal end to the project. In chapter 8, we discuss the experiments with other forms of democracy and the increasing participation in governance that emerged around the antinuclear movement. Most important among them was a local shift in governance practices that occurred in Różan, a site of a nuclear waste disposal, and in the Gdańsk region, where a social referendum on the acceptance and future of Żarnowiec was held. Organized in barely one week, the referendum is perhaps one of the most interesting untold episodes of Poland's democratic transition. However, it also illustrates the limitations of such democratic experimentation, as the results of the referendum were not formally acknowledged by the central government, and it took further, transnational protests for the Żarnowiec construction to finally be closed. The conclusion then brings together all the thematic threads of the book and tries to provide answers to the main research questions posed earlier, while also connecting the history of the antinuclear struggle with Poland's recent energy policy discussions and the observed democracy backsliding after 2015.

References

Arndt, Melanie, ed. 2016. *Politik und Gesellschaft nach Tschernobyl: (ost-)europäische Perspektiven*. Kommunismus und Gesellschaft, Band 1. Berlin: Ch. Links Verlag.

Augustine, Dolores L. 2018. *Taking on Technocracy: Nuclear Power in Germany, 1945 to the Present*. Protest, Culture and Society, volume 24. New York: Berghahn Books.

Bermeo, Nancy. 1997. "Myths of Moderation: Confrontation and Conflict during Democratic Transitions." *Comparative Politics* 29(3): 305–22. https://doi.org/10.2307/422123.

Borewicz, Tomasz, Kacper Szulecki, and Janusz Waluszko. 2019. *Bez Atomu w Naszym Domu. Domu: Polskie Protesty Anty-Atomowe Po 1985*. Biblioteka ECS. Gdańsk: Europejskie Centrum Solidarności.

Chafer, Tony. 1985. "Politics and the Perception of Risk: A Study of the Anti-nuclear Movements in Britain and France." *West European Politics* 8(1): 5–23. https://doi.org/10.1080/01402388508424510.

Codogni, Paulina. 2009. *Okrągły Stół, Czyli Polski Rubikon*. Wyd. 1. Warszawa: Wydawn. Prószyński i S-ka.

Dalton, Russell J., and Manfred Kuechler, eds. 1994. *Challenging the Political Order: New Social and Political Movements in Western Democracies*. Reprint. Europe and the International Order. Cambridge: Polity.

Della Porta, Donatella. 2013. *Can Democracy Be Saved? Participation, Deliberation and Social Movements*. Cambridge: Polity.

———. 2014. *Mobilizing for Democracy: Comparing 1989 and 2011*. First edition. Oxford: Oxford University Press.

Della Porta, Donatella, and Mario Diani. 2006. *Social Movements: An Introduction*, 2nd edn. Malden, MA: Blackwell Publishing.

Goldfarb, Jeffrey C. 2007. *The Politics of Small Things: The Power of the Powerless in Dark Times*, Paperback edn. Chicago, IL: University of Chicago Press.

Inglehart, Ronald. 1994. "Values, Ideology, and Cognitive Mobilization in New Social Movements." In *Challenging the Political Order: New Social and Political Movements in Western Democracies*, ed. Russell J. Dalton and Manfred Kuechler, 43–66. Cambridge: Polity.

Joppke, Christian. 1991. "Social Movements during Cycles of Issue Attention: The Decline of the Anti-Nuclear Energy Movements in West Germany and the USA." *The British Journal of Sociology* 42(1): 43–60. https://doi.org/10.2307/590834.

Mayer, Margit, and John Ely, eds. 1998. *The German Greens: Paradox between Movement and Party*. Philadelphia: Temple University Press.

Milder, Stephen. 2019. *Greening Democracy: The Anti-Nuclear Movement and Political Environmentalism in West Germany and beyond, 1968–1983*. Cambridge: Cambridge University Press.

Radkau, Joachim. 2009. "The Anti-Nuclear Movement in Germany." Presented at the Lecture at Université Paris 7—Denis Diderot, Paris, February 25.

Scott, James C. 2008. *Seeing like a State: How Certain Schemes to Improve the Human Condition Have Failed*. New Haven, CT: Yale University Press.

Skórzyński, Jan. 2014. *Krótka historia Solidarności: 1980–1989*. Wyd. 1. Gdańsk: Europejskie Centrum Solidarności.

Szulecka, Julia, and Kacper Szulecki. 2013. "Analysing the Rospuda River Controversy in Poland: Rhetoric, Environmental Activism, and the Influence of the European Union." *East European Politics* 29(4): 397–419. https://doi.org/10.1080/21599165.2013.836701.

Szulecki, Kacper. 2011. "Hijacked Ideas: Human Rights, Peace, and Environmentalism in Czechoslovak and Polish Dissident Discourses." *East European Politics and Societies* 25(2): 272–95. https://doi.org/10.1177/0888325410387643.

———. 2013. "'Freedom and Peace Are Indivisible': On the Czechoslovak and Polish Dissident Input to the European Peace Movement 1985–89." In *Entangled Protest: Transnational Perspectives on the History of Dissent in Eastern Europe and the Soviet Union*, ed. Robert Brier, 199–229. Osnabrück: Fibre.

Szulecki, Kacper, Tomasz Borewicz, and Janusz Waluszko. 2015. "A Brief Green Moment: The Emergence and Decline of the Polish Anti-Nuclear and Environmental Movement." *Interface* 7(2): 27–48.

Tarrow, Sidney. 1995. "Mass Mobilization and Regime Change: Pacts, Reform and Popular Power in Italy (1918–1922) and Spain (1975–1978)." In *Democratic Consolidation in Southern Europe*, ed. Richard Gunther, Nikiforos Diamandouros, and Hans-Jürgen Puhle, 204–30. Baltimore: The Johns Hopkins University Press.

———. 1996. "The People's Two Rhythms: Charles Tilly and the Study of Contentious Politics. A Review Article." *Comparative Studies in Society and History* 38(3): 586–600. https://doi.org/10.1017/S0010417500020065.

———. 2012. *Strangers at the Gates: Movements and States in Contentious Politics*. Cambridge: Cambridge University Press.

Tompkins, Andrew S. 2016. *Better Active than Radioactive! Anti-Nuclear Protest in 1970s France and West Germany*. First edition. Oxford Historical Monographs. Oxford: Oxford University Press.

Touraine, Alain. 1983. *Anti-Nuclear Protest: The Opposition to Nuclear Energy in France*. Cambridge: Cambridge University Press.

Waluszko, Janusz. 2011a. "Wspomnienia Tomasza Burka, Współorganizatora Kampanii Przeciw Budowie Elektrowni Jądrowej Żarnowiec: Spisane i Opracowane Przez Janusza Waluszko." https://www.siemysli.info.ke/kampania-przeciwko-elektrowni-atomowej-w-zarnowcu-wspomnienia-tomasza-belfra-burka/.

———. 2011b. "Żarnowiec—Wczoraj i Dziś Protestu Przeciw Budowie Elektrowni Jądrowej w Polsce." *Przegld Anarchistyczny* 12: 40–42.

———. 2013. *Protesty przeciwko budowie Elektrowni Jądrowej Żarnowiec w latach 1985–1990*. Publikacje Gdańskiego Oddziału IPN 10. Gdańsk: Instytut Pamięci Narodowej, Oddz.

Chapter 1

Ignoring the Atom

The Parallel Developments of Poland's Democratic Opposition and Western "New Social Movements"

As massive street protests against industrial pollution and against the construction of nuclear power plants sprang up across Western European cities in the second half of the 1970s, in Poland there was no visible environmental movement to speak of. When hundreds of thousands of Germans, Britons, and other Westerners fiercely protested the military buildup that brought the world to the verge of nuclear Armageddon in the first half of the 1980s, the question of nuclear weapons was hardly raised by the Polish independent underground media. This may lead to the conclusion that the Poles were careless, lacking both environmental awareness and a more global and cosmopolitan imagination. Or we might attribute these differences to the "totalitarian" nature of the communist state, which suppressed any form of dissent. However, neither of these explanations is true. To understand why an independent environmental movement did not emerge in Poland until the 1980s, and why the first antinuclear protests were staged only in 1985, we have to first go back a bit further, tracing the evolution of Poland's democratic opposition—the political challengers to the communist regime—all the way to March 1968. This chapter looks at the process that shaped the Polish opposition from 1968 until the early 1980s and contrasts this with the emergence and evolution of antinuclear (i.e., antibomb, and later antireactor) movements, as well as with the rise of "new social movements" in the West, until a common platform of East-West, human rights–based activism and the space for political environmentalism was found in the mid-1980s.

Different 1968, Divergent 1970s

The year 1968 became a symbol of social upheaval, one of the most iconic dates in modern history. For scholars of protest and dissent, its significance is perhaps on par with 1789, 1848, 1917, and later 1989. There were visible commonalities between events that took place in 1968 across the Global

North—both in the Western and Eastern Blocs. From Berkeley to Warsaw, and from Rome to Prague, young people took to the streets and challenged their respective political establishments, whether capitalist or communist (Klimke, Pekelder, and Scharloth 2011; Klimke and Scharloth 2008; Konarzewska, Nakai, and Przeperski 2020; Kurlansky 2003). This was the first postwar generation, people without a living memory not only of the prewar world but also of World War II (Clifford, Gildea, and Mark 2013).

The participants of the transnational "1968" were alike in many ways. In the words of one of them, a Polish student who later settled in the US, the common elements were "the very mixture of anarchy and seriousness, playfulness and cheek. We were innocent—as in lacking experience, unafraid—as in lacking imagination. But trying to prepare ourselves for a meaningful life, we had to break out of a corset imposed on our world by the terrible secrets of World War II" (Grudzińska-Gross 2020, 223). This, however, is where the easy parallels end and things become nuanced, to the extent that the upheavals on both sides of the Iron Curtain can be viewed as "opposing kinds of civilizational critique of the modern project" (Andělová et al. 2021, 8).

In Poland, student protests erupted in March 1968, following a long process in which increasingly boiling revisionist dissent met with the intra–Communist Party struggle between a more liberal wing and a more hard-headed clique, which drew on nationalist and anti-Semitic tropes to increase its power within the state apparatus (Junes 2015, chap. 6; Szulecki 2019, chap. 4). The anti-Semitism, camouflaged as "anti-Zionism," was partly tactical: following the 1967 Six-Day War between Israel and the Arab states, a critique of Israeli "Zionist" militarism was widespread in the Eastern Bloc. Furthermore, there were many party members of Jewish descent occupying attractive and central positions—playing the anti-Semitic card helped the second-rank Polish "natives" to change the balance of power. But when Pandora's box was opened, it turned out that anti-Semitic allusions simply resonated well with large parts of society.

In parallel to those backstage processes within the party, a relatively liberal period of the mid-1960s helped raise a whole generation of students, often children of the urban middle class and party nomenclatura, who began to question the party line, often from revisionist and leftist positions. In early 1968, the party's decision to suspend a play at the National Theatre in Warsaw sparked student-led protests against censorship. Arrests and expulsions from the university led to a large protest on the Warsaw University premises held on 8 March, which was brutally dispersed by police and workers armed with batons. The protests at Warsaw University and other campuses had their own dynamics but merged with the internal party games into one political phenomenon following the brutal crackdown, as student leaders too became targets of an anti-Semitic campaign, and soon many of them were exiled and deprived of their citizenship, alongside over one hundred thousand other Poles with Jewish roots (Junes 2015, chap. 7; Szulecki 2019, chap. 5).

The experience and memory of 1968 conditioned the path of Polish opposition for the following decade. Although the main protagonists of the events, most notably the soon-to-be-prominent dissident Adam Michnik, as well as the slightly older left-wing revisionist heretics, Jacek Kuroń and Karol Modzelewski, were all very much people of the Left, March 1968 marks the end of hopes for reforming communism from within. The opposition that emerged from the scattered pieces of the student movement in the 1970s no longer saw itself as left wing in any meaningful way, and it began to perceive "socialism with a human face" (the ideal of the Prague Spring, which was also crushed later that year) as a naïve and perhaps even dangerous utopia.

Meanwhile, for a generation of Western European activists, 1968 became a foundational myth of an engaged and radical New Left. This divergence would lead to important differences along the way, even if individual activists—like Michnik and Daniel Cohn-Bendit or Rudi Dutschke—could become friends and discover that on some fundamental level they were all tuned to the same generational frequency (Szulecki 2019, 124).

But the memory of 1968 would also haunt Polish politics, particularly the opposition to communist rule. Although among the 2,732 arrested during the protests the largest single group was young workers, the propaganda denunciation campaign focused on the students and had a strong anti-intellectual and anti-elite flavor. As a result, the myth of workers' betrayal of the dissenting students caught on. When factory workers went on strike in 1970, they could not count on the students to join them. And if the crackdown on students—with beatings and expulsions—was harsh, the authorities' reaction to workers' dissent was even harsher. During the December 1970 wave of protests that spread through the shipyards and factories on the Baltic coast, 41 people were shot (18 in Gdynia, where the military opened fire on workers on their way to work from a train station; 16 in Szczecin; 6 in Gdańsk; and 1 in Elbląg) (IPN 2021). There were also 1,164 wounded.

Due to this divergent experience, for most of the 1970s the directions taken by Western activism and Polish *democratic opposition* (a generic term used to describe all the currents of independent social movements and dissenters aiming at reforming or overthrowing the communist regime) were also different. An important element of the Western protest landscape of the 1970s was radical leftist organizations, including those that relied on terrorist tactics (Gehrig 2011; Pekelder 2011). The Eastern European dissenters, looking for a platform that would allow them to transcend both their ideological differences with the West and the West's own internal political divisions, turned around the mid-1970s to the language of *human rights* (Szulecki 2011; 2019, chap. 6). This "lingua franca of the détente" allowed them to frame their domestic struggles in universal ways and mobilize transnational support. Toward the end of the decade, the human rights activist replaced the armed revolutionary as the main icon of radical politics, in what Horvath called the "demise of the revolutionary privilege" (Horvath 2007).

Following the painful experience of the thwarted student protests of 1968 and the bloody events of December 1970, the democratic opposition was looking for a new formula of action. They found it in grassroots activism where workers and intellectuals could collaborate. The intellectual groundwork was done, among others, by Kuroń and Michnik, but the actual window of opportunity for testing these ideas in practice came in 1976, when workers' protests in Ursus, an industrial suburb of Warsaw, and Radom, a provincial capital some one hundred kilometers away, led to mass arrests of the strikers. The Warsaw democratic opposition circles, left and right, formed the Workers' Defense Committee (Komitet Obrony Robotników, or KOR) to provide legal and financial assistance to the imprisoned workers and their families. Once the campaign of support for the Ursus and Radom strikers was over, KOR did not disband, but instead broadened its activity under the new banner of the Social Self-Defense Committee "KOR" (Komitet Samoobrony Społecznej "KOR"), using the original acronym as a brand name, by that time already widely recognized. As the movement expanded and built its brand, it mobilized new groups into various forms of oppositional activity. One of them was university students—this time a new generation, those that were too young to take part in the 1968 revolts nearly a decade earlier. Some came into the orbit of KOR, but their activity remained closely monitored by the Security Service (Służba Bezpieczeństwa, or SB). In 1977, one of the KOR student sympathizers from Kraków, Stanisław Pyjas, was murdered under suspicious circumstances. From the outrage following his death grew the Student Solidarity Committee (Studencki Komitet Solidarności, or SKS) (Junes 2015, chap. 9). The SKS would become a breeding ground for opposition activists born in the 1950s, some of whom would later play an important role in the emergence of new movements in the 1980s.

KOR began to publish its own illegal "alternative circulation" or samizdat newspapers like *Robotnik* (The worker); it also organized a clandestine university, built up a network of activists around the country, and won support abroad. The focus on the worker-intelligentsia alliance also resulted in the emergence of the Free Trade Unions (Wolne Związki Zawodowe, or

WZZ) in Gdańsk, soon joined by a young electrician already seasoned as a leader at his shipyard in the tragic December 1970 events—one Lech Wałęsa.

By the end of the 1970s, the Polish democratic opposition had firmly adopted this dual focus: domestically, on trade union issues, workers' self-government, and expanding the spaces of political freedom, while monitoring violations of the rule of law; and in international communications, on human rights activism and rhetoric. The emphasis on the intellectual-worker alliance was a conscious strategy promoted by the dissident elite, who saw both untapped potential for mobilization among the workers, shop stewards, and lower-level technocrats and managers in Poland's numerous industrial centers, and who were also aware that "hijacking" the working class would be a painful symbolic blow to the communist system. In that context, the KOR leaders saw little space for other issues, at least for the time being.

Meanwhile, the student movement in the West, which also began to consolidate in the 1960s, marked the beginning of a broader wave of social change. What was unique in the 1968 upheaval in the West was, according to Alain Touraine, that it was less about those excluded from the social system and more about those "at its very heart." The "revolutionary thrust" of collective action came from "the most modern sectors of economic activity, where the role of knowledge is most important: the advanced industries, centres of research or advanced technology, the universities, information media, etc." (quoted in Taylor 2017). The year 1968 became an important symbol, but the process already underway had its most important political results in the 1970s. Drawing upon the New Left ideology of the student movement and the unconventional political tactics of student protests, these new groups and protest movements marked a fundamental change from the prevailing norms and political style of Western democracies (Dalton and Kuechler 1994). West German sociologists coined the term *Neue soziale Bewegungen*—new social movements—to describe this phenomenon, and it was arguably in Germany where the rupture between the politics of the 1960s and the 1970s was starkest.

Bombs and Powerplants: Nuclear Technology and Societal Resistance

One galvanizing political issue that gained prominence in Western European societies was the question of nuclear weapons—and with time, also nuclear power. In the aftermath of the first nuclear bombs dropped at Hiroshima and Nagasaki in 1945, the realization began to dawn that humanity had just mastered a technology that has the capacity to destroy the entire planet. It became more pronounced after the Soviet Union obtained its own bomb in 1949 and the nuclear arms raced between the new rival superpowers accelerated.

In the 1950s, a social movement based on this realization began to grow and institutionalize. This occurred in parallel on two levels. Internationally, concerned scientists and experts created a transnational advocacy network, which in 1957 led to the first Pugwash conference, creating a "rare channel of communication between scientists from East and West" (Kraft, Nehring, and Sachse 2018, 4). Domestically, citizen movements targeting national as well as global nuclear armaments began to spring up in Europe. The development of thermonuclear weapons and the dangers of nuclear testing brought "emerging environmental groups together with peace advocates to demand that governments ban the bomb" (Gavin 2015, 6).

Following some earlier expert and lobbying groups that opposed nuclear warfare in general or the British hydrogen bomb in particular, the Campaign for Nuclear Disarmament (CND) arose, which "expressed the manifold fears of the British population about nuclear war" (Nehring 2013, 65). A similar process, though for slightly different historical reasons, occurred in West Germany, where the "geographical position on the frontline of the Cold War and its recent experience of utter destruction during World War II" made nuclear weapons protesters feel that the "dangers coming from the military use of nuclear energy were imminent" (Nehring 2004, 151). The British movement, in turn, drew on the pacifist tradition of the Labour Movement and the Anglican Church.

While these two national movements were strong and vocal, in France nuclear weapons did not spark a similar controversy, as apparently they were "perceived as a national symbol and as securing French independence" (Chafer 1985, 5). In Poland, the situation was different still. During the Stalinist period, roughly 1946–1956, no bottom-up opposition to state military policies was possible or even imaginable. Unlike Great Britain and France, Poland was not developing nuclear capabilities of its own, so protesting nuclear warfare implied resistance to the brotherly relationship with the Soviet Union, which was a political taboo. As domestic relations eased in the so-called Thaw period following the deaths of Josef Stalin (d. 1953) and later Poland's leader Bolesaw Bierut (d. 1956), open dissent in the form known from Western European democracies was still not an option.

However, de-Stalinization opened the space for official diplomatic actions towards disarmament. On 2 October 1957, Polish Foreign Minister Adam Rapacki proposed the denuclearization of Central Europe (East and West Germany, Poland, and Czechoslovakia) (Wilson Center 2021). Actively discussed over the following two years, the Rapacki Plan had two longer-term outcomes. First, it opened a dialogue on the question of regional disarmament, with Polish politicians and diplomats together with other Central European and Western counterparts at its heart. This made disarmament an official Polish policy. It also led to the creation of official, i.e., state-sanctioned, "peace movements," often composed of party members, who were portrayed as a genuine bottom-up response of the Eastern Bloc societies to the Cold War and as a counterpart to Western movements like the CND (Evangelista 1999). The outcome of that latter fact was that the language of peace and disarmament became associated with communist propaganda and was not considered relevant by the nascent political opposition—which also felt that interfering with matters of security was beyond its scope and capacity (Szulecki 2013).

"Atoms for Peace": Civilian Nuclear Energy Use

In the meantime, a new question gained salience—that of the nonmilitary use of nuclear technology. In 1942, the exiled Italian physicist Enrico Fermi constructed the first reactor—an atomic pile—at the University of Chicago, and according to the constructor himself it was literally "a crude pile of black bricks and wooden timbers." After World War II, the first reactors began to be tested for civilian uses, although their primary purpose was to produce plutonium for nuclear weapons. Electricity was in a sense a byproduct of the reaction—reactors were being cooled with water and vapor was used to produce electricity in turbines.

Under President Dwight Eisenhower's "Atoms for Peace" program, the US Navy provided a bridge between using the energy of nuclear fission for civilian use and for mass destruction (in 1952 Americans tested "Mike," their first thermonuclear bomb). On Eisenhower's order, Admiral Hyman Rickover began overseeing research into the use of nuclear reactors in the Navy. Thanks to his persistence, by 1954 construction of the *USS Nautilus*—the first nuclear submarine—had begun. In 1958, the submarine traveled 1,400 miles under the North Pole without surfacing.

Paradoxically, "Atoms for Peace" began as a means of propelling navy vessels, while the first truly "civilian" reactor was constructed in the USSR in 1954, in Obinsk near Moscow, and its energy was used to power a scientific facility. A power plant with six nuclear reactors was also constructed in Troitsk, Siberia, between 1958 and 1963. Simultaneously, work was underway on civilian reactors at the INEEL (Idaho National Engineering and Environmental Laboratory, later renamed the Idaho National Laboratory) near Idaho Falls. There, engineers developed "Mark"—a pressurized water reactor (PWR), used to power *Nautilus* and other submarines, which used water for moderation and cooling—and "Borax," a boiling water reactor (BWR). Both became prototypes for the most popular reactors used in nuclear power plants today: the PWR, powering around 65 percent of power plants, and the BWR, powering around 23 percent. In 1955 Borax-III started supplying power to the town of Arco, Idaho, with a population of 1,200 souls.

Calder Hall, opened in 1956, is considered the first commercial nuclear power plant, even though it also produced plutonium for the military. The second commercial nuclear power plant was Shippingport, which opened in 1957 in the US. By the end of the decade, the nuclear energy club consisted of the USSR (1954), Great Britain (1956), the United States (1957), and France (1959) (France's entry dates to the opening of the commercial power plant in Chinon, though the first French reactor was already built in 1948 and the first one to produce power opened in 1956). Because the United States had a monopoly on enriching uranium, power plants in other Western states, i.e., Great Britain, France, and Canada, all relied on natural uranium.

According to the head of the American Atomic Energy Commission, Lewis Strauss, nuclear energy would be "too cheap to meter." However, these dreams turned out to be very far from reality: for a long time, the production of electricity in nuclear power plants was not profitable at all and was in fact a by-product of military activity rather than a business venture. That situation changed with the oil crisis in 1973, when the Organization of the Petroleum Exporting Countries (OPEC) put an embargo on Western countries and Japan, all of which supported Israel in an ongoing war (Claes 2018). The embargo resulted in long-term gasoline shortages and in a dramatic increase in the price of oil in the United States, Western Europe, and Japan—giving rise to the term "energy security" (Szulecki 2018). Interestingly, the unprofitability of nuclear energy was also underscored in the USSR, which did not have a market economy and made its technological decisions based on a central planning system. Nuclear energy only became profitable thanks to economies of scale around 1985, on the eve of the Chernobyl catastrophe.

The Emergence of Antinuclear Protest

As noted, the earliest initiatives protesting the militarized atom involved scientists advocating for disarmament and peace. These include the Pugwash Conferences on Science and World Affairs and the Campaign for Nuclear Disarmament. The CND's emblematic protest event was the "Easter Marches," an annual protest that covered the eighty-five kilometers from London to the nuclear research facility in Aldermaston. However, while the debates in Great Britain and West Germany highlighted the dangers related to the military uses of nuclear energy, most supporters of the anti–nuclear weapons movement did not extend their skepticism to the civilian use of "the atom," at least initially (Nehring 2004, 163; Rothwell 2007). This was true even of the intellectual leaders of the anti–nuclear weapons movement, and of figures who shaped this mindset. Robert Jungk, later a member of the Austrian Green Party and coiner of the critical term "the atomic state," was initially an enthusiast of atomic sciences, ending his book on the Manhattan Project and German bomb development efforts with the words: "Let fireworks, brighter than a thousand suns and lit by the hand of man, burn only in a controlled manner, bringing vital energy for the benefit of humanity" (Jungk 1967, 297).

Another eventual nuclear sceptic, Joachim Radkau, described the atmosphere in West Germany: "As long as nuclear energy was a vision for the future, one could project all kinds of wishes and fantasies onto it (and in fact, the Germany of the 1950s, like many places in the world, experienced a veritable nuclear euphoria). That stopped precisely at the moment when nuclear power plants became a looming reality" (2009, 168). Not surprisingly, the student protest leaders of 1968, both in France and Germany, by and large embraced nuclear energy as an element of progress in the "atomic era."

The military use of nuclear energy—as well as early accidents at power plants and other locations (e.g., submarines) and coverups of those accidents, even in democratic countries—gradually led part of the public to become wary of nuclear energy. With the 1973 oil crisis, which sped up the heretofore quite languid (due to high costs and lack of experience) nuclear projects, the question of civilian use of nuclear energy came to the fore. This provided an impulse for the creation of new protest movements focused not on the bomb per se but on the risks related to the mass use of nuclear fission technology. It was only in the 1970s that the anti–nuclear energy movement turned "from an elite quarrel to a mass movement" (Mitchell 1981).

However, fears of radiation and nuclear safety issues were from the start only one part of the story. The other was explicitly political, resulting from the tension between technocracy and democracy, between the "nucleocrats" and civil society (Nelkin and Pollak 1981a). The spark igniting this kind of dissent was the authoritarian and "police state" practices occurring in some countries, even including state-sponsored terror: for instance, the French attack on the Greenpeace vessel *Rainbow Warrior* on 10 July 1985 in response to Greenpeace's protests against nuclear testing in the Mururoa atoll. Combined with a blatant disregard for the natural environment (dumping radioactive waste straight into the ocean at La Hague in France and Sellafield in England), these factors led to the development of movements that objected to both military and civilian use of atomic energy, and to the popularization of the notion of an "atomic state."

In his seminal essay under that title, Jungk moved to very different positions that became characteristic for the Western antinuclear movement from the 1970s onward. "Atoms for peace," he argued, are in practice no different from "atoms for war." Declarations on their use for constructive purposes in no way change the character of the life-threatening energy. "All the efforts to tame this risk can only partly lessen the danger" (Jungk 1982, 17). The unbearable levels of danger would require such levels of control that they would make the "atomic state" inherently incompatible with democratic governance, causing it to deteriorate into a dictatorial security state. Together with his other work, Jungk's essay, first published in German in 1977, both reflected and helped shape the intellectual underpinnings of the antinuclear movement.

A wave of antireactor protests swept across capitalist countries in the 1970s. As Milder argues, the first protests against nuclear power plants along the Rhine were not motivated by reactor safety but instead by local environmental, agricultural, and climate concerns, including changing sun exposure due to massive water vaporization (Milder 2019). However, by the second half of the decade, the antinuclear movement was launching its critique along several lines that were universal across the West:

1) the relationship between civilian and military use of nuclear energy
2) the centralization of management required by nuclear energy, which lent itself to antidemocratic practices
3) the high costs of nuclear energy, not only in terms of the construction and maintenance of power plants but also their deconstruction and the storage, for hundreds or thousands of years, of radioactive waste
4) the negative effects on health and the environment
5) the neglect of energy-saving and renewable energy sources
6) the need to import nuclear technology and nuclear fuel.

The antinuclear movement took on many forms in the West. For instance, in the US and Great Britain, the counterculture dimension of the protests was very strong, which shaped their relationship with mainstream political forces and the broader society and led to a shift towards localized rather than mass nationwide protest. US opponents of the atom organized thousands of people to march on and occupy power plant construction sites. Later, their focus shifted to lobbying. Key to limiting the expansion of atomic energy was the Three Mile Island accident in 1979, whose costs are estimated at USD 2.5 billion in property damages alone.

In light of Prime Minister Pierre Messmer's announcement of plans to create a giant network of nuclear reactors that would not only satisfy domestic demands for energy but also be used to export electricity, nuclear technology, and fuel, the French antinuclear movement mobilized thousands of people. Unlike nuclear weapons, which back in the 1950s resonated with national pride, nuclear reactors' construction pushed an eclectic alliance of social and vocational groups to protest for a variety of reasons, safety concerns being only one among many (Tompkins 2016, 36–37). Beginning with the Alsatians, who in 1972 protested the construction of a power plant in Fessenheim, the coalition of opponents grew wider. Since the Rhine River was envisaged as Europe's "atomic valley," with reactors planned in dense intervals by the Swiss, French, and German authorities (Milder 2019, 15), and since the projects were often transnational investments, so too was the protest—with French and German reactor opponents joining forces (Tompkins 2016). Surprisingly perhaps from today's point of view, it was the French movement that mobilized larger numbers of protesters and appeared more powerful and determined in the second half of the 1970s (Radkau 2009).

The former 68ers moved to critical positions regarding the nuclear industry once antinuclear protest became a truly mass phenomenon. According to Radkau:

> [They] initially had to ground this effort theoretically, insofar as it at first sprang only from a spontaneous emotional sympathy for protesters. Amongst the neo-Marxists of the New Left, and not only amongst them, the outlook was widespread that the progress of productive forces furthers societal progress, and this progress is grounded in a growing scientization of industry and technology. This theory was therefore popular amongst intellectuals in the East and the West, if nothing else because it flatteringly credited them with a pioneering role. (Radkau 2009, 179)

An important element of this new theorization was the notion of *technocracy*—the conflation of political power with expertise and the ability to control complex technological systems. Touraine situates new movements in the context of a technocratic "postindustrial" society (Touraine 1974). In such a society technology is able to "penetrate" the social, overriding custom and tradition (Taylor 2017). That new theoretical grounding resulted in the emergence of new social movements. Learning from the experience of 1968 and the limits of a revolutionary approach, new social movements challenged political orders in the West from within, calling for democracies to change, adapt, and open the political process to a more diverse and citizen-oriented set of interests (Dalton and Kuechler 1994, 3). Although environmental, feminist, and peace organizations had taken a variety of forms, at the core of these groups was a qualitatively new aspect of citizen politics in Western democracies. The alliance of grassroots antireactor protests (often launched on narrow and conservative "not in my backyard" grounds) with earlier conservationist groups and the new social movements evolving from the student movement resulted in the emergence of a *political environmentalism* and *green politics* (Newell 2020, 21) that would shape environmental policy into what we know and perceive almost as given from today's perspective, and that would shape democracy more broadly (Augustine 2018; Milder 2019).

However, the other important group was the scientists. In February 1975, four hundred representatives of the world of science issued an appeal that criticized Messmer's decision. By the end of that year, the appeal had been signed by over four thousand scientists. The scientific community also assumed responsibility for shaping public opinion about the risks related to atomic technology, especially through the *Gazette nucléaire* published by the Association of Scientists for Information on Nuclear Energy (*Groupement de scientifiques pour l'information sur l'énergie nucléaire*). Because the French nuclear issue was national in nature, resistance to it also quickly spread beyond the immediate vicinity of the planned power plants, as evidenced by the fact that the coalition against the atom was joined by the main French labor union, the Democratic Labor Confederation (*Confédération française démocratique du travail*). Although initially enthusiastically supportive of nuclear energy rollout, German scientists also gradually began to dissent (Radkau 2009) and challenged "the political decisions regarding how knowledge was presented and applied" (Augustine 2018, 75).

Antinuclear protests also became a way for certain parts of society to express their dissatisfaction with the manner in which decisions were made in their country. France was becoming increasingly centralized and authoritarian, and its nuclear program was a good example of that tendency. However, the same factor that motivated thousands of people to protest also doomed the mass movement. In the absence of any other option, the main tool of resistance was demonstrations, which in that period often ended in brutal clashes with the police that symbolized the authoritarianism of the Gaullist state. The French protests culminated in a demonstration of sixty thousand activists on 31 July 1977 in Creys-Malville, which ended in a massive battle with law enforcement officers. One man was killed and three seriously wounded, as the police used stun grenades (Tompkins 2016, 1). Due to a lack of political coordination and a questionable choice of objectives, key groups gradually abandoned the coalition, which allowed the determined authorities to embark on a massive program of nuclear expansion (Touraine 1983).

In decentralized West Germany, the resistance was more grassroots in nature. Its main tools were local governments, courts, referendums, and peaceful protests. This was especially the case in the Rhine valley; in Baden-Wuerttemberg, for instance, three investments were blocked between 1972 and 1977 (Milder 2019). Some of the most interesting elements of the German resistance were the kilometers-long "tractor demonstrations" organized by farmers from nearby villages, a petition signed by around 90 percent of adult inhabitants of the villages surrounding the planned power plant construction site in Breisach, and a local government session open to the public.

The longest protests were related to the construction of a power plant in Wyhl, where ninety thousand people signed a protest petition (Augustine 2018, chap. 4; Milder 2019, chap. 3; Morris and Jungjohann 2016, chap. 2). After many years, the local administrative court revoked the construction permit, showing antinuclear movements around the world that persistent, peaceful, and effective grassroots resistance was possible.

In the north, in Brokdorf near Hamburg, the protests took on a more brutal character, resembling a "civil war" (Augustine 2018, chap. 5). Occupations of the construction site ended in pacifications. On 11 November 1976, a battle described in the media as a "civil war" took place: police dropped chemical agents onto protesters from helicopters, eventually leading to one hundred people being arrested and five hundred injured. Having learned from this experience, activists came to subsequent demonstrations equipped with helmets, shields, gas masks, and even aluminum kites that scrambled police radio communication and made it more difficult to use helicopters. However, many demonstrations, some gathering over one hundred thousand participants, were peaceful, partially due to the involvement of the Evangelical Church. The first strategies bordering on performance, which would later grow in popularity, also appeared at this time. For example, in Grohnde, around one thousand activists occupied a construction site and threw flowers and confetti at the police. Soon violence as a tool of protest became a divisive issue within the antinuclear movement, with an overwhelming majority of activists advocating peaceful methods.

Although the antinuclear movement enjoyed not only a common set of ideas and a repertoire of protest tactics but also a high level of societal sympathy and support, its impact on national policies differed across Western states, primarily due to political and institutional differences. Two-party systems in Great Britain and the US offered little space for political contestation of nuclear energy, and so the movements remained outside the arena of high politics. In Germany, Switzerland, and Sweden, "the existence of official channels through which the public could influence substantive policy decisions gave the opposition the means to delay the expansion of nuclear power and to sustain a level of conflict over time" (Nelkin and Pollak 1981b, 37). Pressure and the convergence of political factors led to referendums and parliamentary decisions to abandon atomic energy first in Austria (1978) and Italy (1987), and then after 2000 in Germany, Switzerland, and Belgium. At the same time, the most powerful antinuclear movement—in France—entered the 1980s weakened and divided, and ultimately failed to achieve its goals.

If political structures were unfavorable to antinuclear dissent in democratic countries like Belgium, France, or the US, and there were limited opportunities for protest, in the Eastern Bloc of the 1970s such opportunities were virtually nonexistent. As a US expert noted: "In the West there is a nuclear debate; in the East there is a nuclear dictate. Nuclear energy is challenged on economic, environmental, and sociopolitical grounds in the West; but it has been given the official imprimatur in the East. . . . This received view is apparently derived from ideology (the connections between science, technology, and progress) and political-economic necessity" (Pilat 1981, 10).

Poland in the Early 1980s: Solidarity, Martial Law, and the "Second Cold War"

On 14 August 1980, a strike broke out in the Lenin Shipyard in Gdańsk. It was sparked by the firing of a charismatic worker, Anna Walentynowicz, who was also an activist of the Free Trade Unions (WZZ). Along with rehiring her, the strikers called for rehiring another WZZ member, Lech Wałęsa, and they also launched other demands: the construction of a monument to the workers murdered in the violent December 1970 events, pay raises, and guarantees of safety for the strikers. Learning from the tragic lesson of street protests ten years earlier, they launched an occupation of the shipyard, and Wałęsa, who joined them later that day, became the leader of the strike (Machcewicz 2015). Strikes and protests spread all over the country, which ground to a complete halt. On 31 August, Wałęsa was leading a delegation of workers who signed a twenty-one-point agreement with the party, which combined economic, social, and political demands. One of them was the creation of a free, independent, and self-governing trade union—Solidarity. Soon after its creation, the trade union had as many as ten million members, some of them coming from the PZPR itself (Skórzyński 2014).

The period following the establishment of Solidarity was marked by unprecedented liberalization in many aspects of life in Poland, most notably the significant lifting of censorship, which led to a cultural boom. The wave of social enthusiasm and "actorness"—the feeling of regaining political agency and the power to change political reality—was such that the months between August 1980 and December 1981 are referred to as the "carnival" period. Grassroots activism and the energy it unleashed led to the emergence of new groups, organizations, and social currents—including countercultural ones, for example around the nascent punk rock scene. This period also saw the rise of an environmental movement focusing on the most drastic cases of industrial pollution, to which we will return in detail in chapter 2.

However, the threat of communist backlash or worse—a Soviet intervention, similar to the one in Czechoslovakia in 1968—was tangible. Despite the enthusiasm, Poland was also undergoing a deep economic crisis, and the recurring strikes did not make the situation better. Dark clouds began to gather in the second half of 1981, and finally, on the night of 13 December 1981, martial law was declared. Military units entered cities, while police forces arrested some five thousand senior unionists and opposition figures (overall the number would reach ten thousand). A curfew was introduced, and while many Solidarity leaders remained free—or, rather, in hiding—the backbone of the union was broken, and so were the hopes for change. The effective dictator of Poland was now General Wojciech Jaruzelski (1923–2014), who combined the functions of the first secretary of the Polish United Workers' Party, the prime minister, and the supreme commander of the People's Army.

Martial law would last until July 1983, though repressions were eased already by 1982. Opposition activity moved underground, and the clandestine structures of the delegalized and persecuted trade union were only a shadow of the official network it boasted during the "carnival" period. There was very little space for any sort of independent social activity, much less dissent.

"I Hope the Russians Love Their Children Too"

At the same time, important changes in the international arena were taking place. In 1976, the USSR began deploying a new model of mobile middle-range nuclear missiles, known under their NATO code name SS-20. Following the logic of their military doctrine, emphasizing "balance" in arms and threat, in 1979 NATO officials came up with the so-called "double track" decision, which meant that Pershing and Tomahawk middle-range missiles would in turn be deployed in Western Europe. Together with two other circumstances—the Soviet invasion of Afghanistan and the US presidential election won by the hardheaded "hawk" Ronald Reagan—the turn of the decade saw a definite move from the politics of easing of tensions—détente—towards what many call the "Second Cold War" (Gassert, Geiger, and Wentker 2011). Under the emerging nuclear crisis in Europe, the new buzzwords were "disarmament" and "peace."

As a result, a massive movement of protest against the new missiles, as well as against the nuclear arms race in general, formed in Western Europe. The "peace movement" was a diverse coalition of societal and political groups. On the whole it was visibly left leaning, which, combined with its critical attitude towards the immediate actions of the Western governments, NATO, and its apparent anti-Americanism, made it a very popular topic of Eastern European media coverage (Ziemann 2009). What is more, the official (state-sponsored) East European peace organizations were perceived as legitimate partners for a dialogue about peace issues, as the legitimacy of the communist governments was not questioned (Śliwa 1992, 27; Burke 2004, 111–12).

Although large parts of the Western peace movement were suspicious of the USSR, the dominant policy demand was reversal of the "double track" decision or even unilateral nuclear disarmament. To the critical rejoinder that the Soviets maintained conventional arms supremacy in Europe, and that they would strategically benefit from such a move, the proverbial reply was the slogan "better red than dead" (Szulecki 2013). It was the fear of nuclear Armageddon that provided a justification for the peace movement's policy demands.

Conclusions: Why Did Poland Have No Antinuclear Movement until 1985?

With that attitude, so well suited for use by communist propaganda, the Western peace movement was highly problematic for the Polish opposition. The latter, as we have seen, was concerned with very different issues throughout the 1970s, and even more so since 1980. The Solidarity trade union was to a great extent preoccupied with domestic affairs. This was not only because of the salience of immediate domestic problems, which was indeed high. It was also the result of a certain geopolitical taboo. Foreign and security issues were considered off bounds for the democratic opposition in Poland, as they would inadvertently lead to a confrontation with Cold War geopolitics, and thus to a controversy over Soviet policy (Szulecki 2015).

As a result, Poland had no real anti–nuclear weapons movement. The "Second Cold War" and particularly the nuclear crisis that escalated in 1983 left little mark on Polish society and its democratic opposition—in stark contrast to the cases of East Germany or Czechoslovakia, where different forms of dissent or at least alternative cultural responses to the overwhelming threat of nuclear annihilation could be seen (Szulecki 2013). Similarly, there was no antireactor movement or even coordinated dissent among technocratic and scientific elites. Part of the reason was that the Polish nuclear program, although launched formally in the early 1970s, did not reach the localization and permitting stages until 1982, when they were hidden behind a wall of censorship and secrecy (see chapter 5). Another reason is that the dissidents and activists forming the core of Poland's democratic opposition were not interested in questions of technology or environmental conservation.

The only area of agreement between Polish opposition movements and Western European environmental and peace movements was human rights. However, for this common platform to be effective, the Western movements had to undergo a transition of their own. The merger of environmental, antireactor, and disarmament protest currents into a new broad movement in the 1980s, and the emergence of Green politics, particularly with the institutionalization and rise of the Green Party in Germany (Mayer and Ely 1998; Sarkar 1993), were necessary enablers for a dialogue articulated in the language of human rights (Szulecki 2011). But to be able to "localize" the agenda of environmental and peace movements in Poland, and to "glocalize" their own domestic struggles with the help of international human rights talk, a new generation of opposition activists had to enter the stage.

References

Andělová, Kristina, Wendy Bracewell, Irena Grudzińska-Gross, Krzysztof Jasiewicz, David Ost, and Nina Witoszek. 2021. "Re-Enchanting Modernity in the East and West: Comparative Perspectives on the Legacy of 1968. An Author Meets Her Reviewers: A Symposium." *East European Politics and Societies* 35(3): 525–567. https://doi.org/10.1177/08883254211005182.

Augustine, Dolores L. 2018. *Taking on Technocracy: Nuclear Power in Germany, 1945 to the Present*. Protest, Culture and Society, volume 24. New York: Berghahn Books.

Burke, P. D. M. 2004. "European Nuclear Disarmament: A Study of Transnational Social Movement Strategy." Ph.D. dissertation. London: University of Westminster. https://westminsterresearch.westminster.ac.uk/item/93155/european-nuclear-disarmament-a-study-of-transnational-social-movement-strategy.

Chafer, Tony. 1985. "Politics and the Perception of Risk: A Study of the Anti-nuclear Movements in Britain and France." *West European Politics* 8(1): 5–23. https://doi.org/10.1080/01402388508424510.

Claes, Dag Harald. 2018. *The Politics of Oil. Controlling Resources, Governing Markets and Creating Political Conflicts*. Cheltenham: Edward Elgar Publishing.

Clifford, Rebecca, Robert Gildea, and James Mark. 2013. "Awakenings." In *Europe's 1968*, ed. Robert Gildea, James Mark, and Anette Warring, 20–45. Oxford: Oxford University Press. https://doi.org/10.1093/acprof:oso/9780199587513.003.0002.

Dalton, Russell J., and Manfred Kuechler, eds. 1994. *Challenging the Political Order: New Social and Political Movements in Western Democracies*. Reprint. Europe and the International Order. Cambridge: Polity.

Evangelista, Matthew. 1999. *Unarmed Forces. The Transnational Movement to End the Cold War*. Ithaca: Cornell University Press. https://www.cornellpress.cornell.edu/book/9780801487842/unarmed-forces/.

Gassert, Philipp, Tim Geiger, and Hermann Wentker. 2011. *Zweiter Kalter Krieg und Friedensbewegung. Der NATO-Doppelbeschluss in deutsch-deutscher und internationaler Perspektive*. Berlin, Boston: De Gruyter Oldenbourg.

Gavin, Francis J. 2015. *Nuclear Statecraft—History and Strategy in America's Atomic Age*. Ithaca: Cornell University Press.

Gehrig, Sebastian. 2011. "Sympathizing Subcultures? The Milieus of West German Terrorism." In *Between Prague Spring and French May: Opposition and Revolt in Europe, 1960–1980*, ed. Martin Klimke, Jacco Pekelder, and Joachim Scharloth, 233–50. Protest, Culture and Society, volume 7. New York: Berghahn Books.

Grudzińska-Gross, Irena. 2020. "Final Remarks. 1968 Again." In *Unsettled 1968 in the Troubled Present: Revisiting the 50 Years of Discussions from East and Central Europe*, ed. Aleksandra Konarzewska, Anna Nakai, and Michał Przeperski, 223–25. Routledge Studies in Modern History 60. London: Routledge.

Horvath, Robert. 2007. "'The Solzhenitsyn Effect': East European Dissidents and the Demise of the Revolutionary Privilege." *Human Rights Quarterly* 29(4): 879–907. https://doi.org/10.1353/hrq.2007.0041.

IPN. 2021. "Lista ofiar Grudnia '70." Polskie miesiące. https://polskiemiesiace.ipn.gov.pl/mie/wszystkie-wydarzenia/grudzien-1970/ofiary/114890,Lista-ofiar-Grudnia-03970.html.

Junes, Tom. 2015. *Student Politics in Communist Poland: Generations of Consent and Dissent*. Lanham: Lexington Books.

Jungk, Robert. 1967. *Jaśniej Niż Tysiąc Słońc. Los Badaczy Atomu*. Warszawa: PIW.

———. 1982. *Państwo Atomowe*. Warszawa: PIW.

Klimke, Martin, Jacco Pekelder, and Joachim Scharloth, eds. 2011. *Between Prague Spring and French May: Opposition and Revolt in Europe, 1960–1980*. Protest, Culture and Society, volume 7. New York: Berghahn Books.

Klimke, Martin, and Joachim Scharloth. 2008. *1968 in Europe: A History of Protest and Activism, 1956–1977*. New York: Palgrave Macmillan.

Konarzewska, Aleksandra, Anna Nakai, and Michał Przeperski, eds. 2020. *Unsettled 1968 in the Troubled Present: Revisiting the 50 Years of Discussions from East and Central Europe*. Routledge Studies in Modern History 60. London: Routledge.

Kraft, Alison, Holger Nehring, and Carola Sachse. 2018. "The Pugwash Conferences and the Global Cold War: Scientists, Transnational Networks, and the Complexity of Nuclear Histories." *Journal of Cold War Studies* 20(1): 4–30. https://doi.org/10.1162/jcws_e_00799.

Kurlansky, Mark. 2003. *1968: The Year That Rocked the World*. First Edition. New York: Ballantine Books.

Machcewicz, Anna. 2015. *Bunt: Strajki w Trójmieście. Sierpien 1980*. Wydanie pierwsze. Gdańsk: Europejskie Centrum Solidarności.

Mayer, Margit, and John Ely, eds. 1998. *The German Greens: Paradox between Movement and Party*. Philadelphia: Temple University Press.

Milder, Stephen. 2019. *Greening Democracy: The Anti-Nuclear Movement and Political Environmentalism in West Germany and beyond, 1968–1983*. Cambridge: Cambridge University Press.

Mitchell, Robert Cameron. 1981. "From Elite Quarrel to Mass Movement." *Society* 18(5): 76–84. https://doi.org/10.1007/BF02701330.
Morris, Craig, and Arne Jungjohann. 2016. *Energy Democracy: Germany's Energiewende to Renewables*. Basingstoke: Palgrave Macmillan.
Nehring, Holger. 2004. "Cold War, Apocalypse and Peaceful Atoms. Interpretations of Nuclear Energy in the British and West German Anti-Nuclear Weapons Movements, 1955–1964." *Historical Social Research / Historische Sozialforschung* 29(3): 150–70.
———. 2013. *Politics of Security: British and West German Protest Movements and the Early Cold War, 1945–1970*. First edition. Oxford Historical Monographs. Oxford: Oxford University Press.
Nelkin, Dorothy, and Michael Pollak. 1981a. *The Atom Besieged: Extraparliamentary Dissent in France and Germany*. Cambridge, MA: MIT Press.
———. 1981b. "Nuclear Protest and National Policy." *Society* 18(5): 34–38. https://doi.org/10.1007/BF02701324.
Newell, Peter. 2020. *Global Green Politics*. New York: Cambridge University Press.
Pekelder, Jacco. 2011. "The RAF Solidarity Movement from a European Perspective." In *Between Prague Spring and French May: Opposition and Revolt in Europe, 1960–1980*, ed. Martin Klimke, Jacco Pekelder, and Joachim Scharloth, 251–67. Protest, Culture and Society, volume 7. New York: Berghahn Books.
Pilat, Joseph F. 1981. "Communist Nuclear Practice." *Society* 18(5): 10–16. https://doi.org/10.1007/BF02701321.
Radkau, Joachim. 2009. "The Anti-Nuclear Movement in Germany." Presented at the Lecture at Université Paris 7—Denis Diderot, Paris, February 25.
Rothwell, Susan L. 2007. "Anti-Nuclear Movement." In *Encyclopedia of Activism and Social Justice*, ed. Gary Anderson and Kathryn Herr, 165–67. Thousand Oaks, CA: SAGE. https://doi.org/10.4135/9781412956215.n67.
Sarkar, Saral K. 1993. *Green-Alternative Politics in West Germany*. Tokyo: United Nations University Press.
Skórzyński, Jan. 2014. *Krótka historia Solidarności: 1980–1989*. Wyd. 1. Gdańsk: Europejskie Centrum Solidarności.
Śliwa, Maciej. 1992. "Ruch 'Wolność i Pokój' 1985–1989." MA Thesis. Krakow: Jagiellonian University.
Szulecki, Kacper. 2011. "Hijacked Ideas: Human Rights, Peace, and Environmentalism in Czechoslovak and Polish Dissident Discourses." *East European Politics and Societies* 25(2): 272–95. https://doi.org/10.1177/0888325410387643.
———. 2013. "'Freedom and Peace Are Indivisible': On the Czechoslovak and Polish Dissident Input to the European Peace Movement 1985–89." In *Entangled Protest: Transnational Perspectives on the History of Dissent in Eastern Europe and the Soviet Union*, 199–229. Osnabrück: Fibre.
———. 2015. "Heretical Geopolitics of Central Europe. Dissidents Intellectuals and an Alternative European Order." *Geoforum* 65 (October): 25–36. https://doi.org/10.1016/j.geoforum.2015.07.008.
———, ed. 2018. *Energy Security in Europe: Divergent Perceptions and Policy Challenges*. Energy, Climate and the Environment. Palgrave Macmillan. https://doi.org/10.1007/978-3-319-64964-1.

———. 2019. *Dissidents in Communist Central Europe: Human Rights and the Emergence of New Transnational Actors*. Palgrave Studies in the History of Social Movements. Palgrave Macmillan. https://doi.org/10.1007/978-3-030-22613-8.

Taylor, Dylan. 2017. *Social Movements and Democracy in the 21st Century*. 1st ed. 2017. Cham: Palgrave Macmillan. https://doi.org/10.1007/978-3-319-39684-2.

Tompkins, Andrew S. 2016. *Better Active than Radioactive! Anti-Nuclear Protest in 1970s France and West Germany*. First edition. Oxford Historical Monographs. Oxford: Oxford University Press.

Touraine, Alain. 1974. *Post-Industrial Society*. London: Wildwood House Ltd.

———. 1983. *Anti-Nuclear Protest: The Opposition to Nuclear Energy in France*. Cambridge: Cambridge University Press.

Wilson Center. 2021. "Wilson Center Digital Archive." https://digitalarchive.wilsoncenter.org/collection/619/rapacki-plan.

Ziemann, Benjamin. 2009. "A Quantum of Solace? European Peace Movements during the Cold War and Their Elective Affinities." *Archiv Für Sozialgeschichte* 49: 351–89.

Chapter 2

Polish Political Environmentalism before Chernobyl

In the early 1980s, as the military junta of General Wojciech Jaruzelski took power in Poland, thwarted the Solidarity trade union, and dispersed any illusions regarding the regime's possible liberalization from the bottom up, it could seem that Poles had no time or energy for environmental protection. In reality, nothing could have been further from the truth. The state of the natural environment in the 1970s and 1980s became so grave that these issues could simply not be left unaddressed. Although Poland had a long-standing tradition of conservationism and a "green" ecology, the catalysts of political environmentalism that started to pick up pace in the first half of the 1980s were considered to be "gray" ecology. They were not so much nature as the environment around human beings, affecting public health and threatening lives. However, the environmental movement in Poland, as in the other Eastern Bloc countries, emerged in the context of a peculiar discourse on nature, culture, and power—a "communist environmentality."

In this chapter, we discuss the key premises of that environmentality, which also determined the relationship between scientific experts and technocrats on the one hand and society on the other—an issue that would gain salience in the context of nuclear power. We then discuss the environmental crisis that motivated a variety of different groups to act: among these were official and state-sanctioned organizations, as well as opposition groups and movements that occupied a gray zone in between. Finally, we introduce Freedom and Peace—Poland's first new social movement, which merged the agenda of the political opposition with peace and environmental issues, thus becoming a natural partner for Western independents. The participants of that movement were also behind the first antinuclear protest event staged in Poland in 1985.

Nature, Progress, and Technology: How Communism Approached the Environment

"Throughout history," writes Zygmunt Bauman, "communism was modernity's most devout, vigorous and gallant champion. . . . Indeed, it was under communist, not capitalist, auspices that the audacious dream of modernity, freed from obstacles by the merciless and omnipotent state, was pushed to its radical limits: grand designs, unlimited social engineering, huge and bulky technology, total transformation of nature" (1992, 179).

Communism had two major roles for nature: as a resource and as a decoration. Its ultimate ideal was modernization and subjection of the world to human beings—an area where it matched well with conservative instrumentalist views of nature (Ziemińska 2008), according to which humans were to "replenish the earth, and subdue it" (Genesis 1.28). Both Karl Marx and Vladimir Lenin were clear about the ultimate goal of communism in the rationalization of the use of nature as resource, a point that capitalism was not able to achieve in full (Topiński 1983, 154; Debardeleben 1985). That ideological and utilitarian attitude toward nature, building nature's relation with individuals as well as state power, can be referred to as the "communist environmentality." Edward Snajdr, who coined the term, notes that under communism "nature was not a political subject, such as literature, or a trade union, or religion" (2008, 22). This explains the initial lack of interest from the communist authorities in environmental movements, which helped those movements develop. "In fact, the communist regimes of the Soviet Union and East Europe," Snajdr continues, "considered their primary battle to be not with nature but, rather, with culture" (22). Nature, with its utilitarian or aesthetic role, was also not perceived as dangerous due to its recreational function and remoteness.

In consequence, state socialism was characterized by a complete disregard for the natural environment as a separate system (of beings and values), and by a far-reaching arrogance in remodeling it in an arbitrary manner. While grand engineering projects, forever changing or completely demolishing entire ecosystems, also took place in the capitalist world, it is probable that never in history were they achieved at such scale as in the Soviet Union (and to a lesser extent in its satellite states in Eastern Europe) (Kapuściński 2008; Siegelbaum and Sokolov 2000). "Raped and crippled, nature failed to deliver the riches one hoped it would; the total scale of design only made the devastation total. Worse still, all the raping and crippling proved to be in vain. Life did not seem to become more comfortable or happy" (Bauman 1992, 179).

This created a peculiar socialist landscape, in which elements of culture (architecture, urbanization patterns, collectivization of agriculture, heavy industry) were blended with natural decoration. Snajdr notes that it was through education and state-run media that "people were encouraged to view industrial complexes that sprang up at the edges of cities as monuments of the progress of socialism. Out in the countryside, giant grain elevators and huge tractor houses defined the new profiles of agricultural life"

(Snajdr 2008, 25). That socialist landscape saw both native environmental formations as well as older, historic ("backward") cultural elements as alien to its modernizing goals and thus redundant, worthless, and at times even dangerous. A focus on landscape as a major frame for the understanding of the environment also affected ecological studies, as in the 1970s the so-called "Soviet landscape school of thought" dominated Eastern European scientific ecological discourse (Jehlicka and Smith 2007, 6).

Inasmuch as the system was designed to monitor the activity of humans, it was also interested in monitoring nature. The socialist state "created bureaucratic departments whose purpose was to monitor and protect nature, alongside institutions designed to improve knowledge and develop technologies to exploit it," since "[nature] was, in the state-socialist imagination, a concern of the scientist and the engineer" (Snajdr 2008, 22–23). Experts, who according to the famous slogan "mastered technology," were to "decide everything" (Siegelbaum and Sokolov 2000, 128). They were, however, not to inform the general public of the state of nature, especially since it began to deteriorate rapidly due to the numerous interventions and the development of heavy industry. Petr Jehlička and Joe Smith provide a description of the way environmental knowledge was generated and how the expert elites were reproduced in East European communist societies.

> Communist institutional understandings of ecological problems were founded in scientific/technical worldviews. Hence ecological problems were interpreted by the regime as a mere temporary aberration that was to be resolved by ever more vigorous application of scientific and technical advancement. The dominance of science and technology in problem solving . . . was reflected in all aspects of intellectual life including the curricula at all levels of the educational system, in publishing policy and in research priorities. . . . [E]nvironmental studies at the tertiary level of education were taught within university departments and faculties of science and at polytechnics. The limited number of students allowed to enroll in these programmes was required to study a range of highly specialized scientific analytical methods and the (technical) management of protected areas. (2007, 5)

Insulated from the public, the environmental experts gained a considerable degree of freedom, as long as they stuck to the rules. Their specialized education made ecological experts on average incapable of wider critiques because "expertise was almost exclusively directed to ever better recording and understanding of the process of environmental deterioration rather than to developing policy proposals as to how these trends could be reversed or prevented" (Jehlicka and Smith 2007, 6). The authorities, on the other hand, were willing to withhold all potentially disturbing information, as was the case with the Chernobyl catastrophe.

Within this context, societal practices towards the environment were shaped differently in public and in private. The former was marked by a habitual disregard for both urban space and the natural environment, the latter by an absolutely opposite attitude toward all private space, including privatized nature, such as the small suburban garden plots and the countryside vacation cabins (Polish *działka*, roughly the equivalent of Russian *dacha*) (Bren 2002). These retreats gave socialist urban populations an experience of "nature" in its recreational role. Many were not interested in moving beyond that aspect or in noticing any further value of the environment. They were, however, very interested in the quality of the environment in general if it had a direct connection to their health. That was the minimal understanding of environmentalism that the opposition movements would build on, and which would become additionally politicized in the aftermath of Chernobyl.

The Environmental Crisis of the Late 1970s and 1980s

After World War II, Poland underwent rapid urbanization and industrialization, which had a significant impact on its natural environment. The apogee of destruction was reached during the Edward Gierek era (1970–1980). That was when numerous chemical conglomerates were created, particularly the chemical plants in Puławy on the Vistula River, in the town of Police on the mouth of the Oder River, as well as Gdańsk's Siarkopol chemical plant and its petroleum refinery on the Baltic coast, which generated pollution that turned the immediate vicinity into a moon-like landscape, sometimes irrevocably.

By the turn of the 1980s, the entire Eastern Bloc had sunk into an ecological crisis, with an alarming level of water, air, and soil pollution. At this point, the state of the environment could no longer be separated from the issue of public health, because industrial pollution, acid rain, and undrinkable water were directly affecting people's health and quality of life.

From today's perspective it may perhaps come as a surprise that the government of the People's Republic of Poland considered environmental protection to be an important issue. Already in 1972 a Ministry of Land Administration and Environmental Protection was created, making it one of the first such bodies in the world.[1] Many prewar nature reserves were turned into national parks. By 1981, Poland had fourteen national parks (only two were established before World War II), as well as a large number of natural reserves, landscape parks, and other protected areas. Despite formal protection, these areas were sites of extensive resource extraction and mass tourism (Hicks 1996). Nevertheless, the wide membership of the League for Nature Protection (Liga Ochrony Przyrody, or LOP), exceeding one million, made that official organization a significant force in shaping society's environmental discourse. From this emerged a dissonance between the preached "love of nature" and the visible state of the environment.

This does not change the fact that the natural environment was being systematically and mindlessly destroyed, mainly because the socialist model of extensive economy and the communist environmentality not only treated nature as an instrument and saw it as a resource for industry but also because it did not factor in environmental costs or even bother to measure the impact of heavy industry on the environment. Although the Centers for Environmental Research and Control existed, their inspectors only had manual equipment that was difficult to use for measurement (Nowicki 2014). In 1988, 75.8 percent of the rivers were classified as excessively polluted (Millard 1998). Similarly, soil pollution was severe, with some areas designated as zones of "environmental catastrophe" (Millard 1998, 146).

In the mid-1970s, the so-called "Poznań Pit" affair stirred up much controversy. The government was planning to create an industrial zone consisting of several factories and power plants and a large opencast brown coal mine. This investment was to extend into Wielkopolski National Park. Among the protesters of this idea were local government representatives, who had not been consulted on the plan, as well as scientists from the University of Poznań and the Poznań Society of Friends of Science (Poznańskie Towarzystwo Przyjaciół Nauki). They pointed out that the investment would lower the groundwater level and endanger Poznań's drinking water supply, as well as lead to the relocation of several villages. The government eventually abandoned the plan, citing economic concerns (Piotrowski 2017). This controversy is an early example of a nascent trend that united a broader network, including academics as well as local activists (Piotrowski 2015, 245).

In the 1980s, Polish society gradually became more aware of the dangers related to pollution, thanks to the growing "tangibility" of the apparent ecological crisis as well as the educational activities of various groups. The abolishment of censorship of ecological content during the Solidarity carnival (1980–1981) played an important role here. *Tygodnik Solidarność* (Solidarity weekly), the union's main weekly magazine, and other independent and later samizdat media featured many materials about actual environmental damage, often through the prism of resulting working conditions and health risks. Thereafter, despite the introduction of martial law, both the official governmental media and the underground publications of the political opposition discussed and wrote about environmental matters.

The Chernobyl disaster of 1986 spurred a breakthrough in these discussions, but ecology had become popular—and therefore increasingly troublesome for the government—even before that. The citizens of the People's Republic of Poland were learning about it through self-education and underground publications, and even the state-run TV inadvertently inspired homegrown ecologists by covering the antigovernment protests of green movements in the West. One of the leaders of the environmental protests in the 1980s explained: "Environmentalism was an obvious idea, it's popular among the youth, and close to many people's hearts. . . . The huge colorful Western demonstrations shown on TV, which everyone attended with their kids, seemed like one big picnic, and in our drab communist reality, we yearned for something this glorious."[2]

The First Environmental Movement Organizations: The Polish Ecological Club and "I Prefer to Be"

A degree of ecological awareness in Poland was not a novelty or fashion that came from the West but one that drew on a well-established national tradition (Kozielecki 2016; Szulecki 2011). Gliński and Koziarek argue that "the tradition of nature protection in Poland goes back at least to the thirteenth century" (2008, 187), although environmentalism in its modern form appeared only in the mid-nineteenth century (Urban 2016, 411–12). That said, while conservationist ideas neither appeared only during the communist era nor were fully overwritten by that experience (Ziemińska 2008), the societal context in which Polish political environmentalism emerged was characterized and conditioned by the communist environmentality.

The first modern nature protection organization in Poland was established in 1873 to protect the Tatra Mountains, and the country's regained national independence in 1918 quickly spawned a protoministerial Temporary State Commission for Nature Protection in 1919, which was replaced by a State Council for Nature Protection in 1925. Already in 1928, LOP emerged as the first nationwide general conservationist organization, bringing together members from all over Poland (Kozielecki 2016). In the eyes of the ruling power, the educational activities of LOP and the Nature Protection Watch (Straż Ochrony Przyrody, or SOP)—a volunteer-based organization set up in 1957 to enforce and control environmental protection measures—did not pose a direct threat to the regime (Gliński and Koziarek 2008, 191). Yet as the emphasis of the authorities was on economic efficiency and development, environmentalists often encountered hostility and ostracism from the state.

Despite the existence of official ecological organizations and a handful of independent circles interested in the subject, until 1980 there was no ecological movement to speak of in Poland. The democratic opposition, which developed over the latter half of the 1970s, did not address the issue of environmental protection, unlike the dissidents in Czechoslovakia or East Germany, for example. The "old" opposition was reluctant to take up such issues (Szulecki 2011).

The idea of dealing with environmental issues alongside purely oppositional activity originated in the Student Solidarity Committees (SKS) among young activists who worked closely with the older members of the Committee for Social Self-Defense "KOR" (the successor of KOR, the ad-hoc Workers' Defense Committee discussed in chapter 1). The creation of the Independent Self-Governing Trade Union Solidarity in 1980 opened a window of opportunity for all forms of bottom-up engagement and civic initiatives. Then SKS activist Jarosław "Jarema" Dubiel recalled discussing with his friend Mariusz Wilk the idea of creating a new organization whose scope would include not just the workers, as did Solidarity, but also other issues: the environment, young people, education. At that time, despite the enthusiasm, all ideas had to go through the opposition's semi-official central office, the head of which was the veteran dissident Jacek Kuroń. When Wilk went to him and presented this project for his approval, Kuroń laughed him off. "What, you want to fight for lab mice?" As Dubiel noted, "today when someone wants to fight for lab mice, it doesn't seem particularly funny, but back then it was code for 'get lost, there's nothing to talk about here.' So that got shot down."[3] Then came martial law and the idea got buried for years.

However, the Solidarity carnival period allowed for new forms of action and organization on the environmental front, especially due to the loosening of censorship and increased transparency, as well as moving the borders of what was acceptable by the party and the Security Service. A lot of the initiatives that took off at the time were not technically illegal according to Polish law—before 1980 nobody seriously considered using the legal means available as they would lead to politically contentious outcomes. As a result of the loosening control during the 1980–81 liberalization, LOP regained some of its independence, while other ecological organizations entered the scene.

In 1980, Kraków was a city where "water was undrinkable and the air unbreathable" (Topiński 1983, 148). Out of that catastrophic state of the environment grew the Polish Ecological Club (Polski Klub Ekologiczny, or PKE), an organization of concerned environmental experts and natural scientists. It became the first organized current of the environmental movement not inspired by and not controlled by the state (Kozielecki 2016). The first issue that mobilized environmentalists in Kraków was the local polluter—an aluminum smelter in Skawina, responsible for the horrific air quality, smog, and acid rain that gradually destroyed the medieval city's landmarks. A report issued by PKE experts on the state of the environment in Kraków, combined with other forms of pressure—including a lawsuit against the plant's administration and meetings with local and central government officials (Hicks 1996, 124)—led to the eventual closure of the Skawina plant. That was a major and rapid success for PKE but also the only such case where swift expert pressure prevailed (Topiński 1983).

In May 1981, PKE, which had been operating informally since the fall of 1980, was officially registered. The club, consisting for the most part of Solidarity members and sympathizers, modeled itself after the labor union: it, too, was structurally divided into sixteen regions (Hicks 1996). PKE played a key role in formal (and still legal) opposition activity, which consisted of using existing law and the expert status of members of the club to question governmental decisions that harmed the environment.

The club focused on expert-based efforts, e.g., undermining governmental policies and decisions through legal action, scientific analyses, and popularizing ecological problems using official channels. It avoided engaging with the public, though there was some internal debate on that subject. However, starting in the mid-1980s, the ecological movement began drawing its political strength from less formal groups that operated on the fringes of legality and openness, to the point of being somewhat "clandestine."

Expert-based activity was only part of the nascent environmental movement (Szulecka and Szulecki 2017, 2019). The environmental movement was created mostly by scientists, experts, journalists, young people (often associating in their own strictly youth-based groups, but also entering official organizations and revitalizing them in the process), farmers (especially those dealing with eco-friendly crops), and, to a lesser degree, workers (who participated actively in local conflicts). It is difficult to gauge the scale of the movement, as membership was informal. One of the main students of the environmental movement in Poland has identified 40 ecological organizations, 60 organizations that incorporated ecology into their activities, 40 ecological groups, 20 groups that dealt with ecological issues, and a dozen or so foundations (Gliński 1996).

Gliński's list suggests that the term "organization" means a formal group while "group" indicates an informal one. But gauging the membership or number of sympathizers of the entire environmental movement is difficult—one can only offer numbers for formal bodies. Aside from official organizations such as the LOP and SOP, which had many members (1.6 million and 42,000, respectively) but were not particularly active, the biggest independent active organization was the Polish Ecological Club (2,000–4,500 members) (Ostolski 2009).

The state-run media sometimes even inspired people to form ecological movements, as was the case with the "I Prefer to Be" Peace and Ecology Movement (Ruch Ekologiczno-Pokojowy "Wolę Być"), which grew out of the scouting magazine *Na przełaj* (Cross country) in 1984 (Kenney 2002). The name of the organization referred to Erich Fromm's "to have or to be?" dichotomy, where *being* signified moving beyond consumerism and materialism. The "I Prefer to Be" movement, due to its legal and semiofficial character, was able to establish a network far beyond the reach of opposition organizations, and it benefited from synergies with both scouting and official organizations like LOP. Although undoubtedly monitored by the Security Service, the movement could even count on the support of official party structures and access to mainstream media. For instance, one of its participants, Marcin Stoczkiewicz, who joined "I Prefer to Be" early in high school (and would remain an environmental activist for good), recalled a TV program in which he took part on behalf of the movement, representing "the youth."[4] However, for those reasons democratic opposition activists, as well as the independent and often illegal environmental groups that emerged in the second half of the 1980s, often treated "I Prefer to Be" with a degree of reticence, or even with open hostility—which is ironic, because the student activists, who later became the backbone of KOR, benefited from a very similar semiofficial status in the 1960s.[5]

Historians of the youth opposition from that period claim that the government initially saw new forms of youth activity such as environmental activism, rock music (and punk in the 1980s), counterculture groups, and football fan associations as "safety valves" (Vaněk 2002; Kasprzycki 2013). They allowed young people to blow off some steam, giving them an opportunity for controlled and very narrowly defined rebellion, thus turning their attention away from more political forms of opposition. That is why these initiatives were tolerated—though begrudgingly, as their participants were still sometimes persecuted. On the other hand, in Poland both during martial law and after it was called off in 1983, many opposition sympathizers viewed any form of collaboration with the institutions of the regime as highly suspicious.

In mid-1982, the military dictatorship of General Jaruzelski created the Patriotic Movement for National Rebirth (Patriotyczny Ruch Odrodzenia Narodowego, or PRON), a popular front bringing together all procommunist organizations, including the political parties and official trade unions. It was a reply to the dwindling communist party (PZPR) membership, and an attempt to create a constructive alternative to the delegalized Solidarity, which was still fresh in memory, even if its disbanding after an initial outrage led to sweeping apathy to social and political engagement. As it was organizations, not individuals, who entered PRON, many environmental experts found themselves on the new front, even though they were also members of the then unofficial PKE or even former members of Solidarity. The national scouting organization (ZHP) was also part of the front and so by consequence were its affiliated organizations, including "I Prefer to Be."

The Apolitical Politics of Nature: The Rise of Political Environmentalism and the Freedom and Peace Movement

With the introduction of martial law in December 1981, and the subsequent delegalizing of Solidarity, a search began for more neutral arenas in which one could attempt to confront the government. As Leszek Budrewicz, a student activist close to KOR who became one of the leaders of the young opposition in Wrocław, explained, "If I'm an anti-communist, and want to topple the government, and they beat me up for it—maybe it's wrong, but everyone thinks: 'Well, he had it coming.' But when I start focusing on parks, on leaves, people go 'Oh hell, why are they beating him up? It's just leaves.'"[6] Environmental protection, as a "politics-free" area, allowed for more freedom in organizing social initiatives (Kenney 2002).

Environmental protest never directly challenged the communist regime on ideological grounds and yet proved to be lethal for the totalitarian system because it gathered people, made them ask difficult questions and demand explanations, created situations of visible nonconformity, and enhanced civic activity in ways difficult to mute. Szerzyński points to that characteristic of environmental protest when he claims that "while being a highly culturalized form of politics, it cannot easily be categorized under many of the theoretical labels used to understand such politics" (1999, 221).

Increasing local conflicts accompanied the rise of ecological awareness in society, as the government's arrogance led to growing tension. The ostensible political neutrality of issues related to environmental protection caused many to flock to the burgeoning environmental movement, making it very ideologically diverse. During the mid-1980s, participants in and sympathizers with formal, half-formal, and entirely oppositionist ecological organizations varied in terms of their attitudes towards the government, the legality of their actions, their civilizational paradigms, and the circles that they came from, be they expert, professional, religious, youth-based, regional, or local.

Nothing illustrates that variety better than a look at the city of Gdańsk after martial law. The cradle of Solidarity, Gdańsk and the neighboring and connected cities of Gdynia and Sopot (together forming the Trójmiasto or "Tricity") were a stronghold of the workers' movement, which raised labor-related issues but had a visible conservative twist. In Catholic Poland, religion and politics intertwined in peculiar ways, and the alliance between the lay Left and the Church (not just its liberal wing) was an important driver of the 1970s opposition and Solidarity. In Gdańsk, there were also more openly conservative groups, all the way to neo-Nazi football hooligans. However, in parallel or perhaps precisely in response to that, the city also became a nest of some of the most radical movements in the country. Around 1983 a group of friends gathered together and in 1984 became the core of the Alternative Society Movement (Ruch Społeczeństwa Alternatywnego, or RSA), an anarchist milieu whose name was perhaps boastful compared to its initially modest numbers, but the group turned out to be important in the way it influenced the broader opposition.

In 1985, the Freedom and Peace (Wolność i Pokój, or WiP) movement was established. Evolving out of the campaign against mandatory military service and the oath of Polish-Soviet friendship, in time it expanded into other areas and soon became the main engine of Polish political environmentalism. Its intellectual eclecticism was not unusual in Central Europe at the time (Kenney 2002). WiP mastered quite well the skill of articulating its positions in the universally acknowledged language of human rights, helping their struggle to resonate well at home and abroad, and across the political spectrum (Szulecki 2011).

Under these new circumstances, Jacek Kuroń changed his mind about the eclectic themes championed by young opposition activists and, alongside another prominent KOR member, Jan Józef Lipski, became one of the few "old guard" oppositionists to support WiP and acknowledge its potential. Individual branches of the WiP movement that sprouted in various Polish cities had different ideological profiles: for example, the Wrocław and Gdańsk WiP, whose members were more closely affiliated with anarchist circles and with the flamboyant, quasi-artistic Orange Alternative movement, put a much bigger emphasis on ecology, while for those in Warsaw (more politically oriented) and Kraków (more conservative) it was a marginal issue. Gdańsk WiP activist Wojciech "Jacob" Jankowski, who was also linked to the anarchist RSA, recalled: "In 1984–1985, at a hippie convention, I met Wergilla—Beata Matuszak. She was firmly against nuclear power plants, and she knew people from the Polish Ecological Club. She inspired us—meaning RSA—to get into this issue."

Indeed, WiP—influenced by the Gdańsk and Wrocław anarchists—put a chapter on environmental protection in its *Declaration of Ideas,* a document meant to systematize the movement's eclectic agenda. Under point 4 of that chapter we read that although "Poland isn't at risk of dynamic development of nuclear power, attempts to transplant it onto Polish soil should be viewed—in light of experiences from other countries—with distrust." The declaration was published on 17 November 1985 in Machowa near Tarnów, before the Chernobyl disaster.

The new movements, WiP in particular, were skeptical of the "expert-based" tactics of PKE. They were looking for tangible, "concrete" issues around which they could mobilize people, not only those that were already involved in opposition activity. A similar strategy was adopted by the Silesian Ecological Movement, a group originating in the coalmining region of Upper Silesia and its sprawling industrial-urban areas.

As a result, the authorities considered these groups to be particularly dangerous. The Freedom and Peace (WiP) movement was especially so because of its combination of scope (national), topics related to the military (national security), degree of organization (WiP published a significant number of underground publications and attracted the attention of Radio Free Europe and the foreign media), and because it addressed many issues that excited young people. Therefore, these groups were combated by the authorities even during the limited liberalization of the late 1980s. The communist Security Service set up a reconnaissance operation code-named "Alternative," aimed at WiP. The operation had been closed only at the end of March 1990, while materials from the Office for State Protection, the democratic heir of the communist secret police, were transferred to the Institute of National Remembrance only after 1997.

Transcending the Iron Curtain at Last: Mrzeżyno—Poland's First Antinuclear Campaign

In 1985, vacationers in the seaside town of Mrzeżyno encountered giant, incredible sand sculptures along the shore. Whether walking from the town to the workers' holiday resorts, or the other way, they could not miss them on the beach. Massive, expressive shapes on a patch of sand thirty meters wide and thirty meters long. Some of them were humans, bodies twisted horribly in what looked like grotesque embraces resembling mass tombs. Faces screaming. The strong wind blowing from the land towards the Baltic Sea eroded the figures and shapes, and made the entire scene look even more surreal, like a glimpse of a nuclear Armageddon.

The sculptures were made by young activists from Silesia to bring attention to the nearby Soviet military base, to which nuclear warheads were soon to be transferred from the Soviet Union. The mastermind of this event was Wojtek Jaroń. In 1982, during martial law, he objected to his obligatory military service—for which he served thirty months in prison. When he got out, he joined the newly formed Freedom and Peace movement, setting up its Silesian branch, and later he initiated the Silesian Environmental Movement.

In the evening, Wojtek and his three friends would discuss the plan: what to do on the beach the next day. Not bold or crazy enough to try and barge into the guarded Soviet base, instead they wanted to reach the unaware majority around them, reach the people with their message about the warheads that were to be stationed nearby. But not just reach them with facts: they wanted people to *feel* the threat of nuclear war, of which the warheads were a part, a tool. They wanted people to reflect on the danger, the mutually assured destruction, and the senselessness of it all. Who were the warheads aimed at, really? The West? Or Poland? Who was the enemy? The West, or the Soviets who put the missiles there? This became the key theme, and the recurring slogan that they wrote in the beach sand and put on their banners was "Where are you, enemy?" They wrote it in Polish and German—as the town had a significant number of East German tourists—as well as in English and Russian. They wrote it in Russian because of the base nearby, which they treated as Soviet-occupied territory, and the pairing of English and Russian touched the essence of the Cold War conflict. Though on a microscale, they made their art experiment into a transnational protest event.

Until 3 PM a team with shovels would work on preparing a large space all the way up to the shoreline. After the groundwork was prepared, they sculpted. Every day something new, but all the time reflecting on similar themes. Jaroń explains:

> We'd use this part of the beach to create some archetypical forms that would communicate the danger of tactical nuclear warheads. Because it was 1985 and we couldn't just say it directly, we created an outdoor installation and made sand sculptures that expressed the theme of disarmament, then themes of Siberia, persecution, and other images closely related to the results of a nuclear conflict or the detonation of an atom bomb.

Another time, they built a huge sand wall to represent the East-West divide, and next to it was a large mast and a blue WiP flag.

It turned out that this installation was an ingenious idea: within hours of its completion, the wind did an incredible job on the sand, adding some dramatic flair to the sculptures. People would come from the nearby church

a b

c d

Figure 2.1a–d. (a) Mrzeżyno, sand sculptures. Photograph provided by Wojciech Jaroń. (b) Onlookers and tourists looking at the sand sculptures on the beach in Mrzeżyno. Photograph provided by Wojciech Jaroń. (c) Nuclear Armageddon depicted in sand. Photograph provided by Wojciech Jaroń. (d) Universal forms and writings in three languages, Mrzeżyno. Photograph provided by Wojciech Jaroń. As the original photographic negatives for these images have been lost, the quality of reproduced photographs is poor.

after mass, some would even lay flowers by the sculptures, so strong was the association with war and death. The parish priest encouraged those attending mass to "remember and visit the nuclear weapons boys."

The public was not a passive audience. Jaroń and his friends were eager to get people involved. They handed out shovels and asked passersby to help, so that every time at least four or five young people would be working together with the activists, and they also invited others to join in by expressing their feelings about the sculptures, while hundreds passed by, watched, and asked questions.

The happening was so successful that Jaroń organized it again in two consecutive years. Initially a bit undecided, by 1986 the activists were underlining their affiliation with WiP, wearing T-shirts with the movement's symbol (a hand showing the Solidarity victory sign but shaped like a peace dove). On large pieces of cardboard, they wrote some information about the Freedom and Peace movement, its motivations and goals—in Polish and, for the GDR visitors, in German. They also created an antinuclear book: on a sand table they put some pieces of paper bound with a piece of string, like a huge tome. In it they wrote information about the presence of atomic weapons, about the possible ramifications of a nuclear explosion, and about the necessity of disarmament both in the West and the East, which was an important argument that WiP introduced into the East-West peace dialogue (Szulecki 2013). They would stop people coming home after a day at the beach or strolling after dinner and ask them to sign the book, which meant that they had to read it first. This created new relationships, even friendships.

Tourists coming to Mrzeżyno often visited the site every day, and according to Jaroń, some were undergoing a change, as evidenced by the letters they wrote later, or by their coming back next year. Something inspired them, and they would think about it over the course of that year. In this seemingly carefree holiday resort, they were shown in a very vivid and dramatic way what lurked a mere two kilometers away. Women would come with strollers to show it all to their babies, people would sign the book and then start crying.

Jaroń had an explanation for these emotional reactions to their messages and to the form of the sculptures.

> In Mrzeżyno, another example of Polish absurdity manifested itself. Among these hundreds if not thousands of simple people, who came there for their summer holidays, many were members of Solidarity during the 16 months of the so-called Solidarity carnival and carried within them the defeat of martial law. It turned out that talking to

> them in the context of holidays, in a relaxed atmosphere . . . worked wonders on their psyche. . . . It was an anti-nuclear protest and a seaside gallery all rolled into one. There was this element of a shared awareness—it was probably the first time that these people saw and felt what a nuclear power plant is, what a nuclear disaster might look like, what it meant to have nuclear weapons in their country, and to have nothing to say about it. To know that in the event of a nuclear conflict, Poland would be turned into a crater. Everyone understood that, but no one was saying it aloud aside from WiP.

A Security Service assigned "guardian" came over every day, asking about the signs, writing down everything that was written on them. The WiP activists were just accepting his presence, they had to carefully balance the direct message with what they communicated between the lines, knowing that if the police decided to put an end to it, they could do it any day. But at the same time, they would prove them right and only legitimize their protest. In fact, it later turned out that there were no tactical warheads in Mrzeżyno, though there were nuclear missiles in the Pordborsko base, some sixty kilometers away.

The Mrzeżyno sculptures were the first protest against nuclear weapons, and also the first open *antinuclear* protest event in Poland. As we have seen, the Second Cold War and the nuclear crisis of the early 1980s hardly left a mark on Polish society, which was first preoccupied with Solidarity and then thwarted by martial law. The Freedom and Peace movement took up the issue of bilateral disarmament and engaged in transnational dialogue with Western peace and environmental movements. Some of that engagement was instrumental. Transnational contacts were empowering, they brought new resources (also financial) for domestic opposition activity, and no less important was the propaganda effect. The creation of Freedom and Peace introduced a true partner to talk with Western pacifists and a means to fight the communist propaganda at home. In public declarations, this exchange was to be reciprocal. But in internal statements, it was far more instrumental. Maciej Kuroń, the son of the KOR leader Jacek, argued at a hunger strike where the idea of a peace movement was first discussed: "We have to think how the Western peace movement can help us here, and not how we can help the Western peace movement." This instrumental view was especially clear among the Warsaw WiP activists gathered around the samizdat magazine *Czas Przyszły* (Future tense), who made transnational politics their specialty. One of the leaders of that group, and later Poland's minister of foreign affairs, Jacek Czaputowicz, pointed out:

> The political slogan of the peace movements in the West is unconditional disarmament, the postulate of the reduction of armaments. The entire cunningness of such a movement in Poland could be . . . to put forth identical claims. Our propaganda uses the peace movements for its own interest . . . By siding with them, we bring back a kind of political balance.[7]

However, instrumental motivations should not outweigh the genuine interest of young Poles in peace issues, especially the questions of conscientious objection, alternative military service, and pacifism more broadly. Talking the talk of Western independent organizations was a way to engage them and keep them interested, while among Western activists dialogue with unofficial (and in practice illegal) East European organizations was a contentious issue. Many older generation leftists in the West were very skeptical of such overtures, seeing them as striking the détente out of balance. But others, particularly the 1980s generation, including peace movement and Green leaders, wanted to see a "détente from below" (Szulecki 2015).

In a similar way, the growing environmental awareness could be framed in ways that resonated well with Western partners, thus expanding the audience to which WiP could address its message of human rights. Among environmental issues, nuclear reactor safety was perhaps the most resonant of all. And so, when "Jacob" Jankowski approached Czaputowicz with a list of antinuclear demands developed by the Gdańsk RSA and WiP circles, the latter rubbed his hands together, saying, "the Western peaceniks will love this."[8]

Notes

1. In the same year, the European Community adopted its first Environmental Action Plan in response to the UN Stockholm Conference and the so-called Club of Rome report "Limits to Growth." By comparison, the US equivalent of this ministry, the Environmental Protection Agency, was established in 1970, the French Ministry of the Environment in 1971, but the German Federal Ministry of the Environment, Nature Conservation, and Reactor Safety only in 1986, and the Swedish Ministry of the Environment and Energy in 1987.
2. L. Budrewicz in Kenney 2007, 122.
3. J. Dubiel, personal communication with K. Szulecki, Szczecin, 11 June 2010.
4. M. Stoczkiewicz, personal communication with K. Szulecki, 16 June 2021.
5. As a matter of fact, Seweryn Blumsztajn, one of the leaders of the rebellious students of 1968, and later a KOR and Solidarity activist, was also invited to talk about their discussion club on state TV.
6. L. Budrewicz in Kenney 2007, 122.

7. Quoted in "Społeczeństwo polskie a ruchy pokojowe" *Vacat [samizdat]* (32/33), 19 March 1985, pp. 69–76, here p. 70.
8. W. Jankowski's account in an email to K. Szulecki, 9 October 2018.

References

Bauman, Zygmunt. 1992. *Intimations of Postmodernity*. London: Routledge. http://www.dawsonera.com/abstract/9780203414934.

Bren, Paulina. 2002. "Weekend Getaways: The Chata, the Tramp, and the Politics of Private Life in Post-1968 Czechoslovakia." In *Socialist Spaces: Sites of Everyday Life in the Eastern Bloc*, 123–40. London: Bloomsbury.

Debardeleben, Joan. 1985. *The Environment and Marxism Leninism: The Soviet and East German Experience*. London: Routledge.

Gliński, Piotr. 1996. *Polscy Zieloni: Ruch społeczny w okresie przemian*. Wyd. 1 edition. Warszawa: Wydawn. IFiS PAN.

Gliński, Piotr, and Małgorzata Koziarek. 2008. "Nature Protection NGOS in Poland. Between Tradition, Professionalism and Environmentalism." In *Protecting Nature: Organizations and Networks in Europe and the USA*, ed. Kris Van Koppen and William T. Markham, 187–212. Cheltenham, UK: Edward Elgar Pub.

Hicks, Barbara E. 1996. *Environmental Politics in Poland: A Social Movement between Regime and Opposition*. New York: Columbia University Press.

Jehlička, Petr, and Joe Smith. 2007. "Out of the Woods and into the Lab: Exploring the Strange Marriage of American Woodcraft and Soviet Ecology in Czech Environmentalism." *Environment and History* 13(2): 187–210. https://doi.org/10.3197/096734007780473546.

Kapuściński, Ryszard. 2008. *Imperium*. Warszawa: Biblioteka Gazety Wyborczej.

Kasprzycki, Remigiusz. 2013. *Dekada Buntu. Punk w Polsce i Krajach Sąsiednich w Latach 1977-1989*. Krakow: Libron. https://lubimyczytac.pl/ksiazka/197726/dekada-buntu-punk-w-polsce-i-krajach-sasiednich-w-latach-1977-1989.

Kenney, Padraic. 2002. *A Carnival of Revolution. Central Europe 1989*. Princeton: Princeton University Press.

———. 2007. *Wrocławskie Zadymy*. Wrocław: Atut.

Kozielecki, Mateusz. 2016. "Historia Ruchu Ekologicznego w Polsce." Zielona Zmiana. http://www.zielonazmiana.pl/polska-i-swiat/polska/historia-ruchu-ekologicznego-polsce/.

Millard, Frances. 1998. "Environmental Policy in Poland." *Environmental Politics* 7(1): 145–61. https://doi.org/10.1080/09644019808414377.

Nowicki, Maciej. 2014. Przemiana truciciela Interview by Marek Józefiak. Tygodnik Powszechny. https://www.tygodnikpowszechny.pl/przemiana-truciciela-25210.

Ostolski, Adam. 2009. "Krótki kurs historii ruchu ekologicznego w Polsce." In *Ekologia: przewodnik Krytyki Politycznej*, ed. Michał Sutowski, 401–24. Warszawa: Wydawnictwo "Krytyki Politycznej."

Piotrowski, Grzegorz. 2015. "The 'Other' Democratization in Poland: The Case of Environmental Protection Movement." In *Democratization Through Social Activism:*

Gender and Environmental Issues in Post-Communist Societies, 235–64. Bucharest: Tritonic.

———. 2017. "Żarnowiec-Grobowiec. Opozycja Ekologiczna w Polsce i Kampania Antynuklearna." *HistMag*. https://histmag.org/Zarnowiec-grobowiec-Opozycja-ekologiczna-w-Polsce-i-kampania-antynuklearna-15099/3.

Siegelbaum, Lewis, and Andrei Sokolov, eds. 2000. *Stalinism as a Way of Life: A Narrative in Documents*. Translated by Thomas Hoisington and Steven Shabad. New Haven, CT: Yale University Press.

Snajdr, Edward. 2008. *Nature Protests: The End of Ecology in Slovakia*. Culture, Place, and Nature. Seattle: University of Washington Press.

Szerzynski, Bronisław. 1999. "Performing Politics: The Dramatics of Environmental Protest." In *Culture and Economy after the Cultural Turn*, ed. Larry Ray and Andrew Sayer, 211–28. London: Sage.

Szulecka, Julia, and Kacper Szulecki. 2017. "Polish Environmental Movement 1980–2017: (De)Legitimization, Politics & Ecological Crises." *ESPRi Working Papers* 6. https://doi.org/10.2139/ssrn.3075126.

———. 2019. "Between Domestic Politics and Ecological Crises: (De)Legitimization of Polish Environmentalism." *Environmental Politics*. https://doi.org/10.1080/09644016.2019.1674541.

Szulecki, Kacper. 2011. "Hijacked Ideas: Human Rights, Peace, and Environmentalism in Czechoslovak and Polish Dissident Discourses." *East European Politics and Societies* 25(2): 272–95. https://doi.org/10.1177/0888325410387643.

———. 2013. "'Freedom and Peace Are Indivisible': On the Czechoslovak and Polish Dissident Input to the European Peace Movement 1985-89." In *Entangled Protest: Transnational Perspectives on the History of Dissent in Eastern Europe and the Soviet Union*, 199–229. Osnabrück: Fibre.

———. 2015. "Heretical Geopolitics of Central Europe. Dissidents Intellectuals and an Alternative European Order." *Geoforum* 65 (October): 25–36. https://doi.org/10.1016/j.geoforum.2015.07.008.

Topiński, Piotr. 1983. "Ekolog w Polsce Ludowej." *Aneks* 31: 148–55.

Urban, Sergiusz. 2016. "Wilderness Protection in Poland." In *Wilderness Protection in Europe: The Role of International, European and National Law*, ed. Kees Bastmeijer, 409–31. Cambridge: Cambridge University Press. https://doi.org/10.1017/CBO9781107415287.

Vaněk, Miroslav. 2002. *Ostrůvky svobody: kulturní a občanské aktivity mladé generace v 80. letech v Československu*. Praha: Ústav pro soudobé dějiny AV ČR: Votobia.

Ziemińska, Julia. 2008. "Greening the New EU: A Constructivist Analysis of the Europeanization of Environmental Norms." MA Thesis. Amsterdam: Vrije Universiteit.

Chapter 3

The Chernobyl Catastrophe and Its Aftermath

The Chernobyl meltdown is widely acknowledged as a catalyst of civil mobilization in Eastern Europe, especially of those protest movements that focused on environmental issues (Kenney 2002). This effect is hard to deny across the region, where the second half of the 1980s was a period marked by a change in protest methods and causes. One crucial shift was the emergence of environmental protection as an issue that mobilized vast sectors of society—far beyond the traditional opposition in the various countries of the region. In Poland, this effect is perhaps most clearly visible. Before the Chernobyl catastrophe, environmental issues were discussed, as we have seen in the previous chapter, and some protests were held, but political environmentalism lacked a mobilizing potential. Conservationism was a domain of scholars and passionate, apolitical circles. Even the more contentious problems of health hazards related to pollution were mostly taken up by scientists and experts, such as those forming the Polish Ecological Club (PKE).

Following Chernobyl, the environment became an immediately recognizable problem and provided a new integrating arena of dissent. Environmental issues encouraged open opposition in the second half of the 1980s, after a period of communist backlash and the decline of the Solidarity trade union, which was forced to operate as a clandestine network and lost some of its societal appeal. Environmental mobilization, despite its seemingly apolitical nature, constituted an important field of political activity for old and new activists, combining a tangible issue with an opportunity to protest the communist regime. But thanks to the apparently apolitical nature of the problem, the risks involved in protests were perceived as lower, which encouraged broader groups to take part. The innovative protest repertoire, which was inspired by Western and non-Western nonviolent protest and civil disobedience actions, became a trademark that also increased the attractiveness of the post-Chernobyl opposition for new participants and onlookers.

In this chapter we look at the way the Chernobyl catastrophe affected Poland and the way the handling of the issue became a spark for initial dissatisfaction that led to spontaneous acts of protest. Once the initial anger faded, the public awareness of nuclear safety issues made the activists change their focus to domestic infrastructure, which we discuss in the following chapters.

Keep Calm and Avoid Spinach

On 26 April 1986, an accident during a test conducted in reactor 4 at the Chernobyl Atomic Energy Station in Soviet Ukraine led to the largest nuclear disaster in history (Higginbotham 2019; Leatherbarrow 2016; Plokhy 2019; Brown 2020). An explosion in the reactor room created a radioactive cloud that then spread over large parts of Europe. However, the Soviet government was reluctant to acknowledge the scale and disastrous nature of the incident even to itself (Brown 2020), and it was in fact the Swedish government that announced that an accident had probably taken place, once the radioactive cloud reached Scandinavia and high levels of radiation were recorded at Swedish nuclear facilities (Higginbotham 2019). Under international pressure, the Soviets were eventually forced to acknowledge the fact that something terrible had happened in Chernobyl, but the public statement was made only on 28 April (Plokhy 2019, 177).

Already in the early morning of 26 April, only some hours after the explosion, the radiation monitoring station in Mikołajki, in northeastern Poland, showed that the radioactivity in the air was 550,000 times higher than normal (Cymerman 2021). Later that day, the Swedish authorities published their findings, and once the source of radiation was identified as the USSR, Western-based Polish-language radio stations (e.g., the Polish section of the BBC and Radio Free Europe) broadcast the information to Poland, where news began to spread by word of mouth in the morning of 28 April.

The news of the alarming readings from Mikołajki reached the chairman of the Scientific Council of the Central Laboratory for Radiological Protection in Warsaw, who also heard the BBC broadcast and quickly connected the dots. With the help of his wife, who was affiliated with the Polish Academy of Sciences, he managed to directly inform the prime minister of their findings. Polish scientists and apparatchiks alike started contacting their Soviet counterparts with difficult questions.

However, like Soviet citizens, the Poles officially learned about the problem only two days after the explosion, on 28 April, through a laconic remark on the evening news. It was only on 30 April that *Trybuna Ludu* (The people's tribune), the party's flagship daily, and other national newspapers mentioned "an accident in Chernobylsk [*sic*]" and used a downright Orwellian tactic by suggesting that the matter "had already been described in the press."[1] The readers were also informed that a special commission, furnished with cutting-edge equipment, was monitoring the situation and that although a radioactive cloud was in fact moving over northeastern Poland, it was already almost gone and was never a threat to human health.[2]

Aware of the fact that Polish society might not be inclined to trust its own experts, the paper also quoted "Scandinavian scientists" who claimed that the radiation is so low that no special measures need to be taken.[3] Over the next few weeks the topic was widely discussed, with voices of reassurance ("the radiation is absolutely not harmful for pregnant women and children"), expert panels (one of which finally admitted when the accident occurred and when the cloud reached Poland), condemnation of Western governments and the United States for spreading "ridiculous misinformation," and reporting about seventeen historic nuclear accidents (in the US, West Germany, Japan, Great Britain, and Canada).

The weather in the region—both in Poland and the most affected Soviet republics—was unusually warm (21–23 degrees centigrade on 28 April), so before realizing the gravity of the situation, many people spent time outdoors, and Communist Party members were eagerly preparing May Day parades in cities and towns. The PZPR leadership toned down the rapidly rising popular anxiety, but the credibility of official media was very limited in the eyes of regular Poles.

It was also obvious that the authorities were saying one thing but acting as if they did not believe it themselves. On 29 April, the PZPR authorities appointed a government commission to combat the crisis, and the first priority was to reduce the risk of thyroid cancer inflicted by radioactive iodine I-131. Rapidly administering iodine, which began on the afternoon of 29 April, was later seen as exemplary governmental response in the event of a radioactive crisis (Cymerman 2021). It was the largest preventive measure in the history of medicine: in merely three days, 18.5 million people were given iodine. The pharmacies and local medical centers were open almost around the clock, and iodine solution was also distributed in schools.

While nuclear energy and radioactive safety authorities later praised Poland for the effective and speedy move, the broad distribution of iodine had a psychological effect with political consequences. The stable iodine solution, popularly known as Lugol's liquid and also dubbed "Russian Coca-Cola," would remain the symbol of the nuclear disaster for most Poles born between the early 1970s and early 1980s, leaving memories of the truly disgusting iodine liquid, which they were forced to drink in an atmosphere of general panic. Despite the official version of events, people across Poland, especially parents of small children, learned about the invisible danger of radioactive fallout, and Chernobyl changed from a far-off event into something close and frightening.

The authorities also issued food safety guidelines, and all fresh spring vegetables were removed from the market, alongside dairy products. Milk and butter, which were generally in short supply, first disappeared from the shops as panic buying followed the news, and then did not reappear as new safety regulations stopped new supplies. Powdered milk was handed out only to mothers of small children, who waited in long queues and received only one package "per one pair of hands" (Kietliński 2021).

But the contaminated vegetables were not simply thrown away. Tomasz Burek was an Independent Students' Association activist, studying history at the Pedagogical University in Słupsk on the Baltic coast, when on 26 April 1986 he was arrested for possession of illegal publications and printing materials. To help their investigation and to soften him up for interrogation, the police put him in a "stiff cell"—a maximum security unit, where he joined hard criminals, including some serving time for murder. The maximum security unit was cut off from the rest of the world, without access to radio, TV, and press. What he noticed, however, was that suddenly in May the food visibly improved. They were getting all the fresh vegetables they could eat, and never-before-seen volumes of milk and cheese.

He only understood what had happened when he left prison some months later. On a train he took on the way home, people were constantly mentioning the name "Chernobyl" as well as other strange names such as "Lugol"—and they seemed to understand each other perfectly. "What's Chernobyl?" Burek asked, only to see fellow passengers' astonished faces. "It pissed me off that I was not informed, that something was hidden from me," said Burek, adding that at the time his partner was pregnant.[4] That was his private path to antinuclear protest; following influence from the Gdańsk RSA and WiP circles, he would soon turn to environmental themes and the issue of their local nuclear power plant, under construction at Żarnowiec. Thanks to these experiences, Burek made an internal pledge to protest against the plant until its construction was stopped. For many others it was also a wake-up call.

"You Knew, but You Did Not Tell Us!"—The Wave of Spontaneous Protests across Poland

On 27 April 1986, the semiofficial youth environmental movement "I Prefer to Be" was preparing for a meeting with the official experts and the party bosses from the Patriotic Movement for National Rebirth (PRON). The meeting, planned for Monday, 28 April, was about the national nuclear energy program, and the movement's activists were invited to present the "youth's point of view." Their standpoint was highly critical and featured both economic arguments (e.g., on the profitability of investing in energy efficiency and new technologies) as well as ones related to reactor safety. Knowing that the battle would be hard, they read up, going through foreign antinuclear literature and the cases of known nuclear disasters.

In Warsaw the weather was particularly hot, and on Sunday afternoon the streets were almost empty. It was just a short walk—barely a mile from the YMCA building that housed the editorial office of the scouting magazine *Na przełaj* (Cross country), where youth movement members met—to the PRON headquarters in the governmental district at Aleje Ujazdowskie. They decided to put on a show, even though the meeting was supposed to be held only the next day. They prepared banners, primarily aimed at the most advanced nuclear energy facility in the country—the Żarnowiec Nuclear Power Plant, which was already being built near Gdańsk. Although the demonstration was, technically speaking, illegal, they did not expect to be stopped. They were, after all, representing an official organization and had been invited by PRON. Indeed, on their way, a policeman watched bemusedly as a group of young people carried posters and chanted antinuclear slogans—but he decided that nothing could be done about it (Wyka 1988).

They had no idea that while they sat at the editorial offices and prepped for their meeting, a radioactive cloud was in fact passing over Poland, and that as a result their protest stroll was perhaps more dangerous because of the contamination than because of the police. One of the founders of the movement, economist and environmentalist Ewa Charkiewicz, does not remember what the result of the meeting was, only that when she returned home that evening, her father, who was listening to Radio Free Europe, told her that "some nuclear power plant blew up in Sweden."

The next day, "frowning gentlemen" from the Security Service showed up at her apartment. On Monday morning, the activists were not allowed to enter the YMCA building and the editorial offices. Charkiewicz also noticed a policeman suspiciously interested in her car, and she received an unusual ticket for double-parking. These small acts of harassment were softer than what the political opposition groups would get but still a clear indication that the party was not happy with their sudden interest in nuclear energy at that particular time. Charkiewicz went down the escarpment on which the YMCA building stands, heading for a meeting with a friend on the bank of the Vistula River. She felt a strange taste of metal in her mouth but still did not know what it was—the official news would mention Chernobyl only that evening.

After they learned of Chernobyl, they gathered again at the offices of *Na przełaj* on Tuesday afternoon, picked up their banners and posters, and marched again to the PRON headquarters, but this time the reason was more obvious, and the anger quite real. That was the first recorded protest event following the Chernobyl disaster, though in the governmental district of Warsaw, few people could witness the short antinuclear march.

Anna Koczut, a Freedom and Peace participant, recalls that the scariest part of the entire situation was the disinformation. "People were wondering what they should really do, what they should give to their children. . . . Should they give them milk, or not? Or powdered milk? Feed them lettuce, or not? For political reasons we were cut off from sincere information."[5] That is why the situation had both an environmental and a directly political edge. And indeed, the anger at the authorities was most visible among women, especially mothers. "They loudly spat out phrases no worse than those on [underground] leaflets: a boycott of the communist parade [May 1], and refusing to support a regime which takes care only of itself and its militia. . . . They sounded like a threat. Little groups of women—strangers to one another—in front of stores, on the sidewalks, all talking about one thing" (Kenney 2002, 72).

The May Day parades were fast approaching—since the 1981 crackdown on Solidarity, that communist ritual festival was also an occasion for opposition counterdemonstrations. Usually, Solidarity sympathizers or members of the newer, more radical groups would attempt to sneak into the official parades and disturb them in some way, e.g., by unveiling their own banners when they passed by the party grandstand, and by chanting a few slogans before the police inevitably picked them up. The authorities were not sure what to do with the parades in 1986. They realized that these gatherings were a health hazard, and they also knew that in the wake of Chernobyl, the atmosphere in the crowd could be more tense. But they decided to follow the plan, pretending everything was under control and generally normal.

In Wrocław, "Jarema" Dubiel had something of an "I told you so" moment. He was one of the handful of oppositionists who were aware of environmental problems, and for some years now he was also trying to raise awareness of the risks of nuclear energy. He was one of the proponents of adding an environmental and antinuclear agenda to the *Declaration of Ideas* of the Freedom and Peace movement back in 1985. And then Chernobyl blew. "To every thinking person, Chernobyl showed you that borders don't really exist, which is something every self-respecting anarchist had been saying for ages," recalled Dubiel. "It's such a massive problem that it can go wherever it wants, and it's also downright deadly. So people started thinking, though very slowly at first." Dubiel's attempts to get the opposition circles interested in reactor safety and nuclear waste risks had mixed results. To his surprise, many in the Polish Ecological Club (PKE) were supportive of nuclear energy. "I attended their meeting once, there were something like seven people there, all midlevel ministry civil servants, and it was clear that they had no common view on the issue. When someone from PKE showed up at an event you never knew what to expect from them—will they support you or be against you."

He hoped that the opposition in Wrocław would jump on the opportunity to hit the government during the May Day parade with something related to the Chernobyl disaster. But at the parade there was not a single slogan referencing the current situation. As a matter of fact, the clandestine Solidarity did not manage to organize any larger demonstration on May Day that year, let alone adapt it to the recent news from Ukraine. The Ministry of Internal Affairs was watching the situation as anxiously as Dubiel, but from the opposite perspective—they were fearing mass unrest. Nothing of that was visible, and as the State Atomic Agency reported to the Security Service, the radiation levels on 1 May were already back to normal, though food remained hazardous.[6]

Dubiel came up with the idea of a small-scale peaceful protest—a sit-in (or "sitting," as it would become known in Polish opposition circles). At the time, this form of protest was still only experimented with. Apparently, Jacek Kuroń, the prominent KOR leader, had the idea of organizing an impressive sit-in featuring dozens of authority figures in defense of political prisoners—but in the end, nothing came of it, everyone had some excuse not to show up. Dubiel was not discouraged. He pitched the idea after the May Day parades, in a Freedom and Peace group meeting at the home of Marek Krukowski, a former medical student and Independent Students' Association activist, expelled for refusing to take the military oath. Leszek Budrewicz was also present, and he was initially very skeptical of the idea. They managed to convince him, but he forbade his wife Krystyna from taking part, apparently afraid of the police reaction to such a bold open act of protest. But Małgorzata Krukowska decided to join.

Budrewicz, Dubiel, the Krukowskis, and a group of friends sat down in Wrocław's top political demonstration spot—on the low stairs on one side of Świdnicka, a pedestrian street connecting the city's historic Market Square with one of its main communication hubs, with many shops and department stores. This was a natural spot, thanks to a modernist clock, which was a landmark and an easy meeting point, and to an underground passageway next to it that would keep up the flow of onlookers. The spot's inaccessibility by car made it safer from rapid police intervention. They unveiled banners demanding full transparency, identifying themselves as Freedom and Peace, and asking why the information on Chernobyl was kept from the public. The placards they held said, for example, "We demand full access to information," "Żarnowiec will be next," and "Is nuclear death from the East any different?" (Podsiadło 2010, 31). Krukowski recalls:

> We sat down, people were looking at us from afar. The police didn't react. It's interesting that they did not. . . . There were a number of people who supported WiP, from these, shall we say, alternative circles. . . . I was much more in contact with that sort of "underground" back then—the cultural one, not the political one. Several people from that scene came to the demonstration, even though I hadn't particularly been trying to talk them into it.

The sit-in protest organized by WiP was a novelty in terms of its form and, perhaps more importantly, its course. It was nonviolent, building on a rich tradition of civil disobedience previously known in Poland mostly from television. It was open, spontaneous, and bold—street actions were rarely taken up by the opposition after the imposition of martial law, and if they were, they more often than not ended in riots. Although the protesters were joined by some passersby and were surrounded by several hundred mostly sympathetic or indifferent onlookers, the police did not intervene. They sat out there for a long while before peacefully wrapping up and leaving.

Street demonstrations are a particular type of protest. According to social movement scholars, they can be aimed at persuading the authorities, at venting frustration, and at consolidating the participants (Van Stekelenburg, Klandermans, and Walgrave 2018). However, in a nondemocratic regime, they also aim at informing, persuading, and reaching out to the nonparticipants, making them aware of the frustration in the first place.

And so there were two surprising discoveries made thanks to that protest experiment. The first one was the positive reaction of the onlookers, as well as sympathizers who spontaneously joined—if not by sitting together, then at least by approaching the protesters, talking to them, and asking questions. As Krukowski explains, "It was the first public independent action. Before that everything was organized through informal channels someone can be told about and invited into, or someone can't. What we [WiP] were doing prior to that was only echoed by the mass media, you could hear something about it on Radio Free Europe. This was the first brawl, where people could touch us" (Smółka 1994, 52).

The other one was the police reaction, or lack thereof. No one was arrested, no one was beaten up. Although the authorities rejected the claims of protesters in the official rhetoric and the media, they did not suppress the growing dissent. This gave a totally new meaning to the opposition's slogan "Come with us, they are not beating today." WiP adopted the chant

Figure 3.1. The sit-in organized by WiP on Świdnicka street, Wrocław, 2 May 1986. Photograph: NAF Dementi, Archive Pamięć i Przyszłość.

as one of its trademarks because, in the case of the movement, this was indeed true.

Encouraged by these discoveries, the Wrocław WiP activists organized another protest a week later. This time they focused on the group that seemed most enraged by the handling of the Chernobyl disaster: the mothers. A group of female WiP participants (in fact only around five or six) marched down Świdnicka street with strollers, accompanied by their partners and childless activists, holding banners—this time specifying the potential risks for children. The crowd walked holding placards such as "Why were we informed so late?" and "We demand powdered milk for all the children." Numerous policemen watched the demonstration, but no one was detained. Despite the modest size—altogether, some twenty to forty people actively took part in the march, while a crowd of onlookers gathered to hear the speeches they gave once they reached the Market Square—Dubiel remembers that "there was this electricity in the air."

Radosław Gawlik, an environmental engineer trained in Czechoslovakia, also joined the two demonstrations and gave one of the speeches on nuclear fallout risks. His wife, Anna, by then a committed WiP activist and a veteran of a protest hunger strike, was one of the protesting mothers, pushing their child in a stroller, though the couple had second thoughts about protesting the risks of radioactivity by walking with an infant. Like Krukowski, the Gawliks were positively surprised by the lack of police crackdown, and Anna felt that "she hadn't risked much" (Kenney 2002, 72). All this made them consider the possibilities of environmental protests. Radosław would soon become Wrocław's main environmental protester, leading the struggle against the Siechnice smelter and other local polluters, in marches that would by 1988 reach the then unthinkable size of ten thousand participants. But the technicalities of the march had to be reconsidered: while the sit-in allowed the audience to interact, the march "kept passersby at bay" (Kenney 2002, 72).

The Chernobyl anniversaries also became occasions for staging protests. A year after the catastrophe, Krukowski and others blocked the city's main communication artery, Grabiszyńska street, with a twenty-meter-long banner with just one word: Chernobyl. It was as if there were nothing more that needed to be said, and the word itself conveyed the deeper message—*we remember that you knew, but you never told us.*

Krukowski prepared flyers for that event, to be handed out to drivers of the cars they stopped and to people boarding nearby trams. He made these not in the usual samizdat fashion, in clandestine printing houses of Solidarity, or on homemade press, but in a legal copy shop with a Xerox machine. They must have been forwarded to the police and the Security Service, but the authorities again did not react.

Figure 3.2. Protest march of mothers with strollers, organized by WiP in Wrocław, 9 May 1986. Photograph: NAF Dementi, Archive Pamięć i Przyszłość.

Another demonstration was organized by university students from the Gdańsk-Sopot-Gdynia Tricity as part of Gdańsk University's "University Days." On 7 May 1986, a large group of students, dressed up in costumes and holding banners, marched down the streets of Gdańsk to the embankment where they boarded a ship, which then took them to Sopot. There, the protest march was continued on the city's main boardwalk, the Monte Cassino Heroes boulevard. The organizers were linked to the university's chemistry club, established in 1981, and some of the posters they used were already present at demonstrations during the Solidarity carnival period. This event too—though illegal—was ignored by law enforcement. No one was arrested, no one was sentenced by a misdemeanor court, which was the go-to way of punishing open oppositionist activity in that period.

Less than a month later, post-Chernobyl protests spread to Kraków. A group of women activists had wanted to organize an environmental demonstration there for some time—the city was suffering from water pollution, smog, and acid rain. But Chernobyl provided an even more powerful frame. They set the date of the protest on 1 June, Children's Day, to "keep that for-the-future-generations vibe" as Dubiel puts it. They showed up at the historic Market Square with dried flowers, meant to symbolize the death of nature (Kenney 2002, 72). As this was the conservative old capital city, the event started with a Holy Mass at the iconic St. Mary's cathedral. The church was packed, and as the worshipers stepped outside, they were greeted by another group, including many WiP activists, holding banners and distributing fliers. The "Mothers of Kraków" were demanding the truth about radiation risks and the nuclear power plant accidents. Other banners read "The lives of Polish children born in 1980 will be at least 10 years shorter than those of their Western counterparts," "We demand compensation from the USSR," and "I'll trade in a large apartment in Kraków for a sleeping bag in New York." The crowd grew, some accounts claim it reached ten thousand people, and the police appeared around them but did not intervene. Then the march headed to the royal castle on Wawel hill, chanting, among other things, "We don't want iodine from the East!" Dubiel sums it up: "I think it was a great success—ten thousand people marching in the name of Chernobyl. . . . Just let the police try to use force here. Seeing that ZOMO [riot police] wasn't reacting, everyone felt more confident. After all, there were ten thousand of us there."

Budrewicz, described the nascent environmental protest movement as benefiting from the "luxury of small disobediences" (Budrewicz 1987), although in terms of numbers of protesters, these disobediences were becoming quite large. The visibly positive and impressive results of the protest popularized the Freedom and Peace movement, especially in Wrocław, and opened many doors within the "older" opposition. Before establishing its own samizdat network, WiP used Solidarity's channels and just days after the sit-in issued an appeal for "gathering all possible information on the Chernobyl threat" through the high-circulation Solidarity journal *Tygodnik Mazowsze* (Mazowsze weekly).

The Chernobyl Effect: Elements and Impact

On 15 May 1986, major Polish papers reprinted, in full, the text of the fatherly television address by Mikhail Gorbachev, who assured viewers that both Soviet and allied citizens were informed "as soon as we got the full picture of the situation," sniped at the US and NATO for their "unworthy lies," and claimed that "the worst is already behind us."[7] He was gravely mistaken: for the leadership of the Soviet bloc states the worst was still to come.

The way the Chernobyl disaster was handled ended up being a key factor in the subsequent development of the environmental movement, as well as other independent opposition initiatives in Eastern Europe. We can even speak of a "Chernobyl Effect," which is discernible across Eastern Europe (Arndt 2016), but which had a particularly strong effect on Poland due to a confluence of factors. The disaster posed an immediate danger to people's health, but the authorities decided to hush it up, or at least to delay the information for several days so as to not derail the May Day celebrations. A protest against this type of governance—with power wielded against society, at its expense—did not require any ideological coloring. At the same time, the fallout from the disaster, as well as the entire growing ecological crisis, affected children, adults, and seniors alike, even if they worked for the authorities. It was impossible to ban talking about these issues, so the protests could not be stopped easily. A good example of this is a Wrocław demonstration against the Siechnice industrial plant, which was polluting the Oder River, where people yelled "The police drink the same water!" at law enforcement officers. This new situation allowed for new forms of opposition to emerge on an unparalleled scale. The nuclear energy issue became the linchpin, as it was directly responsible for the Chernobyl disaster and could be linked to nuclear disarmament, which was a hot topic in the 1980s.

In Marek Krukowski's view, Chernobyl was an important spark, which started a larger fire that would otherwise not ignite. "We didn't really know how to start this fight. I think our success in combatting Żarnowiec owes much to the fact that Chernobyl redirected our attention to other nuclear infrastructure that was already there, not just the Żarnowiec power plant, but also the issue of nuclear waste." This is echoed by other activists' accounts. Małgorzata Górczewska, who was close to the anarchist RSA and the Gdańsk WiP circle, emphasizes that "the Chernobyl accident was, not only for me, but for many people in our milieu, a breaking point in environmental awareness and led to our active involvement in a lot of activities, from printing leaflets, making posters, and gathering signatures to direct street protests."[8] The movements established around 1984–1985 provided preexisting mobilization structures when the Chernobyl accident suddenly opened a new window of opportunity for protest.

Following the collapse of the Solidarity opposition during martial law, a new wave of independent groups cropped up in the mid-1980s. They were initially anarchist and pacifist in nature, and thus generally belonged to the counterculture. These new social movements were populated by a new generation of activists, born mainly in the 1950s and 1960s, though younger members had joined by the end of the decade. These new activists were geared toward resistance against the communist system, but also against the politics of the leaders of the old Solidarity movement, which was considered to be too conciliatory and lacking momentum.

This trend also spurred new arenas of oppositionist activity and new forms of action. As far as new arenas go, the biggest issue was the fight to abolish mandatory military service, started by anarchists from the Alternative Society Movement and continued by the Freedom and Peace movement. They changed the thrust of their protest from the contents of the military pledge—advocating for the removal of a passage about alliance fidelity to the USSR and the key role of the PZPR—to requesting a civilian service option, in keeping with the RSA's demands.

Ecology became a second new and important arena. Various topics were taken up, including the pollution of drinking water by the Siechnice steelworks near Wrocław and by the chemical plant at Police. However, the main fight was against the construction of nuclear power plants and the resultant expansion or construction of new radioactive waste disposal sites, as we will describe in detail in the following chapters. This led to the creation of groups dedicated mostly to this topic, such as the Green Federation (Federacja Zielonych), the Franciscan Ecological Movement (Franciszkański Ruch Ekologiczny, or FRE), the revived (following martial law) Polish Ecological Club, and the "I Prefer to Be" movement, which was gradually growing independent from the government. Their activities varied in nature, from discussion among a closed circle of experts (akin to PKE) to educational activities (FRE, for instance, organized meetings in churches), all the way to various types of legal and illegal demonstrations (Szulecka and Szulecki 2017).

The forms of protest—and, more broadly speaking, independent activity—likewise varied. The most common techniques, which provided information and reminded people that the opposition was still alive and kicking, were traditional samizdat publishing and a new form of communication—graffiti. In the second half of the 1980s, radical opposition groups, such as the Fighting Solidarity (Solidarność Walcząca) or the Federation of Fighting Youth (Federacja Młodzieży Walczącej), made riots with stones and even petrol bombs their trademark. The state security apparatus challenged these with the notorious Motorized Citizens' Militia Reserves—Zmotoryzowane Odwody Milicji Obywatelskiej, or ZOMO, antiriot police units armed with plastic shields, long truncheons, water cannons, and tear gas. In the midst of that, nonviolent protests also appeared, drawing inspiration from the teachings of Mahatma Gandhi and events such as the American Civil Rights Movement. It was an alternative that was welcomed both by many opposition sympathizers and by the police, who were inclined to treat peaceful protesters with respect.

We can identify two main forms of nonviolent protest. One was passive protest, first in the form of the aforementioned sit-ins, or "sittings": protesters would sit down in the street with banners explaining the reason for their protest in order to amplify their message and make it more difficult for law enforcement to intervene. In time they also included versions of what goes under the name "monkeywrenching" in Western environmental movements: *daching* (from the Polish *dach* ["roof"]), in which participants occupied the roof of a newsstand, a bar, a pharmacy, etc., as well as *ruszting* (from the Polish word for "scaffolding"—*rusztowanie*), in which protesters climbed scaffoldings and tied themselves to them with rope. The second technique was *happenings,* performance events that were initially the domain of the Orange Alternative—a surrealist, artsy protest movement originating from Wrocław—but which were soon adopted by other groups, not only anarchists and pacifists but also groups advocating for independence. At times, the happenings parodied the official work of the government; other times they took on a more artistic quasi-theatrical character (as in the already mentioned case of Mrzeżyno), where the medium became part of the message to make it more attractive or more resonant by amplifying its emotional impact.

One thing that set these new movements apart from underground post-Solidarity opposition was their overwhelmingly overt nature (Szulecki 2019). Members of WiP worked openly, revealing their names, addresses, and telephone numbers to the samizdat press. The human rights committees, the source for some of the founding members of WiP, followed suit. This approach wasn't specific to just WiP: the Workers' Defense Committee (KOR) and the Movement for Defense of Human and Civil Rights also acted openly, and even those Solidarity and radical militant Fighting Solidarity members who were in hiding gave out their names. It was a breath of fresh air after years spent "underground." Indeed, it was important to risk and even court repression in order to humiliate the government and its impotence. This was a conscious nod to the tradition of passive resistance and the ideas of Mahatma Gandhi and the Reverend Martin Luther King.

Refusal of military service was one of the early fundamental acts of protest, followed by a boycott of military studies at universities (analogous to traditional strikes, except that they did not always include an occupation of the workplace or school), sit-ins, and hunger strikes. That last, most radical form of nonviolent protest usually had a deadline and was dedicated to a specific cause, such as defending detained colleagues. But there were also open-ended hunger strikes. The most publicized objector, Sławomir Dutkiewicz, whose case was the initial spark for the formation of WiP, was detained for refusing military service. Dutkiewicz began an indefinite hunger strike and was eventually forcibly fed. All these elements became part of WiP's "oeuvre" and were therefore also used in the antinuclear campaign.

As we can see, the evolution of political environmentalism in Poland was similar to that in the West, though delayed by about a decade. Official ecological institutions and associations of natural scientists were gradually transformed and enriched with wider movements grouped around certain environmental concerns or acting in accordance with the spirit of deep ecology (Kozielecki 2016). The dominant trend in the 1980s was the so-called protective ecology, sometimes called the "ecology of fear," which underscored the necessity of preventing further ecological disasters that would make life on Earth even harder, and eventually impossible.

Alongside the ecology of fear, in terms of strictly ecological movements, there was "deep ecology," which advocated for the protection of nature not just because it is our habitat, but for the sake of nature itself. This more radical form of ecology rejects industrial capitalism and modern civilization. In the West, radical ecological organizations often took on a distinctly countercultural character, creating a platform for criticizing society and civilization. In Poland, even though proponents of "deep ecology" were growing in popularity among young activists, the movement did not turn into a rebellion against civilization as such. Instead, it was mostly a tool used to resist the authoritarian policies of Communist Poland. It was only after 1989 that more radical and deeply ecological (but also mostly fringe) organizations set their sights on industrial civilization itself (Szulecka and Szulecki 2019).

That said, the year 1985 also saw the establishment of the first Polish animal rights organization, Gaja. There were also certain local activist groups and initiatives facing environmental threats emerging in their area, as well as countercultural movements promoting an ecological lifestyle such as the Living Architecture Workshop (Kożuchowska 2007). Although officially registered in the 1990s, the Workshop for All Beings (Pracownia na rzecz Wszystkich Istot), was already functioning in 1988–1989. Its members organized local protests in Southern Poland over the Wapienica Valley, against urban forestry cuttings in Bielsko-Biała, against a coke fuel plant in the neighboring Czech Stonava, and against the Żarnowiec Nuclear Power Plant. Issues such as the pollution of the Baltic Sea as well as global warming were beginning to be discussed, although the environmental movement lacked the capacity to act internationally due to difficulties with traveling and interacting across the Iron Curtain.

In sum, by the second half of the 1980s, Poland boasted a full spectrum of environmental organizations, from official ones linked to the state, through independent elite and expert groups and semiofficial youth associations, to unofficial and openly political dissident movements (Szulecka and Szulecki 2017; Hicks 1996; Kozielecki 2016; Ostolski 2009).

Environmental activists focused on studying the issues related to environmental protection, educating organization members and the general public, publicizing ecological issues, organizing interventions, putting pressure on the government, and attempting to change people's attitude towards nature (in the spirit of deep ecology and promoting vegetarianism). Activists attempted to combine various types of actions in the spirit of the famous rule: "think globally, act locally." Young people especially appreciated WiP's actions for their spectacular nature and exceptional effectiveness, which stood in stark contrast to the impotence of Solidarity or official organizations.

Notes

1. "Awaria elektrowni atomowej na Ukrainie" *Trybuna Ludu*, 30 April–1 May 1986, p. 1.
2. "Komunikat Polskiej Komisji Rządowej" *Trybuna Ludu*, 30 April–1 May 1986, pp. 1–2.
3. "Opinie ekspertów skandynawskich" *Trybuna Ludu*, 30 April–1 May 1986, p. 2.
4. T. Burek in Waluszko 2011.
5. A. Koczut in Kenney 2007, 154.
6. See: IPN BU 0296/146/3, k. 188–189.
7. *Życie Warszawy*, 15. May 1986, pp. 1–*passim*.
8. M. Górczewska's Account in an e-mail to K. Szulecki, 2 June 2021.

References

Arndt, Melanie, ed. 2016. *Politik und Gesellschaft nach Tschernobyl: (ost-)europäische Perspektiven.* Kommunismus und Gesellschaft, Band 1. Berlin: Ch. Links Verlag.

Brown, Kate. 2020. *Manual for Survival: A Chernobyl Guide to the Future.* London: Penguin Books.

Budrewicz, Leszek. 1987. "Luxus zu kleinen Unverantwortlichkeiten: Interview mit Leszek Budrewicz." Interviewed by Helene Konstantin. *Die Tageszeitung,* 6 May. https://taz.de/I-N-T-E-R-V-I-E-W-Luxus-zu-kleinen-Unverantwortlichkeiten/!1866702/.

Cymerman, Beata. 2021. "Chernobyl 35 Years on—the 'Polish Puzzle.'" Heinrich-Böll-Stiftung. https://eu.boell.org/en/2021/04/26/chernobyl-35-years-polish-puzzle.

Hicks, Barbara E. 1996. *Environmental Politics in Poland: A Social Movement between Regime and Opposition.* New York: Columbia University Press.

Higginbotham, Adam. 2019. *Midnight in Chernobyl: The Untold Story of the World's Greatest Nuclear Disaster.* Reprint edition. New York: Simon & Schuster.

Kenney, Padraic. 2002. *A Carnival of Revolution. Central Europe 1989.* Princeton: Princeton University Press.

———. 2007. *Wrocławskie Zadymy.* Wrocław: Atut.

Kietliński, Marek. 2021. "1986—Wybuch w Elektrowni Atomowej w Czarnobylu." Miasto Białystok. https://www.bialystok.ap.gov.pl/arch/kalendarium/26_04.htm.

Kozielecki, Mateusz. 2016. "Historia Ruchu Ekologicznego w Polsce." Zielona Zmiana. 2016. http://www.zielonazmiana.pl/polska-i-swiat/polska/historia-ruchu-ekologicznego-polsce/.

Kożuchowska, Olga. 2007. "Jak Widzisz Ruch Ekologiczny w Polsce i/Lub Na Świecie?" *Zielone Brygady.*

Leatherbarrow, Andrew. 2016. *Chernobyl 01:23:40: The Incredible True Story of the World's Worst Nuclear Disaster.* Milton Keynes: Andrew Leatherbarrow.

Ostolski, Adam. 2009. "Krótki kurs historii ruchu ekologicznego w Polsce." In *Ekologia: przewodnik Krytyki Politycznej,* ed. Michał Sutowski, 401–24. Warszawa: Wydawnictwo "Krytyki Politycznej."

Plokhy, Serhii. 2019. *Chernobyl: The History of a Nuclear Catastrophe.* London: Penguin Books.

Podsiadło, Jarosław. 2010. *Krótki Kurs Historii Ruchu Wolność i Pokój.* Gdańsk: Maszoperia Literacka.

Smółka, Anna. 1994. "Miedzy Wolnością a Pokojem." MA thesis. Warsaw: Warsaw University.

Szulecka, Julia, and Kacper Szulecki. 2017. "Polish Environmental Movement 1980–2017: (De)Legitimization, Politics & Ecological Crises." *ESPRi Working Papers* 6. https://doi.org/10.2139/ssrn.3075126.

———. 2019. "Between Domestic Politics and Ecological Crises: (De)Legitimization of Polish Environmentalism." *Environmental Politics* 0(0): 1–30. https://doi.org/10.1080/09644016.2019.1674541.

Szulecki, Kacper. 2019. *Dissidents in Communist Central Europe: Human Rights and the Emergence of New Transnational Actors.* Palgrave Studies in the History of Social Movements. Palgrave Macmillan. https://doi.org/10.1007/978-3-030-22613-8.

Van Stekelenburg, Jacquelien, Bert Klandermans, and Stefaan Walgrave. 2018. "Individual Participation in Street Demonstrations." In *The Wiley Blackwell Companion to Social Movements: New and Expanded Edition*, ed. David A. Snow, Sarah Anne Soule, and Hanspeter Kriesi, 371–91. Hoboken: Wiley.

Waluszko, Janusz. 2011. "Wspomnienia Tomasza Burka, Współorganizatora Kampanii Przeciw Budowie Elektrowni Jądrowej Żarnowiec: Spisane i Opracowane Przez Janusza Waluszko." https://www.siemysli.info.ke/kampania-przeciwko-elektrowni-atomowej-w-zarnowcu-wspomnienia-tomasza-belfra-burka/.

Wyka, Anna. 1988. "Ruch Wolę Być." *Państwo i Kultura Polityczna*, no. 4.

Chapter 4

"No Atom in Our Home"

Targeting Domestic Nuclear Facilities

As we have seen in the previous chapter, the Chernobyl catastrophe was not only a massive industrial disaster with tragic environmental consequences. It was also an unprecedented blow to communist governance, exposing its opaque decision-making, poor technological oversight, and the direct dangers that controlled information flows create in such emergency situations. All this led to political fallout that the regime found impossible to clean up, and that radiated dissent.

Chernobyl anniversaries continued to be occasions for smaller-scale demonstrations across Poland, particularly in big cities that were home to larger opposition structures, especially WiP circles. But protests spread to other urban areas too. On the second anniversary of the disaster in 1988, there were demonstrations in several cities, including a 28 April rally outside a department store in Opole, a regional capital in southwestern Poland with some 120,000 inhabitants. The rally was followed by a banner march through the city center. The next day, six people were arrested at a similar rally in Szczecin, a major industrial hub in the northwest of the country, home to some 400,000 people.

The scale and character of the new post-Chernobyl protests were in many ways unexpected and created new opportunities for mobilization and for challenging the regime in relatively safe ways. It is therefore not surprising that as the immediate post-Chernobyl momentum faded, new issues were adopted, and the most pressing question that many, not only the activists, asked themselves was whether a similar accident could happen in Poland. That is when they turned their attention to domestic nuclear facilities, the potential Chernobyls in their own backyard, and found many causes for concern.

Already in October 1985, Beata Matuszak (under the pen name Kaya) published an article entitled "Nuclear Energy: Fiction and Facts" in the anarchist RSA magazine *Homek*. Kaya claimed that "peaceful" and "safe" atoms were myths and stressed that much more money is invested in nuclear energy than in renewable energy because the former can also lead to obtaining nuclear weapons. Moreover, radiation is invisible and only harmful in the long term (many victims of Hiroshima and Nagasaki died years after the bombs were dropped, for example, while the French nuclear plant in La Hague led to diseases and mutations among fish living nearby). Nuclear is neither safe nor cheap and it requires special oversight, argued Kaya, which lends the technology to totalitarian practices. These ideas, very much in line with the popular thinking in the Western environmental and antinuclear movement at the time, were a novelty in the Polish context, and the article was an intellectual bomb dropped by the Gdańsk anarchists, who would from that time become a leading force in the emerging antinuclear protest.

In a subsequent article in *Homek*, written in May–June 1986, Matuszak emphasized that in the aftermath of Chernobyl it was no longer enough to just hypothetically muse about nuclear energy because its cleanness and safety had been proven to be a fiction: "Żarnowiec is the same thing" as Chernobyl, "only much closer." That sentiment would soon become very popular all over Poland, and not just among the most environmentally aware activists.

A narrative deftly constructed by the emerging political environmentalist movements drew a parallel between the Soviet power plants and the ones that were supposed to be built in Poland. Starting in the late 1970s, the PZPR leadership planned to build several nuclear power plants (NPPs): the Żarnowiec NPP, the construction of which was confirmed in 1982 and located near the cities of Gdańsk, Gdynia, and Sopot (the Tricity) on the Baltic coast; the Warta NPP, located on a major river of the same name in Klempicz, in the western region of Greater Poland (*Wielkopolska*), near Poznań, which was planned for 1987–1998; and other potential NPPs on Lake Kopań near Darłowo (on the Western Pomeranian stretch of the Baltic coast) and in Chotcza on the Vistula River (southeast of Warsaw). Additional friction was caused by the existing and planned radioactive waste disposal sites: Różan and Międzyrzecz.

All these sites were quite remote from the centers of Polish political opposition until that time. Warsaw, Gdańsk, Kraków, Wrocław—those were arguably the main hubs of dissent. Yes, workers' protests could erupt in smaller industrial centers, such as the 1976 riots in Radom and the 1980–1981 wave of Solidarity-related strikes that swept through pretty much the whole of urban Poland. However, the smaller industrial towns could not count on the same level of national attention, and sometimes—as was the case with the female textile workers strike in Żyrardów in November 1981—they were not even endorsed by the Solidarity trade union (Leszczyński 2005). Opposition elites could organize meetings in remote locations, as did the KOR leadership who met their Czechoslovak counterparts from Charter 77 in the mountains on the state border, or the core WiP activists who met in the village of Machowa. But the power to mobilize open protest ended roughly at the level of regional metropoles, voivodeship capitals, and medium-sized cities of some one hundred thousand inhabitants. Protests were grassroots, as long as it was urban grass you had in mind.

The dispersed infrastructure of the nuclear program was therefore a new kind of challenge but also a new opportunity to organize protests in places where no open dissent had been seen since the establishment of the People's Republic. Localization of protests, however, meant that they were not geared towards resisting nuclear energy as such but merely opposed its presence in a particular location, like Międzyrzecz, Chotcza, Różan, or Klempicz. The broader context was addressed in the big cities, where protests were partly attached to the NPPs in the regions but framed in national terms, as in Poznań and subsequently—on a bigger scale—in Gdańsk, where already during the first event people protested not only against Żarnowiec but also Klempicz. Local activists also eventually initiated the nationwide Agreement on Alternative Energy (Porozumienie na rzecz Energetyki Alternatywnej).

In this chapter we will first briefly recapitulate the history of the Polish nuclear program, which started in the 1950s but saw the first building permits issued and infrastructure constructed only in the 1980s, and the emergence of a technocratic elite—the "apostles of the atom"—who would later be pivotal in Poland's turn towards nuclear energy. We then go through the initial protests against the most advanced of the NPP projects—Żarnowiec—and focus on the unprecedented and successful example of grassroots mobilization in a small provincial town related to the Międzyrzecz nuclear waste storage facility.

The Polish Nuclear Program

The first preliminary plans for building an "industrial" nuclear power plant appeared in the second half of the 1950s under the leadership of PZPR's First Secretary Władysław Gomułka (1905–1982). At the time, the coal sector was still relatively underdeveloped (Bendyk et al. 2015). Large hard coal reserves and an accompanying industrial complex of mines, power plants, and heavy industry was developed in the Upper Silesian basin, and the "black gold" was also extracted in Lower Silesia—a region taken over from Germany after 1945. However, electrification of the countryside was limited and constituted a major ambition of the communist authorities (Derski and Zasuń 2018). For that, all new sources of energy were explored, and nuclear was certainly seen as the most attractive technology at the time.

The first research nuclear reactor in Poland, "Ewa," was launched in 1958 in the Warsaw suburb of Otwock-Świerk. This high-powered research reactor gave rise to the idea of large-scale atomic energy in Poland. It is, however, a long way from a mere idea to the implementation of even preliminary plans. Toward the end of the 1950s, a nuclear energy section was created at the Warsaw University of Technology (Politechnika Warszawska), which soon yielded its first engineers. According to Jan Ryszard Kurylczyk, a politician, engineer, and former director of, among other things, the Żarnowiec plant complex and Pomeranian voivod:

> [In] the 1960s, Polish nuclear physics reached a new level, thanks to the research reactor in Świerk. There were a lot of publications. Our scientists were very bold. Our theories on the fundamentals of physics were shocking, revolutionary. . . . Thanks to these contacts, Poles were often given scholarships, both young people and postgraduates, as people saw that we brought something new to the table. There was a high demand for Polish physicists in laboratories, on scholarships.

However, the realities of Poland's technological and industrial capacity diverged considerably from the exceptional level reached by its experimental and nuclear physics. Under Gomułka, the country was focused on postwar reconstruction and on reaching modest levels of consumption. While the symbol of Polish technological prowess at the time was the "Syrena" car manufactured in Warsaw, a rather mediocre achievement even by Eastern Bloc standards, Kurylczyk emphasizes that "the country was riding a futurologist wave then. Industrial realities did not matter. That's just us. We're great at abstractions, but not that amazing when you actually have to do something manually."

The late 1950s and the 1960s were indeed an age of faith in progress and technology, of fascination with the conquest of space, and finally, of belief in the power of the human mind, which managed to split the atom. The most internationally renowned Polish symbol of that technoscientific mindset was the novels and short stories by the sci-fi guru Stanisław Lem, who produced his best-known works at the time.

It was also then that a group of highly educated, passionate individuals appeared, soon to become the "apostles of the atom," key experts who would inspire the authorities to choose the path of nuclear energy. They were all—as most technocrats, especially in the Eastern Bloc, were—believers in what James C. Scott calls a high-modernist ideology. This ideology "tends to devalue or banish politics. Political interests can only frustrate the social solutions devised by specialists with scientific tools adequate for their analysis. As individuals, high modernists might well hold democratic views about popular sovereignty or classical liberal views about the inviolability of a private sphere that restrained them, but such convictions are external to, and often at war with, their high-modernist convictions" (2008, 81).

Andrzej Strupczewski, one of the first nuclear engineers to graduate from the newly established WUT program, the lead scientist in the Otwock-Świerk experimental reactor, and later a key nuclear energy lobbyist, recalled the beginnings of his own fascination.

> My father was a very good mechanical engineer. . . . So I naturally gravitated towards that area. During my second year at the Technical University, a new specialization opened: nuclear energy. I decided to study it because it was definitely on the cutting edge of technology. We hardly knew anything about it. I remember, for example, the first time I saw a drawing of a reactor without any slag and ash outlet, which you had to have in coal power plants. I looked at this drawing and wondered why this part at the bottom was closed, and how they were getting rid of the slag. Obviously, there's no need for that in a nuclear power reactor, because you replace fuel every year by opening the top and removing it that way, but I was a regular 1960s engineer who was so used to coal-based thinking. . . . It was all new to us. . . . I was very interested in these new technologies, but I wasn't so emotionally involved in them yet. That came in the 1970s, or towards the end of the 1960s, when during my hikes in the mountains I realized how air pollution had devastated Silesia. I've done all the mountain trails in Poland; I have the gold tourist badge. . . . I saw, among other things, the Izera Mountains, located in the so-called black triangle between Poland, Czechoslovakia, and [East] Germany, which had been terribly affected by emissions. . . . Pines, spruces—especially spruces—die at thirty micrograms of pollution per cubic meter, and the pollution in that area was fifty, sixty micrograms, if not more. That's when I started reading various publications, and found, among other things, one by the Silesian branch of the Polish Academy of Sciences that said that the life expectancy of people in Wałbrzych [the capital of the Lower Silesian coal mining basin] was around four or five years below the Polish average, and the Polish average isn't particularly long either—it's below the European one. People in Wałbrzych were well supplied, they could buy everything they needed, as it was a highly industrialized region, but you couldn't breathe the air. Air pollution was . . . so high that

> there was 40 percent less sunlight than in other parts of Poland. . . . That's when I realized that nuclear energy, which wasn't present in Poland yet, offered a big chance because . . . by definition nuclear power plants don't burn coal, so they don't pollute: they don't emit CO_2, which is very fashionable now, but neither do they emit sulfur oxides, nitrous oxides, dust, and heavy metals, which have an immediate impact on people's health. I started reading more, for example about Łódź, where 40 percent of children suffered from upper respiratory tract conditions because of the polluted air, and about similar situations in other cities, and decided we should try to introduce nuclear energy to Poland. Because it would result in cleaner air. . . . If we're convinced that nuclear energy is safer and will be handled properly—and it seemed like it really would be—then the benefits were very clear: clean air for people, whose life expectancy would be extended by several years.

Jerzy Bijak, the president of Energoprojekt, the company in charge of designing and constructing the Żarnowiec NPP, also remembers the early days of the nuclear sector in Poland.

> In Warsaw . . . I delved into industrial installations, power plants. I had prepared the first design of a nuclear power plant in 1958, at the Warsaw University of Technology. [Andrzej Strupczewski went into the scientific side of things;] meanwhile I was leaning towards the practical side. I found myself at Energoprojekt [as part of a group] that dealt with the location of the first nuclear power plant in Poland on the Narew River, in a place called Gnojno [a village some seventy kilometers north of Warsaw].

This group of engineers and scientists, educated in the 1950s and 1960s, was later expanded to include even younger experts educated in Poland and abroad (especially in Czechoslovakia), and in time they became one of the main forces behind the plans for Polish nuclear energy, lobbying for its further development. These plans were made more specific under the leadership of Gomułka's successor, Edward Gierek (1913–2001), who took power in 1970. NPPs were among the many modernization megaprojects so characteristic of that period in Communist Poland's history. "The reason was simple," explained J. R. Kurylczyk. "Since the world was moving towards nuclear energy, if Poland didn't want to stay behind, she'd eventually have to follow suit."

However, funds were notoriously limited, and even though Gierek launched a large-scale rollout of heavy industry supported by foreign credit and often based on Western patents, nuclear energy was low on the priority list. Gierek came from a family of miners who emigrated to France and later Belgium before the war—as did many Polish and Silesian miners who populated the Ruhr and Saar mining towns in Germany and similar communities in France and Belgian Flanders (A. B. 1933). His primary constituency was Silesian workers and miners, and the coal sector became one of the most powerful lobbies in the country (Kuchler and Bridge 2018). Nuclear energy was seen by many in the government as either irrelevant or as direct competition to coal.

But there were also arguments in favor of nuclear technology. Poland wanted to join the international "nuclear club" for reasons of prestige, and placing this investment on the coast would tie into further futuristic visions of Gierek-era city planners. According to architect and urbanist Mieczysław Kochanowski, the Planning Committee of the Council of Ministers and the Gdańsk Regional Planning Unit envisioned transforming the Tricity into "something akin to the Rotterdam of COMECON [Council for Mutual Economic Assistance—Eastern Blocs counterpart of the European Community]" Aside from developing the harbor infrastructure, investments were also to be made in heavy and energy-intensive industry. This would have meant a direct challenge to the primacy of Upper Silesia as the industrial powerhouse of Communist Poland.

Meanwhile, energy production was located almost exclusively in south and central Poland. There were no (and still are no) large power plants in northern Poland. Therefore, plans were made to either transport coal from Silesia to a great power plant in Tczew or directly to Gdańsk, where a new river terminal was to be constructed for this purpose. "Simultaneously," Kochanowski adds, "people were saying: if we're doing this, we must use modern solutions, in order not to stay behind like we did in terms of the steel industry and mining. At that time, modern meant nuclear. Remember, this was the early 1970s." In 1970, the construction of the second Polish experimental reactor—"Maria"—began at Otwock-Świerk. It was finished in 1974.

The future deputy director of the Żarnowiec NPP construction site, Henryk Torbicki, ten years Strupczewski's and Bijak's junior, recalled:

> When I was deciding to study chemistry, and specifically nuclear chemistry, I received information that a nuclear power plant was to be built somewhere in our region. These rumors were already

> around in the 1960s. It fascinated me because in those times it was a topic that managed to escape the everyday grayness, and my studies tied into it. There were more official rumors about nuclear energy in the 1970s, that was also then that the name Żarnowiec was mentioned for the first time. At one point, they even created a governmental plenipotentiary for nuclear energy. I wrote to him asking about potential employment in this field. He directed me to the planning bureau, which in turn directed me to the investor. That's how I found myself on the team that prepared the construction of the nuclear power plant. At first, there were three people working on it, I was the third one. . . . We had some technical issues to resolve, so we also pushed for the Atomic Law, because we needed the legal situation to be clear.

The long-awaited formal decision to build the first NPP in Poland was made on 12 August 1971, and the decision to put it near the Żarnowiec Lake passed first on 19 December 1972 and then again on 25 June 1979. It had to be updated because the construction still had not begun, and the validity period of the previous location decision had lapsed. The building permit decision for the power plant also had to be renewed, which happened on 18 January 1982. That is also when the construction formally began. It was anticipated that by 2000, Poland would have several power plants with a total nominal capacity of 6,000 megawatts in total. The Atomic Law Act, the first document of this magnitude regulating the use of nuclear energy in Poland, was adopted only on 10 April 1986, four years after the construction of the Żarnowiec Nuclear Power Plant had begun.

Żarnowiec was chosen for several reasons. First, it was to fill the electric capacity vacuum in the north of the country (there were very few larger power plants located north of Warsaw) and support the further industrialization of the port and shipyard cities—Gdynia and Gdańsk. Additionally, the Baltic Sea could be used as an emergency source of cooling water, while the Żarnowiec Lake was to be used as an open cooling pool, part of the secondary cooling circuit (this NPP was not to have any cooling towers, which are emblematic of nuclear facilities). That would increase the temperature of the lake by several degrees, on average, and the idea of populating the lake with warm-water fish was even proposed. The NPP was to be coupled with a pumped-storage hydropower plant, which would provide flexibility to the entire complex (the latter plant was in fact built and works until this day). The permanent staff of the facility was to number over one thousand people.

According to Strupczewski, Poland's nuclear lag stemmed from the fact that decision makers did not want to get WWERs (water-water energetic reactors) from the Russians because they did not meet European norms; they instead preferred RBMKs (which stands for the Russian *reaktor bolshoy moshchnosti kanalnyy*, or high-power channel-type reactors). The Russians did not want to cede the RBMK technology to any of the satellite states, as this type of reactor was directly linked to the production of nuclear weapons. In hindsight, that was also a stroke of luck, as RBMKs used graphite, not water, as the moderator, which meant that in case of a malfunction their power increased instead of decreasing, and there was no way of stopping them—one reason for the disaster in Chernobyl.

Interestingly, the Polish nuclear energy development program received a poor evaluation from the Security Service. In his evaluation draft, the Ministry of Internal Affairs official responsible for issues related to the construction of the power plant mentioned insufficiencies in terms of the resource base (mainly smelting), component production, specialized construction know-how (equipment and resource base), timeliness of implementation, and organization and coordination of the entities responsible for program implementation. All these shortcomings were reflected in the way the Żarnowiec NPP was being constructed—with delays in supply deliveries, which were also often incomplete or not up to standards, as well as in the filing of documents, construction work, and acceptance of individual stages.

The Żarnowiec power plant itself was a typical communist construction project. No serious prognoses of energy demand were made prior to the construction decision, and no environmental impact assessment was required. Neither were social, cultural, and financial costs of the project evaluated. Several workers died in accidents at the construction site; the entire Kartoszyno village, which could have become a seaside resort, was relocated; there was widespread theft of materials from the site; and the government devoted resources to the project that were lacking in other segments of the economy.

The construction began under the umbrella of martial law, which minimized the possibility of any social protest. Kurylczyk talked about the context of adopting this decision at that particular time.

> I had direct contact with General Wojciech Jaruzelski on a number of occasions. . . . He was an enlightened man. I was impressed by his intellect. He realized that the creation of a Polish nuclear energy program would require developing dozens of areas: industry, chemistry, and many other fields, so that the nuclear sector could take off. And he decided to bet on Polish solutions in nuclear technology. [Ninety] percent of the Żarnowiec power plant was designed by Polish companies. [Unlike Edward Gierek, who put an emphasis on loans and foreign licenses] he realized that making Polish com-

> panies design, build and equip the first nuclear power plant, would force Polish industry to ascend to a new level. . . . It was Martial Law. There were military men in the government, army commissioners everywhere. They were convinced that if they took over the economy, things would finally budge. They'd restore discipline, the economy would restart, there would be profits. Because obviously when civilians ran the whole thing, it was hopeless. . . . So with that mindset, they started making decisions in 1981. Only once they realized that this wasn't the way to develop your economy, that you can't just order things to be the way you want them to be, only then did they begin . . . to delegate things to civilians and back away from the fray, but for the first three years there was this conviction that now we're going to make this country run like military barracks.

Indeed, since the end of 1981 many branches of industry had been militarized—workers were treated like employees of strategic sectors, and not reporting for work was treated almost as desertion, while the centralist and high-modernist mindset of Jaruzelski's junta was visible in many areas of the economy. Until the second half of the 1980s, these plans went virtually unchallenged. As noted already in earlier chapters, Poland did not experience any visible anti–nuclear weapons movement, or even organized expert-led dissent in that area. The civilian nuclear sector was also depoliticized, and nuclear safety was not an issue until the Chernobyl disaster. That was despite the rather relaxed approach that the authorities seemed to take, at least initially, and also despite some smaller scale accidents that occurred.

The former director of the unfinished Żarnowiec NPP, Kurylczyk, describes the evolution of the approach towards reactor safety.

> The first approach was: there would be no malfunction. Later it evolved to: if there is one, we have to protect the crew and the surroundings somehow. Only the third one brought us to: if there is a malfunction, let's try to keep it local. So that's when we got malfunction location towers and outer casings that would contain potential sources of radiation, i.e., radioactive vapor (in case of water reactors). The next generations went towards outright avoiding malfunctions, that is towards stopping the reaction in the event of a potential malfunction. . . . There would be no malfunction, that was the initial premise. Why should there be one, if everything's working fine?

There were two major Polish nuclear incidents. The first was the experiment in which cooling was turned off at the "Ewa" reactor in Otwock-Świerk. It involved an experiment conducted by Andrzej Strupczewski. The second, uncontrolled incident happened in 1979 during the startup of the "Maria" reactor, which had been operating at reduced capacity. According to Strupczewski, during an attempt to replicate an earlier experiment and introduce a thermocouple into the core, "the [aluminum] casing, which had been weakened around the incision made to introduce the thermocouple, slid off. We had to stop the experiment." Strupczewski admits that "some products of fission, mainly gases, were released" but contends that "this had no effect." However, the public health expert, Jerzy Jaśkowski, former head of the commission evaluating the radiation effects of Chernobyl, claims that there was a significant increase in radiation, in effect contaminating the entire reactor building, but no one notified the staff of the Nuclear Research Institute about the accident.[1]

Żarnowiec—Our Own Chernobyl?

One account suggests that the first protests against the Żarnowiec NPP occurred already in late 1984, reportedly organized by the Polish Ecological Club (Śliwa 1992). However, this claim does not seem to be supported by archival sources or witness testimony. As Jacek Lendzion, one of the leading activists of the Baltic coast branch of the Polish Ecological Club, recalls, during martial law "the situation was that while we weren't formally on a hiatus, there was no will to get involved." Many former leaders of the PKE were also members of the underground Solidarity and they were preoccupied with clandestine union work. Lendzion and his friends became involved in PKE work again in early 1987 "mostly due to the growing danger exemplified by Chernobyl." The push came from a Danish environmental NGO, which was not linked to any political party, and which contacted the PKE directly about the Żarnowiec issue. However, the primary focuses of the club were chemical works and the Gdańsk petrochemical facility, not the NPP, as according to Lendzion the PKE "generally was not involved in the antinuclear movement." Joanna Radecka, an architect and urbanist, head of the Environmental Protection Commission in the Baltic coast branch of Solidarity, also mentions "thousands of protest letters" regarding Żarnowiec sent to the government between 1983 and 1986, signed by Lech Wałęsa, among others. However, these have not left any trace in the archives.

The expert efforts focusing on popularizing the dangers related to nuclear energy bring us to the mysterious case of Zbigniew Wołoszyn. This employee of the Central Laboratory of Radiological Protection had been doing his own research on the scale of radiation in Poland following the Chernobyl disaster. He would always carry the results of his research with him in a briefcase. On 9 January 1987, he died under mysterious circumstances—supposedly having jumped out of a window at the building across from his workplace, while simultaneously losing the abovementioned briefcase. The matter still has not been explained to this day (Potkaj 2006).[2]

In the beginning of May 1986, right after the Chernobyl disaster, Lech Parell, a WiP movement participant, approached Father Jankowski, the pastor of the Gdańsk shipyard, and Solidarity with the idea to have the union start collecting signatures demanding a stop to the construction of the Żarnowiec NPP. He turned to Father Jankowski because he was such a celebrity in the opposition and at the same time was very approachable and had a good rapport with young people.[3] "I thought it was a brilliant idea that would hit the Communists where it hurts. That it would be an obviously political initiative dressed in apolitical clothing. For me, it was mainly an assault on a flagship communist construction project. It was less about ecology," Parell recalls. He believed that this would allow Solidarity to open another front of confrontation, and that it would help the union, since people were genuinely scared of the Chernobyl fallout.

Father Jankowski gave the idea his blessing, but it soon became obvious that he was not doing anything much in that direction. Some months later "there was a meeting at Father Jankowski's with a dozen scientists who wrote a sort of petition to the government asking about the type of technology that would be used at the power plant, and expressing their general concern, etc. Radio Free Europe mentioned it in passing, but that was it," Parell recalls, expressing his disappointment. The meetings at the St. Bridget Church, however, eventually resulted in the creation of the Franciscan Ecological Movement in the fall of 1986, which filled the space of Catholic engagement in environmental issues and aimed at awareness raising and education. But Parell had a very different kind of activity in mind, and he thought that "poor publicity and sticking to legal forms of protest meant that [the Franciscan Ecological Movement] failed to produce any tangible results."

Ewa Charkiewicz from the semiofficial "I Prefer to Be" movement looks at an undated picture from a demonstration on a Baltic beach, not sure if it was 1987 or 1988: "We had some sort of gathering at the seaside, there was also a march down the beach with slogans protesting against Żarnowiec or—as we called it then—*Żarnobyl*." It is hard to pinpoint the moment when Żarnowiec and Chernobyl were first symbolically blended into the mock name Żarnobyl, though most likely that was an invention of the Gdańsk anarchists—either the RSA or WiP.

In June 1987 a group of WiP activists, including Małgorzata Górczewska and Tomasz Żmuda-Trzebiatowski, met with the latter's friend, a Żarnowiec NPP employee, who answered their questions about the state of the construction, the details of the way NPPs work, and what safety risks they carry. He also let them visit the pumped-storage station near Żarnowiec. After the meeting, the man got in trouble with the Security Service for disclosing classified information to illegal organizations.

Protests against the Żarnowiec NPP only started to intensify in 1987. On 11 March, a meeting between the residents of the Przymorze housing estate, the PRON leadership, and representatives of the Voivodeship Committee of the Polish United Workers' Party was attended by WiP activists, who presented information on the dangers related to the construction of the Żarnowiec power plant. In several places in Gdańsk, signatures were collected under a petition to stop the construction. The final tally was around two thousand.

On 1 May 1987, WiP activists crashed an official May Day parade in Sopot wearing Chernobyl and Żarnobyl T-shirts and holding antimilitary banners. They were stopped before reaching the stand where party officials stood, waving at the crowd passing by. One of the protesters, Krzysztof Grynder, was badly beaten. Later, during an interrogation at a precinct, his beard was set on fire. This is the best documented and therefore most likely the first open protest against the NPP, evidenced by graffiti on Gdańsk walls, photographs, petitions, fliers, and banners that were confiscated during a search of WiP activists' homes. There were also reports about an ecological demonstration in Gdańsk planned for 18 July 1987. Between March and July, WiP activists gathered signatures on a protest petition, which was later sent to the parliament of the Polish People's Republic.

The best-known antinuclear event from that year was also organized, on 16 October 1987, by the Gdańsk WiP, in a manner as unbelievable as the spelling of the place where it was held—Wrzeszcz, a district of Gdańsk. Four followers of the Freedom and Peace movement climbed the rooftop of a local pharmacy dressed in animal costumes. As the Gdańsk Region Solidarity magazine later reported:

> At 3 PM, four costumed WiP activists appeared on the roof of the pharmacy at the intersection of Grunwaldzka and Hibnera in Wrzeszcz: Marek Bik (as a hedgehog), Jarosław Cieszyński (fox), Wojciech Jankowski (fish) and Lech Parell (hare). They put up banners saying "We do not want the power plants in Żarnowiec and Klempicz" and "Freedom and Peace." Onlookers and pedestrians were showered with fliers. . . . [A]fter about fifteen minutes, two law enforcement officers climbed onto the roof and tried to convince WiP activists to come with them because . . . they did not have

> demonstration permits. The activists responded with a shower of fliers, and then sat down on the roof, at which point the Militia officers had no choice but to leave.[4]

In fact, in order to avoid accidents, the human-animal protesters agreed to climb down after fifteen minutes and appeal to the one hundred to one hundred fifty people gathered there to disperse and not intervene. The next day, they were fined around ninety thousand złoty each (more than three times the average monthly salary at the time) and their costumes were confiscated as evidence.

On the same day in different points of the Tricity, their colleagues distributed some ten thousand leaflets. Andrzej Szulc, a WiP activist and later founder of one of the first Amnesty International groups in Poland, who was nicknamed "Theologian" (although he is a political scientist), together with another WiP member, Wojciech Błażek, rode the train from Gdańsk to Gdynia, throwing out fliers on nuclear energy at every stop, and then went back to join the demonstration at the Wrzeszcz pharmacy, participating as spectators. "People saw it as some sort of novelty, they cheered, but treated it kind of like theater or live TV, because the Militia kept trying to negotiate, people were stopping in the street to see how it would turn out," he recalls.

That event-like form of protest—the "happening" in Polish opposition parlance—was indeed something new. Szulc, like many others his age who had been raised in Gdańsk, was used to the typical, almost routine demonstrations-cum-riots outside the St. Bridget church, which would end up with all the young lads—skinheads and football fans of the local "Lechia," punks, and pacifists alike—being beaten by police truncheons. Nothing of the sort happened in Wrzeszcz. The militia was almost apologetic. "People were also intrigued by the disguises, by the animal costumes—it wasn't a typical political demonstration, people were holding banners, but they were also yelling, it seemed like a kind of playful happening," Szulc continues, noting that this new "carnivalesque" style was inspired by the increasingly famous actions of the Wrocław-based Orange Alternative (Kenney 2002). That artsy and flamboyant style of making quasi-political events resonated with people who were previously neither interested nor involved in political action. Szulc recalled meeting a girl on a trip to the mountains who told him of an Orange Alternative demonstration, narrating it as if it were a theatrical play, something that could actually be turned into a story and that left an impression beyond taking a momentary political and moral stance. "It was something new, a breath of fresh air. I think people respond better to images, to moving pictures, to something going on, as opposed to someone just throwing a flier and running away."

On the margins of this radical activity there was also educational activity conducted by the Franciscan Ecological Movement and the Gdańsk Science Society, among others, but they did not venture beyond a small circle of coworkers. Jerzy Jaśkowski wrote that even his official report on the impact of the Chernobyl fallout was never made public—it was announced only in 1992 and remains very difficult to access to this day. The year 1988 saw the creation of the Gdańsk Ecological Forum. It was one of the first Polish associations of official ecological groups that, without abandoning their own actions and methods, united to more effectively fight for their common objectives, including not allowing nuclear power plants to be built in Poland.

"Leave the Bunkers to the Bats!" Protests Against the Międzyrzecz Nuclear Waste Storage

The issue of radioactive waste is very controversial the world over, even in countries with high approval for nuclear power plants. In Poland, discussions engaged questions about what to do with the waste, where it should be kept, and how to handle the enormous cost of transporting and storing it. Although there was not a single "industrial" nuclear power plant in Poland—there were only the reactors at the research center in Otwock-Świerk—the existing and planned radioactive waste disposal sites served as important fodder for the initial protests. The largest and most innovative protests happened in response to the planned construction of a site that was to house most of the waste from the planned NPPs—in the bunkers near Międzyrzecz, in western Poland.

The Międzyrzecz protest constituted the first coordinated antinuclear action that cut across scales—from local grassroots involvement on site to solidarity actions all over the country. Arguably, this was the first *campaign* of the nascent antinuclear movement. It was also groundbreaking in that it saw a rebellion of local party structures against the central authorities in Warsaw. The protest by local people was supported not only by environmentalists but also by local government and political organizations, such as PRON, as well as by PZPR's junior satellite parties—the United People's Party and the Democratic Alliance.

The radioactive waste disposal site was to be constructed in the bunkers of the central part of the Międzyrzecz Fortified Area (Międzyrzecki Rejon Umocniony). Constructed by Nazi Germany in 1934–1944 as the "eastern wall" guarding Berlin, the massive complex consists of some one hundred interconnected bunkers and underground storage compartments. The fortifications are located in a wooded area crosscut by many rivers (the name of the town literally translates to "between rivers") and lie at the water table of the Oder and Warta, two of Poland's largest rivers.

In the spring of 1987, reports started appearing in the press about plans to use the bunkers to store waste from the Nuclear Research Center in Świerk and other scientific facilities, as well as from the planned power plants and those already under construction. As the local government or the population of Międzyrzecz were not consulted about these plans, the news caused anxiety about the waste possibly negatively impacting the groundwater and the health of the residents of nearby settlements. But Międzyrzecz was no nest for opposition. A town of around twenty thousand inhabitants, it had no major industry and that meant no trade union network. Finally, a large part of the population was soldiers, their families or employees providing services to the army.

Stanisław Bożek was a farmer from the Międzyrzecz area. When the Solidarity trade union emerged from the August 1980 strikes, he was one of many in the countryside that also wanted to participate in the new social movement. At the time, over 40 percent of Poles lived in the countryside, and roughly a third of the population was working in the agricultural sector. Some were laborers—the communist term was "peasant-worker"—in large-scale, state-owned farms, but many were working their own land. They set up the Independent Self-Governing Trade Union of Individual Farmers "Solidarity," and Bożek was one of the founding members, setting up both the national structures and the grassroots union cells in the Gorzów voivodeship.

One day, an environmental activist from Poznań visited him and invited him to a symposium organized at the Dominican church about the risks of nuclear power plants and waste storage facilities like the one planned in Międzyrzecz. Bożek went and started participating in PKE meetings regularly. He learned about the risks of nuclear waste and the environmental concerns that the governmental plans raised, but he felt that "this was just talk," and if they really wanted to stop the nuclear waste facility from becoming reality, they had to do more. For that, Bożek had to use the organizational skills he acquired in union work some years before.

"The situation in Poland was such at that point that I decided we should act openly," and so, together with two friends, he organized a committee to protest against the site, which initially consisted of ten people. They prepared fliers that called on the citizens to participate in protests. The tactics were tailored to fit the small-town realities of Międzyrzecz: they would organize a protest on the first Sunday of every month after Holy Mass at noon, in the church near the town hall. The church would be a natural place for people to gather, and the proximity of the town hall made it easy to move quickly to a scene where protests would become visible and meaningful. This regularity was important so that people would get used to the idea that there was a protest in the streets of Międzyrzecz every month. He wanted to keep it nonpolitical and ideally turn the protest event into something resembling a picnic. "We were protesting because we didn't want our children to live in a town threatened by dangerous waste. That was the main reason for our protests," Bożek explains, highlighting the motivation of his committee and the locals that joined.

However, for the environmentalists, like Marek Kossakowski, a WiP affiliate and later Green Party leader from Warsaw, there was also another side to the story. The bunkers were an extremely valuable habitat for bats—a very rare site that deserved to be protected (Kossakowski 1987). "Leaving the bunkers to the bats" turned out to be a good slogan and yet another motivation. WiP and PKE were able to quickly gather independent expert reports, which suggested that the site (the bunkers) was absolutely unfit and the project was highly dangerous for the local population, and that it was also a very important bat habitat (Śliwa 1992, 60).

They started on the first Sunday in May 1987. Bożek prepared the text on the flier. The protest committee members handed out the fliers, and on that first Sunday throngs of people took to the streets. The demonstration on 3 May 1987 gathered around a thousand locals in Międzyrzecz, an outstanding result. There were also external guests, as the Wrocław activist Radosław Gawlik recalls, the number of protesters meant that the militia could merely observe the demonstration. "They got interested in Międzyrzecz because our first demonstration was a success," boasts Bożek. However, external participants were there not only to bask in the reflected glory of the locals. They would turn out to be indispensable as protest fatigue kicked in, and once grassroots resources reached their limits.

On 18 May 1987 five WiP activists climbed up onto the ledge of a department store in Gorzów, the nearby voivodeship capital. A perfect example of the new *daching* monkeywrenching tactics,[5] the activists held banners that said "No nuke waste heap near Międzyrzecz" and "Radioactive waste poses a constant threat," and they scattered leaflets and pasted posters on the building's windows. Firefighters called to the protest location were not able to convince the activists to get down; the riot police were summoned and dragged them down by force. The protesters were detained for forty-eight hours.

Successful protests were held in Międzyrzecz on Sundays in June, July, and August, but the numbers were dwindling. When the protests grew weaker, Bożek reached out to opposition contacts in Gorzów. He met Kazimierz Sokołowski, a dynamic local leader involved in the Independent Youth

Movement (Ruch Młodzieży Niezależnej) and a participant in the Freedom and Peace movement, though Gorzów's WiP was perhaps the most radically conservative and nationalist branch of the movement. Sokołowski recalls:

> Mr. Bożek was organizing the protest in Międzyrzecz, he was most involved, he had ideas, but it turned out that the actions he and his people took were not enough. They thought that if they make and distribute fliers, people would come and get actively involved in the process. Turns out that's not how it works: people were intimidated, so everything needed to be taken to the next level to motivate them to act.

In a town without a history of active and open opposition, people were much more anxious about getting involved. The moment fliers appeared, people "became paralyzed with fear: whoever picked up a flier would immediately put it away, scared"—Sokołowski explains, adding that "because it's such a small town, there weren't enough people to help—there were those who wanted to advise, but too few of those who'd actually go and throw fliers, or engage with the community in some other way."

So Sokołowski called in reinforcements. On 2 September, together with another WiP follower, Marek Rusakiewicz, he invited scouts from the Gorzów patriotic Republican Scouting Union. They prepared several thousand fliers, climbed onto the roof of a bar in the middle of Międzyrzecz, and started throwing the fliers onto the streets below. Barbara Hrywacz, another WiP activist, watched from a distance to tell the story to Radio Free Europe and the independent media. According to Sokołowski,

> We're standing on the roof of a bistro in the rain, throwing fliers. The streets were covered with them. . . . It was a shock: people knew someone was protesting. They also saw our faces, saw that we weren't afraid. They'd pick up these fliers, and then we saw them throw them from neighboring buildings. There was applause, people brought some flowers to the roof we were on. It was like they broke through the fear. I guess you could call it a turning point in what was happening in Międzyrzecz.

But that was not the end. Sokołowski and his team climbed down from the bar rooftop, thinking that the militia would grab them on the spot since they seemed to be waiting for that moment. Suddenly, a crowd surrounded them, taking advantage of the fact that the militia was hesitant. The protesters unrolled a banner and started walking down the street, followed by children and young people. They walked through the entire city, all the way to the church, where Rusakiewicz improvised a speech to thank them for their support (Kenney 2002, 75). Once they arrived there, they put their banners away—and then walked to the bus station. "They grabbed us on our way there [and] put us in Międzyrzecz jail for 48 hours."

After the demonstration on the roof on 2 September, the militia detained six activists. On 6 September, a march of three thousand people was organized. This time, activists from Gorzów, Poznań, Wrocław, and even Gdańsk came. The locals were defending the environmentalists from the police who tried to arrest them, and in the process, the demonstrators blocked the international route passing through Międzyrzecz, stopping the traffic and creating a visible incident. Sokołowski, who had just left jail, was arrested again for another forty-eight hours. There were also other arrests, and misdemeanor courts fined four activists a total of over a half million złoty. "But that was a big thing," explains Sokołowski, "because the papers wrote about the road getting blocked. And there were a lot of people there."

Again they realized that this strategy was becoming obsolete, and that they had to try something new. Sokołowski convinced Bożek to organize a hunger strike in Międzyrzecz. The strike was an overt form of protest. "It's not the same as throwing out fliers from hiding," Bożek explains, echoing the words of Andrzej Szulc from Gdańsk. Indeed, a hunger strike "required you to demonstrate your conviction, to show that one mustn't be afraid. And

Figure 4.1. Protest march organized by WiP in Miedzyrzecz, 4 October 1987. Photograph: NAF Dementi, Archive Pamięć i Przyszłość.

people stopped being afraid. I think the march after the hunger strike was our biggest one. There was no politics here."

On 27 September, twelve people started a week-long hunger strike in a church in protest against the repressions and the planned waste disposal site. The strikers were people from Międzyrzecz and Gorzów, as well as some individual guests from all over Poland. They received a formal Church blessing—not just the premises to hold a strike (churches were often used for hunger strikes at the time) but also a visit by the local bishop, who expressed his support.

That was the first hunger strike of the antinuclear movement, though it would not be the last. Sokołowski explains that it resulted from "determination." The activists felt backed into a corner, because the authorities were using a very painful, even if nonviolent method of repression—high fines. "What else could we do? Marches, *daching*, fliers, we had already done all of that. So how long were we supposed to keep it up? The hunger strike drew people's attention to the protest and showed our determination."

While protests continued in Międzyrzecz and Gorzów, the official and expert organizations—the League for Nature Protection, the Polish Nature Society, "I Prefer to Be," and the PKE—had been writing letters to local and national authorities and conducting awareness-raising campaigns all around Poland (Hicks 1996, 89).

Figure 4.2. *Daching* in Gorzów: a protest held on the roof of a department store, 22 March 1989. Photograph provided by Mirosław Wrąbel.

The combination of local involvement, external help, and expertise, together with the activists' determination, bore fruit. The local newspaper, *Ziemia Międzyrzecka* (Miedzyrzecz Land), wrote a series of articles about the planned facility, putting the emphasis on the contamination of groundwater, which could directly endanger people. Expert analyses provided by WiP and others proved that the contaminated water could reach drinking water intakes. This proved to be a solid argument that also convinced the local PRON governors, who sided with the opponents of the facility.

On 30 September 1987, a resolution against the current placement of the site was adopted by the Municipal and Communal National Council in Międzyrzecz. Sokołowski, who was participating in the hunger strike at the time, recalls, "We got word that for the time being, they were abandoning plans to build the site. I think this was meant to defuse the situation, because the whole thing became very public, and the government saw that these ecological initiatives were directed at them, which meant that the socialist system was taking a beating."

After the hunger strike was concluded on 4 October 1987, there was a march that gathered, according to different sources, between three and seven thousand people—approximately 20–25 percent of the town's population. Małgorzata Górczewska, who came to the protest from Gdańsk, recalls the unbelievable enthusiasm of the local people, who would invite the visiting activists for dinner at their homes. The matter of the protests in Międzyrzecz was discussed at the International Scientific Symposium "Nuclear Energy, Man, Environment" on 5–7 November 1987 in Poznań. On 9 November, another poster/flier operation was organized. In effect, at a meeting with the residents of Międzyrzecz, the chairwoman of the PRON Municipal and Communal Council declared that the preliminary analysis conducted by the State Atomic Agency regarding the potential disposal of radioactive waste in the Międzyrzecz bunkers would not be continued, which was confirmed by a member of the Political Office of the Central Committee of PZPR. The conflict was resolved, and the locals, as well as activists from the local protest committee, led by Bożek and WiP, won.

As Padraic Kenney notes, that was probably the first significant defeat of a government policy by organized civil dissent that Poland had seen since 1981 (Kenney 2002, 75). It was also the first nationwide campaign on an antinuclear issue after the Chernobyl catastrophe and the first-ever opposition action that worked on all scales: from local involvement on site through pressuring local and regional authorities, protesting in the regional capital, and holding solidarity campaigns around the country (Szulecka and Szulecki 2017). It combined radical direct action with expert knowledge, and it saw conservatives and Catholics joining ranks with anarchists and environmentalists as well as with local party apparatchiks.

The protests made a lasting impact. The levels of mobilization seen in Międzyrzecz transformed the local community. Sokołowski emphasizes that "the events organized to protest the waste disposal site unleashed potential in people, suddenly we had new brave people stepping up to the plate, willing to do something, to take on the authorities. A community coalesced, and people started working together." He was able to establish a local structure of his Independent Youth Movement and a network of dissenters that could later be used for other purposes in Międzyrzecz. "That was all because of those environmental protests."

Notes

1. J. Jaśkowski in conversation with T. Borweicz, but see also: http://www.polishclub.org/2013/05/04/dr-jerzy-jaskowski-czarnobyl-fukushima-windscaletree-mile-island-i-co-dalej-cz-3/.
2. The mysterious case is also described in: *Milczący świadkowie*, 13grudnia.pl, http://www.13grudnia81.pl/portal/sw/698/6766/Zbigniew_Woloszyn.html (data dostępu 6 listopada 2018); *Sprawa fizyka W.*, "Sobiepaństwo atomowe," http://czarnobyl.info/page3.html (data dostępu 21 marca 2011); K. Witkowska, *Listy gończe* (odc. 10), magazyn kryminalny, TVP3, Polska, 2010.
3. Some thirty years later evidence would emerge that the priest was a pedophile, using his position to abuse young boys (Klauziński 2019).
4. J. D. *WiP we Wrzeszczu*, "Solidarność" nr 17/183, s. 4.
5. The terms *daching* or *ruszting* come from the Polish words for roof and scaffold and the "-ing" as in "sitting." The idea was to climb a scaffold or a roof and sit there—for increased visibility of the activists and to extend the length of the protest, as the police needed equipment and reinforcements to take the protesters off their "nest." This followed one of the key principles of the movement's nonviolent strategy: "It takes only a single cop to arrest a standing protester, but up to four to arrest a sitting one" (and a whole platoon to surround and climb onto a rooftop if you pull the ladder up).

References

A. B. 1933. "Wśród Bartków i Maćków we Francji." *Światowid*, 1933. http://retropress.pl/swiatowid/wsrod-bartkow-i-mackow-we-francji/.

Bendyk, Edwin, Urszula Papajak, Marcin Popkiewicz, and Michał Sutowski, eds. 2015. *Polski Węgiel*. Wydanie pierwsze. Warszawa: Wydawnictwo Krytyki Politycznej.

Derski, Bartłomiej, and Rafał Zasuń. 2018. *Wiek energetyków: opowieść o ludziach, którzy zmieniali Polskę*. Warszawa: WysokieNapięcie.pl.

Hicks, Barbara E. 1996. *Environmental Politics in Poland: A Social Movement between Regime and Opposition*. New York: Columbia University Press.

Kenney, Padraic. 2002. *A Carnival of Revolution. Central Europe 1989*. Princeton: Princeton University Press.

Klauziński, Sebastian. 2019. "Prałat Jankowski, Czyli Ksiądz Pedofil Modelowy." OKO Press. 2019. https://oko.press/ksiadz-jankowski-pedofil/.

Kossakowski, Marek. 1987. "Zostawcie Bunkry Nietoperzom." In *Leaflet*. Warsaw.

Kuchler, Magdalena, and Gavin Bridge. 2018. "Down the Black Hole: Sustaining National Socio-Technical Imaginaries of Coal in Poland." *Energy Research & Social Science*, Energy Infrastructure and the Fate of the Nation, 41 (July): 136–47. https://doi.org/10.1016/j.erss.2018.04.014.

Leszczyński, Adam. 2005. "Bunt głodnych kobiet." Wysokie Obcasy. 2005. https://www.wysokieobcasy.pl/wysokie-obcasy/1,96856,2998573.html.

Potkaj, Tomasz. 2006. "Co Się Działo w Polsce 20 Lat Temu." *Tygodnik Powszechny*, no. 30 April.

Scott, James C. 2008. *Seeing like a State: How Certain Schemes to Improve the Human Condition Have Failed*. New Haven, CT: Yale University Press.

Śliwa, Maciej. 1992. "Ruch 'Wolność i Pokój' 1985–1989." MA thesis. Krakow: Jagiellonian University.

Szulecka, Julia, and Kacper Szulecki. 2017. "Polish Environmental Movement 1980–2017: (De)Legitimization, Politics & Ecological Crises." *ESPRi Working Papers* 6. https://doi.org/10.2139/ssrn.3075126.

Chapter 5

Kopań and Klempicz

The NPPs That Never Came to Be

The 1986 Chernobyl accident raised societal awareness of the dangers of nuclear energy, and the 1987 wave of protests around the Międzyrzecz waste storage plans made large groups of Poles realize that there was a domestic nuclear sector with safety issues—and that coordinated dissent can block it. What followed in 1988–1989, however, was the peak of Poland-wide anti-nuclear activism in terms of breadth and scale. This time, the focus was on the nuclear power plant projects.

The Żarnowiec Nuclear Power Plant (NPP) was never supposed to be the only power plant of its type in Poland—on 15 June 1987, the government approved the location of the Warta NPP in Klempicz. This plant was to consist of four blocks of WWER-1000/320, which was the Soviet version of the pressurized water reactor (PWR) reactors used around the world. Another location considered was Kopań, a lakeside village outside Darłowo (until 1945 Rügenwalde in German Pomerania), a popular holiday resort on the Baltic Sea coast. Preliminary evaluations were also conducted for six other locations for potential power plant construction. The main factor was a ready supply of water needed for cooling as well as the possibility of connecting to the national electricity system in a way that would ensure a reliable method to transfer energy produced in the power plant and provide backup power in case of an emergency. Before construction began, the government also wanted to gauge the reception of these investments among local communities. According to Security Service reports, these plans were universally opposed by the local population, although the objections did not initially take the form of organized resistance.

However, in the wake of the successful Międzyrzecz campaign and in parallel with increased social turmoil—in 1988 Poland witnessed a new wave of strikes on a scale not seen since 1981—this situation quickly changed and opposition against proposed NPPs consolidated and spawned vocal protest actions. In this chapter, we look at two NPPs that never continued beyond the phase of initial plans and building permits—Kopań and Warta. The localized campaigns against both plants were quite different, with the former displaying similar dynamics to the Międzyrzecz protests, while the latter concentrated not on the actual site in Klempicz, but on the regional capital city, Poznań. The protests against the Warta NPP would also see surprising levels of police violence at a time when the negotiations for a peaceful handover of power began between the PZPR and the political opposition. In the conclusion, we discuss the dilemmas that antinuclear as well as broader environmental activism faced at the beginning of 1989, confronted with the acceleration of regime change and, at the same time, with protest fatigue. Importantly, however, the most important protest campaign—against Żarnowiec, the only NPP that was actually under construction—would only unfold in 1989 and 1990.

Kopań—Combining Direct Action and Expert Pressure

The first center of recurring antinuclear protests was Darłowo, on Kopań Lake, near where the third NPP in Poland (after Warta and Żarnowiec) was scheduled to be constructed. Since 1987, WiP activists from Kołobrzeg, a larger city some eighty kilometers west of Darłowo, had been handing out fliers against the construction of power plants in Żarnowiec and Kopań. They also tried to collect signatures on a petition. These efforts were, however, hindered by the Security Service, which arrested people during flier campaigns, confiscated signature lists, and arranged to have certain activists called up for military service.

In 1988, activists from Kołobrzeg established cooperation with WiP centers in Darłowo and Koszalin (the voivodeship capital roughly midway between the two towns). On 22 June 1988, a meeting of local residents was organized by the Friends of Children Society (Towarzystwo Przyjaciół Dzieci). The main speaker was Jadwiga Gosiewska, then a sixty-two-year-old Darłowo resident, pediatrician, and local activist, who informed people about the dangers posed by the potential construction of a nuclear power plant on the outskirts of the seaside resort. Despite the peaceful and apparently nonpolitical nature of the meeting, police officers detained attendees for several hours.

At another meeting, on 21 July 1988, it was decided that an open letter would be sent to parliament (the Sejm), and the Civic Ecological Club "Vigil" (Ekologiczny Klub Obywatelski "Czuwanie") was created. It was led by Gosiewska, and in just two months the club, aided by WiP, collected around fourteen thouand signatures.

Gosiewska's leadership allowed the Vigil club to borrow from various networks. She was three decades older than the most active WiP generation—in fact, that was the generation of her son, Przemysław, who was a student activist in Gdańsk, and who would later become a prominent conservative politician, deputy prime minister, and leader of the Law and Justice parliamentary club, before his tragic death in the Smolensk plane crash in 2010. She had good contacts in the Solidarity trade union and, as a devout Catholic, was also able to gain the Church's support. Because of that, the Darłowo protests used a wide variety of tactics, pressuring the authorities from all possible sides.

The consolidation of local dissent pushed the authorities to act. On 4 October 1988, in Darłowo, a meeting took place between representatives of the Office of the Government's Plenipotentiary for the Development of Nuclear Energy, governmental experts, and some three hundred Darłowo residents. The protesters received support from Bishop Ignacy Jeż, who wrote a letter to the plenipotentiary, Jerzy Bijak, asking him to reconsider the location decision.

However, no such policy reversal ensued. The antinuclear activists turned to the well-tested repertoire of more direct forms of protest. On 20 January and 19 February 1989, small groups of WiP sympathizers, roughly a dozen activists each, walked down the streets of Darłowo with banners, handing out around three thousand fliers. On 27 February 1989, the Vigil club along with WiP and the Franciscan Ecological Movement organized a legal rally against the construction of nuclear power plants in Poland. They received formal endorsement from the Solidarity unionists, which was the first instance of the trade union taking sides in the nuclear controversy. The rally gathered around a thousand people, including Solidarity unionists from nearby factories. Representatives of Vigil, WiP, and Solidarity delivered speeches, then led a march down the streets of Darłowo with banners saying "We want homes, not atoms," "One, two, three—radiation city," and "Real socialism = nuclear power plants instead of butter." Another rally with around five hundred participants took place on 28 April—on the anniversary of the Chernobyl disaster—and was combined with the election campaign of Solidarity candidates for the semi-open Sejm elections in June 1989 (see chapter 6).

On 14–15 May 1989, the Vigil club organized an International Ecological Symposium in Darłowo devoted to, among other issues, nuclear energy and safety concerns. The three-day-long symposium hosted officials, including the head of the Maritime Authority from Słupsk. He came to Darłowo on Gosiewska's personal invitation, not realizing what he was getting involved in. "I invited him over the phone: 'Will you come? It's a nonpolitical issue. . . .' When he realized what it was, oh God, I remember his terror to this day: 'How could you have invited me here?! Don't you realize what's going on here?'" recalls Gosiewska. When the symposium was nearly over, she in turn received a phone call from the Ministry of Internal Affairs, asking her to provide a list of all the participants including ID numbers, but she declined, claiming that everyone had already left, and it did not even cross her mind to prepare a list like that for such a low-key event. She was eager to protect the participants of the movement, especially since the symposium also hosted foreign guests, making it a more serious matter for the authorities.

According to Gosiewska, the symposium introduced "a sense of rebellion" and a number of new environmental topics going beyond the not-in-my-back-yard antinuclear agenda. A participant from South America talked about dying rainforests and guests from Switzerland spoke of societal environmental awareness. "It's been so long ago, but I still remember them saying that if they tell people not to use a specific brand of washing powder, no one in Switzerland uses that powder. So when they announce that something is poisonous . . . then the company that produced those products goes bankrupt," Gosiewska recalls, unable to hide her enthusiasm. The international meetings were continued in Darłowo and Gdańsk, as the Baltic Ecological Forum, endorsed by the Słupsk diocese.

In order to placate the residents of Darłowo and the entire voivodeship, Minister Aleksander Kwaśniewski, a young PZPR official and later the president of Poland, officially announced in May 1989 that the plans to build the Kopań NPP had been scrapped. Security Service documents reveal that local workers were ill disposed towards nuclear energy and instead believed in energy conservation and efficiency, for which there was a great potential in the underdeveloped and inefficient communist industrial facilities. Their attitudes were influenced by the Vigil club and Solidarity, and especially by Franciszek Sak, who later became an MP of the opposition Citizens' Parliamentary Club and an expert on nuclear energy on the Economic Committee of the Council of Ministers, and by support from Bishop Jeż.

But the story of antinuclear activism in Darłowo and the environmental movement's engagement does not end here. Archbishop Kazimierz Świątek, the last Polish and Catholic priest to be ordained in the Belorussian city of Pinsk before the USSR's invasion in 1939, was caring after children affected by the Chernobyl disaster. There was a large number of children with congenital defects who were also severely malnourished. Jerzy Jaśkowski, who worked with Jadwiga Gosiewska on the Baltic Ecological Forum, received a letter from the archbishop asking if they could offer any help. Jaśkowski and his colleagues loaded up a van with clothes and medicine and went to Pinsk. There, through the archbishop, they met Professor Volkov, who brought maps of radioactive contamination in Belarus. According to the maps, already in the 1960s, in Pinsk and other areas neighboring Poland, the Soviets were testing nuclear mines that contaminated the area much worse than Chernobyl. "These explosions, which ruptured aquifers and resulted in the drying up of Pinsk marshlands, were such that the entire area, probably all the way to Warsaw, became contaminated, even though Polish agencies, be they sanitary or atomic inspection bodies, never said a thing about it," claims Jaśkowski, who was working on a report on Chernobyl's fallout at the time. The Vigil club decided to organize a holiday on the Baltic coast for the Belarusian children and to invite Professor Volkov to a Baltic Ecological Forum conference.

Soon after arrival, Volkov reported to the Belarusian Consulate in Gdańsk, which had at that time still been located at the Russian Consulate. "They held him there, and wouldn't even let him contact us, which is why he didn't come to the first day of the forum. It was only on the second day, precisely on 4 May 1991, that he came to a meeting in Darłowo, and right after his lecture he was taken away again," recalls Jaśkowski. The entire conference, which gathered scientists from Latvia, Lithuania, and Russia, as well as Germans and Swedes, was devoted to Chernobyl, and the topic of Volkov's lecture was the contamination of Belarus. He was also scheduled to deliver two lectures the following week, including one at the Medical University in Gdańsk. As Jaśkowski explains:

> When we called on that day, no one at the Consulate could give us any information: either the line was busy, or someone would say that Volkov is in a meeting. Because the matter seemed very strange, I was put in touch with the officer on duty at the District Police Headquarters, so that I could report a missing person. Volkov came at our official invitation, so we would be responsible if he were to go missing.

Simultaneously, the newspaper *Wieczór Wybrzeża* (Coastal evening) became interested in the matter and ran a series of articles on it. According to Jaśkowski,

> The whole thing went really far up the ladder, because already on Thursday, Polish TV showed some Professor Volkov who came to Poland and was alive and well. Obviously, it was a completely different man who had nothing to do with our guest. I mean, we gave photos of our Professor Volkov to the press, just in case—the one on TV looked at least ten years younger. So it was some masquerade.

Jaśkowski suggests that the Polish authorities were instrumental in this cover-up, as the meeting coincided with the final phase of the antinuclear campaign against Żarnowiec (see the next chapters) and his letters to the authorities remained unanswered.

He was so eager to find out what happened to Volkov that when an opportunity arose, he asked a journalist who was going to Belarus to visit Archbishop Świątek and tasked her with checking Professor Volkov's known address. She reported back that the apartment was sealed shut with tape that made it seem like the police had been around, but that a neighbor from downstairs said that no Volkov had ever lived there. One Doctor Miodoński, a Pole from Switzerland who was involved in supplying aid for children after Chernobyl, went to Belarus and claimed to have met Professor Volkov, but "he was always in the company of some strange gentlemen," in Jaśkowski's words. "Miodoński only managed to ask what happened, to which Volkov replied: 'Well, it's all good now.'" According to Jaśkowski, Volkov was taken from Darłowo, transported directly to the Soviet army base in Legnica and put in the care of the Main Intelligence Directorate (Glavnoye razvedyvatel'noye upravleniye, or GRU). As for the children, the Vigil club looked after them until 1996, when Belarusian president Alexandr Lukashenko introduced the ban on travel to Poland.

Klempicz—Unprecedented Violence in the Streets

The region of Greater Poland became an important center of antinuclear protests, in large part due to the involvement of some of the students and professors at the Adam Mickiewicz University in Poznań. Actions against placing the Warta NPP in Klempicz were taken by independent groups such as the Freedom and Peace movement, the anarchist Alternative Society Movement (RSA), the Independent Self-Governing Trade Union of Individual Farmers Solidarity (Niezależny Samorządny Związek Zawodowy Rolników Indywidualnych "Solidarność," or RI "Solidarność"), and the militant opposition group Fighting Solidarity, the latter not refraining from violence in clashes with the riot police. They were also joined by the semiofficial and government-endorsed environmental movement organizations, such as the Greater Poland's Ecological Seminar (Wielkopolskie Seminarium Ekologiczne), the Polish Ecological Club (PKE), and even by the Catholic clergy. The Security Service also reported about the involvement of activists from Gdańsk—including Jerzy Jaśkowski and environmentalists from Swedish Greenpeace.

In April 1987, RSA and WiP members staged the first protest against the nuclear power plant in Klempicz at the Archeological Museum in Poznań. Simultaneous protests took place at the St. Bridget church in Gdańsk, as well as in Kraków, Szczecin, and Warsaw. On the first anniversary of the

Chernobyl disaster, 27 April 1987, there was a meeting of the Greater Poland's Ecological Seminar, Individual Farmers Solidarity, and several scientists at the Dominican church, which was the meeting place for regular PKE events (those that Stanislaw Bożek from Międzyrzecz attended at the time). Its goal was promoting resistance against nuclear energy and fighting for a clean environment and healthy food. On 28 April 1987, another meeting was organized by the Polish Ecological Club and the Association of Polish Electricians. The expert meeting hosted among others a professor from the Polish Science Academy in Warsaw. The meeting was interrupted by WiP activists protesting the construction of the Warta NPP and plans to create a waste disposal site in Międzyrzecz.

The then-anarchist and later renowned sociologist Jarosław Urbański, who stirred the direct action on behalf of WiP that day, recalls there were one hundred to one hundred fifty people present at the PKE seminar.

> Quite a lot, but not dramatically so. They came to debate. We went in through the front door. Our message was: no more talking, time to hit the streets. So we went in with banners. Turns out, Security Service officers were in the room. Maybe they were there just because, but I think they knew about the protest in advance. I'm not the biggest fighter around, but I didn't want all those weeks of preparation to go to waste.

The Security Service interrupted the meeting, telling everyone to leave. The WiP activists tried to blend into the crowd of seminar participants, while the secret police attempted to arrest them. Afraid of being dispersed and violently treated if separated, the activists staged a sit-in outside the building (in Poznań's market square). "It seems a bit pointless now, but it was due to lack of experience and the fear that they were going to pick us off one by one in that crowd, and we wouldn't even know what's going on," Urbański explains. Thirteen people were arrested, and the meeting was dissolved.

That was the first protest that attracted broader attention: it was reported by Radio Free Europe, and news spread that WiP was stirring up antinuclear brawls in Poznań. Around that time Urbański met another sociologist-to-be, Piotr Matczak, as well as Elżbieta Olędzka. The latter wanted to get involved in WiP's activity, but as a woman, she did not really buy into the antimilitary agenda of the movement—how was she supposed to burn her military identity card if she never got one? Instead, she wanted to focus on environmental issues. The year 1987 was certainly the time for those, and Poznań (located close to both Klempicz and Międzyrzecz) was the place. But there was already a division of labor within the movement. Międzyrzecz was covered by the Gorzów WiP branch, meaning that activists in Poznań had to focus on Klempicz.

The modus operandi emulated that in Międzyrzecz, as Urbański attests: "We'd go there and try to distribute fliers. We tried to establish contact with rural activists in the region—through oppositionist networks." There was also the Greater Poland Ecological Forum, which held monthly meetings where nuclear safety issues were debated. The forum's meetings turned out to be very popular among the region's farmers—they were eager to keep their activity "ecological" and the environmental agenda naturally resonated with them. Olędzka's international contacts also played a role in publicizing the Warta NPP problem.

Much like Stanisław Bożek, Urbański grew impatient with the expertocratic atmosphere of the forum. "They mostly talked about writing letters, working gradually, that it would take years, yadda yadda. We, the young guns, were seen as ragpickers, really. We'd come and say that we needed to march, to distribute fliers. Let's say we disagreed on tactics." However, Klempicz was not a town but a tiny hamlet, and grassroots actions faced limitations of a completely different sort than in Międzyrzecz. Urbański only recalls two visits to the site itself, one a reconnaissance he did together with another WiP activist and a Dutch environmentalist, and another one with Olędzka and Matczak to distribute fliers among the local farmers. They went there by car on a Sunday to distribute fliers to larger crowds leaving nearby parish churches after mass. Some people took the fliers, but the trio was soon arrested.

As the nuclear safety issues became popular across Poland, other local governments also became skeptical, as had Międzyrzecz's. On 29 September 1987 in Obrzycko, a town just eight kilometers south of Klempicz, the agrarian United People's Party (Zjednoczone Stronnictwo Ludowe, or ZSL, a junior party in the communist-dominated political system) proposed a resolution against the construction of the Warta NPP. The resolution was adopted by the Communal National Council (the local governing body) who called on other communes to work together in this regard. It was the Security Service's conclusion that the Obrzycko commune was the most active in the protests. Local PRON and ZSL activists joined in, aided by employees of the Biology Department of the Medical University in Poznań. An attempt was made to mollify them during a meeting between the government's plenipotentiary for nuclear energy, Jerzy Bijak, and a group of eighty residents, which took place on 20 October 1987. However, the preparatory construction works were slowly progressing. The authorities purchased thirty-seven hectares of land and deforested some twenty hectares to clear the construction site (Kiełbasa 2021).

One of the leaders of the Międzyrzecz campaign, Kazimierz Sokołowski from Gorzów, stopped by Klempicz on his way back from a pilgrimage in the fall of 1988. He and his friend had a look around, took pictures, and documented the clear-cuts and the construction of houses for workers. After returning to Gorzów, he asked his friend, who was a catechist in local schools, to informally survey people's awareness of Klempicz. "It turned out that nobody knew anything about it, no one saw any connection [between] atomic power plants and Klempicz," Sokołowski claims. The Gorzów sociologist Marek Rusakiewicz also conducted research that showed there was absolutely no awareness of the issue. Having realized that the locals knew nothing of the plant to be located just a hundred kilometers to the East of Gorzów, Sokołowski launched another local campaign. Again, they began by doing "groundwork" with fliers: every Sunday at every church in Gorzów, after every mass, activists would hand out fliers about the planned construction of the Warta NPP. Then came other actions, like graffiti (using stencils), some small fliers, and information in underground publications of the Independent Youth Movement and WiP.

Sokołowski was a natural talent in social movement mobilization and direct action. He envisaged a specific target for the campaign and kept gauging people's awareness of what this power plant was, where it was supposed to be built, and why it posed a danger to Gorzów. They could make this danger tangible because research had been done by a scientist from Poznań that showed that Gorzów's drinking water supply, which came from drilled wells located along the Warta River, would, in the event of a radioactive event in Klempicz, draw contaminated water from the river. Once again, public health and nuclear reactor safety became the most resonant frames for protest action.

The regular Greater Poland's Ecological Seminar in Poznań was a place where the Poznań, Gorzów, and Piła (another large city in the area) circles mingled. At the seminars, activists could receive updates on new information—both scientific knowledge and news from the other cities on planned protest actions. They signed joint petitions about the Klempicz issue, and also organized collaboration. Sokołowski went to Piła to meet the local Solidarity leaders and to establish lines of communication for joint actions regarding Klempicz. At the seminar they agreed that each city (Piła, Poznań, and Gorzów) would organize a protest march against the NPP. All the activity from the fall of 1988 to April 1989 was geared towards preparing the locals so that people knew why protest marches were held.

Weekly demonstrations began in March 1989. People demonstrated in Poznań, but also in smaller cities across Greater Poland such as Gorzów, Piła, and Wronki. There were also demonstrations in other regions of the country,

Figure 5.1. "Klempicz—NO!—Communists are poisoning us—Radioactive wind will disperse all doubts—John Lennon is dead." Protesters on the roof of the department store in Gorzów Wielkopolski, 22 March 1989. Photograph provided by Mirosław Wrąbel.

e.g., Katowice, Częstochowa, Lublin, Wrocław, and elsewhere. These were the result of the Freedom and Peace movement's convention that took place in Poznań on 4–5 March 1989, during which a decision was adopted to start a nationwide campaign against nuclear energy.

By that time people had learned from Międzyrzecz. Sokołowski suggests that the information campaign was so thorough that "by the end it was almost too much info. People would hear 'Klempicz' or 'nuclear power plant' and go 'enough already!'" The campaign required the involvement of the Independent Youth Movement, WiP, and Gorzów scouts. As part of the preparations for the April demonstration against Klempicz, the activists returned to the tested *daching* strategy, climbing atop the roof of a department store in downtown Gorzów. The police were there to take them down, but in early 1989 things were already different. It was not 1987, negotiations between the government and opposition were ongoing, and under this limited "thaw" protests were generally getting a much lighter treatment.

Sokołowski also comments on the changing atmosphere and relative easiness of conducting protest actions at the time: "We got signatures by just standing around in cities with a guitar or some posters, or banners, the lists laid out on a table. We also did that outside of churches and got a really impressive result. . . . We had to form a committee that would be responsible for registering the march officially." The April demonstrations were therefore the first ones to be legal, but according to Sokołowski, they would have taken place even without a permit.

The foundations had been laid so well that the demonstration in April exceeded everyone's expectations. People came not just because they were against the power plant but out of sheer curiosity. There were also people who thought that it was a demonstration against the political elites (Solidarity and PZPR) that were ignoring citizens. Once the march in Gorzów started, some five to seven thousand people appeared. The demonstration ended at the Voivodeship Office. Sokołowski explains:

> I think the whole thing [was] powerful enough [for] the authorities to really get scared—you need to remember that similar demonstrations took place in Piła and Poznań—and so we didn't have to do another one. It turned out that we picked the right moment, it was the transition period, and the government had already been weakened, so they abandoned plans to build that power plant.

Meanwhile in Poznań, events took a very different turn, ending in the most violent clashes with the police that the city had seen in almost a decade. Poznań, although one of the country's biggest cities, was hardly the opposition capital of Poland, and so a march that gathered a thousand to fifteen hundred people was a good result, and as Urbański attests, "shows that the locals were incensed and moved by this issue." Radosław Gawlik visited the city, invited by Urbanski and Olędzka. He was happy to see the large crowd, but also concerned that there seemed to be equally many riot policemen around. "Suddenly we were being cordoned off, suddenly there's this huge brawl—ZOMO [the riot police] charges in, blocks the march. I think they were trying to redirect us. . . . We're surrounded by ZOMO with their plexiglass shields." Gawlik and Urbański were not involved in the fighting, and the police initially seemed to just be blocking the march and asking the participants to disperse (unlike in Gorzów, the march was illegal). However, clashes with the police erupted on different sides of the main marching column, and eyewitnesses reported some heavy rioting and severely beaten protesters.

A subsequent demonstration called "The funeral of Polish nature," organized by high school students, was held on 15 March 1989. A funeral procession with a casket and banners went down Półwiejska Street and, after it was blocked, down Strzelecka Street, where the first clashes took place. The law enforcement's actions were met with chants of "MO—Gestapo!" and

Figure. 5.2. "The funeral of Polish nature," an environmental protest organized by students on 15 March 1989, Poznań. Photograph provided by Tomasz Borewicz.

the officers were pelted with coins rather than stones. (The Citizen Militia—Milicja Obywatelska, or MO—was the official name of the Polish police under communism.) Upon reaching Wildecki Square, the casket was burnt. After the demonstration was over, the Security Service started arresting participants. A leader of the Fighting Solidarity, Maciej Frankiewicz, was among those beaten up.

Mid-March saw an escalation of protests and violence. On 16 March, at the Old Town Square, a legal rally was organized under the auspices of PKE and the Greater Poland Civic Action (Wielkopolska Akcja Obywatelska), which gathered a record eight thousand people. After the rally was over, some three thousand continued it illegally under the auspices of more radical organizations—Fighting Solidarity and the Confederation for an Independent Poland (Konfederacja Polski Niepodległej, or KPN). The protesters scattered a cordon of ZOMO officers outside the local party headquarters. On 18 March, an event with three hundred people was held, but a strong ZOMO presence forced the young people to capitulate honorably (they kept their banners but handed over their sticks). On 19 March, several hundred people marched again to protest against the construction of the Warta NPP.

Figure. 5.3. Riot police block and disperse the environmental demonstration in Poznań. Photograph provided by Tomasz Borewicz.

Further demonstrations, coordinated with Gorzów and Piła, were announced for 2 April and 26 April. At the time, during the ongoing Round Table negotiations and in the run-up to the semi-free elections in June 1989, the Polish political scene began to be populated by an ever-growing number of radical splinter and offshoot parties, dissenting from the main Solidarity line and not willing to accept the moderate and conciliatory tone represented by Lech Wałęsa. The demonstrations in Poznań were endorsed by some of these, e.g., the Independent People's Movement Solidarity, the "Independence" Liberal Democratic Party, the Independent Students' Union (Niezależne Zrzeszenie Studentów, or NZS), the School Clubs of Social Resistance (Szkolne Koła Oporu Społecznego), the already mentioned right-wing KPN, Fighting Solidarity, and the Polish Socialist Party (PPS).

Around three thousand people gathered on 2 April. The march proceeded to the Old Town Square, where it was surrounded by numerous ZOMO squads. After the speeches, a procession was formed, but the road was blocked by the police. That's when the first clashes happened. In response to beatings and arrests, protesters attacked ZOMO officers, obtaining the first pieces of equipment (shields, truncheons, etc.). A police car was destroyed. The demonstration visibly turned from an environmental protest into an antisystem one. Further attacks by ZOMO officers and continued resistance from the demonstrators led to the destruction of seven police vehicles, and there were many wounded on both sides.

According to Maciej "Metys" Hojak, an anarchist who took part, the police forces had to be brought from all around the region, because blocking the entire Old Town Square required a considerable number of officers. Some twenty policemen were reportedly hospitalized, and Metys recalls metal trash cans flying at the ZOMO squadrons. The rioters even took a whole van full of policemen hostage for a while, before the other police forces were able to liberate them. But the demonstration was experienced differently by people in different parts of the Old Town: while heavy fighting ensued in some streets, in others smaller peaceful marches were uninterrupted by ZOMO.

After the demonstration was over, ZOMO summoned reinforcements and used truncheons and water cannons to attack the people in the Old Town Square. A crowd clustered in front of city hall. Water cannons were brought in. The City Hall and several apartments near it got hit with water. People threw down bandages from windows to help the wounded. Some of the protesters took refuge under the city hall arcades—they were pulled into "health jogs" (forcing people to run between rows of officers who beat them with truncheons). Metys recalls:

> Me and my crew were in a stairwell that was filled with people up to the last floor. We tried blocking the door, but we failed, and they started beating up people inside the entrance and up on the stairs. Some started fleeing using a scaffolding—the next building was being renovated. The police also climbed onto the scaffolding, but people above them started pelting them with metal stuff, like buckets, so they retreated. I was downstairs. The crowd pushed us out into the courtyard. People were being put up against the wall and searched for crowbars and screws (several police officers were wounded with that sort of stuff).

The young hotheads from the radical wing of the already radical and militant Fighting Solidarity were indeed treating these demonstrations as a battleground. Metys explains that "they had some other name, so they wouldn't be associated with Fighting Solidarity. They were hardcore, they'd go to demonstrations with Molotov cocktails, crowbars, rocks, and bolts, and they were the ones who messed those police guys up the most." He continues:

> For talking back to an officer, I was invited into the stairwell of the building on the other side of the courtyard, where they beat the shit out of me. . . . I also hit my head on some pipe (it was dark), so I don't remember anything else. After it was over, some guy found me and led me away. The streets were completely empty. A police van

> soon rolled up and they started giving us trouble, but out of nowhere around thirty people appeared, emerging from nearby buildings—locals, some of them thugs, and quite a lot of older women who formed a wall. They made such a ruckus that the officers backed off, and I was led away. I remember just bits and pieces because I had a concussion and was seeing spots. Someone checked my head, he said he was a doctor, someone else put me in a car and took me to hospital. At the hospital, when the doctor heard that I was from the demo, he locked the door, examined me, did an X-ray, and said he won't fill out any paperwork, so there wouldn't be a trace of me being here. Two floors up, they were bringing in police officers with head wounds, and there were already Security Service officers prowling the halls, looking for wounded demonstrators. There were supposedly eight wounded on our side.[1]

Around two hundred protesters were arrested, and the IDs of a thousand were taken down. The intensity of the fighting was so great that the 2 April riots became something of a Poznań legend, and the words "02.04—we fought here," spray-painted on one of the Old Town buildings where the riots were heaviest, was still visible on the wall for at least another decade.

On 3 April 1989, a dozen young NZS and SKOS activists, along with one representative of the medical services from Solidarity, went to city hall to clear up the issue of the police using force as the demonstrators were trying to disperse. It was suspected to be a provocation meant to influence the Round Table negotiations that were to be finalized the next day. "Someone from the communist brass must have given the go-ahead, because there were reinforcements from the entire voivodeship, if not beyond," claims Metys.

At the same time, in the remaining cities in Greater Poland, peaceful antinuclear marches were held. In Piła and Gorzów, where the demonstration was legal, around two thousand people demonstrated, and around twelve hundred showed up in Wronki. Further demonstrations were planned for 26 April—the Chernobyl anniversary. They were not held because on 22 April 1989 Mieczysław Rakowski's communist government scrapped plans to build the Warta NPP.

From Heyday to Burnout: The Environmental Movement at the Time of the Round Table Talks

The environmental protest movement experienced a period of exceptional growth in 1988, both in terms of numbers and in terms of quality. The most well-known group of deep ecologists—the Living Architecture Workshop/Workshop for All Beings (Pracownia Architektury Żywej/Pracownia na Rzecz Wszystkich Istot)—emerged from isolation and started working with Solidarity and the Freedom and Peace movement. They did so, for example, by engaging in protests against the construction of a coking plant in Stonava in Czechoslovakia, and by sending activists from the ecological settlement in Dąbrówka to participate in the Green Federation, created in 1988.

International contacts intensified, both with independent and environmental movements in the West and, despite some difficulties, with those in other Eastern Bloc countries. WiP became an important element in the European peace movement landscape, and 1987 saw the organization of the first international Peace Seminar in the Eastern Bloc, in Warsaw, followed the next year by another one in Kraków (Kenney 2002; Szulecki 2013). They also partnered with Western ecological movements and green parties. In 1987, WiP activists and representatives of the German Greens signed a joint declaration, and in the fall of 1988 the WiP activist and later diplomat and Eastern policy expert, Mariusz Maszkiewicz, went to Florence as the movement's representative, to attend a large congress called "Europa Verde" (Green Europe).[2]

WiP did not initiate any coordinated actions regarding nuclear energy until the issue of replacement military service was resolved in 1988. The situation changed dramatically in 1989. At a WiP convention that took place in Poznań in March 1989, the issue of nuclear power plants was designated as the main area of interest for the movement. The danger posed by WiP in the field of environmental protection, due to the group's scaling down their pacifist activity following the introduction of replacement military service, was also recognized by General Krzysztof Majchrowski, the Director of Department III of the Ministry of Internal Affairs, in a memo from 11 January 1989.

The gradual consolidation of the environmental movement was accompanied by the strengthening of its cultural resonance, although unlike in the West, it never became a strong subculture or a political party. Piotr Gliński, a leading student of the movement, writes that this was the result of internal disagreements and external pressures, or even provocations. This was confirmed by an official report from the Ministry of Environmental Protection and Natural Resources. Already in the aftermath of Chernobyl, the Jaruzelski administration and prime minister Zbigniew Messner realized the "explosive" potential of antinuclear and environmental mobilization (Hicks 1996, 123) and reacted by expanding the role of ecological issues taken up by official institutions. In the spirit of Mikhail Gorbachev's glasnost policy, they also introduced more transparent reporting in official media.

In 1988–1989 several regional ecological organizations appeared, and even local governments began to venture into ecology. In many regions, social activity and protests were recorded regarding multiple issues.

- the activity of particularly harmful industrial plants, such as Cewiskoza in the Jelenia Góra Valley, Igloopol in the Bieszczady Mountains, Nowa Huta and Skawina near Kraków, and Police near Szczecin
- skiing infrastructure in the Tatra Mountains
- developing green areas in cities (e.g., the Vistula bank in Warsaw and Kraków's Planty park)
- the location of garbage dumps
- and particularly the planned and under-construction nuclear power plants and nuclear waste disposal sites.

These issues were also popularized in many other developing independent and youth movements, including those seemingly far removed from right-wing, patriotic groups. Demonstrations became regular and spread to smaller population centers.

The line between legal and illegal activity was becoming blurry, which is why some demonstrations against the construction of nuclear power plants in the late 1980s were legalized, allowing their organizers to expand social participation. Lower levels of National Councils, PRON, the United People's Party, and the Democratic Alliance also got involved in ecological activity, and particularly in the fight against nuclear energy, even if those actions were illegal and the "higher-ups" were against it.

The line between the "government" and the "opposition" was also being gradually blurred, while new divisions appeared within the oppositionist camp. When activists from the first Solidarity started "emerging from the underground" and the union declared its interest in ecology, there was anxiety about a potential clash between the newly arrived union activists and the people who had been involved in ecological protests for years. That conflict did not materialize, however, because most of the old guard chose politics or legal Solidarity, quickly forgetting about environmental protection.

Instead of sparking an internal struggle, it soon became clear that Solidarity oppositionists, or rather the government they would go on to form, posed an external *threat* to the environmental movement. As Security Service informer "DEL" astutely noted: "many a political force quickly changed its slogans as soon as it came into power." One of the most seasoned WiP activists, Wojciech "Jakob" Jankowski from Gdańsk, explained in an independent TV video at the time:

> WiP was formed in 1985, when the situation in the opposition was quite clear, i.e., all oppositionist activity was simply oppositionist, and we had the support of Solidarity. . . . Currently, the situation is a bit more complicated, the Round Table is underway [and] WiP is now this little orphan no one really knows what to do with. The demonstrations we organize don't end in brawls, but they're probably not supported by Wałęsa and his circle.[3]

Toward the end of 1988 and the start of 1989, there was a radical changing of the guard in young opposition movements, especially in WiP. Social movement theoretician Sidney Tarrow proposed the concept of a "protest cycle" (Tarrow 1998), which explains the changes that took place in 1988 in the Polish opposition, particularly within the environmental movement (Piotrowski 2015; Szulecka and Szulecki 2017). At this stage, many participants of the 1980s opposition movements were reaching burnout in terms of social activity, organizing events, sacrificing their private and/or professional lives, constant pushback from the government, and despite some success, the rather slow pace of progress (Szulecka and Szulecki 2019).

Jankowski's statement showcases how exhaustion, disillusionment with the progress of change, and various life entanglements conspired to remove a significant number of the older WiP activists from the battlefield:

> [In 1988], the Security Service assured me that I'd be detained for longer than the usual forty-eight hours if I show up at the August strikes. I did show up—so they wanted to lock me up, issued a warrant for my arrest under the pretext of collecting an overdue fine for trying to drown General Jaruzelski's effigy. I holed myself up in the mountains, in a cottage with Andrzej Stasiuk, another WiP activist [and later a famous writer]. But they found me even there—it was only by chance that I wasn't home when they got there, and since they had already put Krzysiek "Gal" Galiński away for a month, I went to Gdańsk and just allowed them to take me. I sat down outside the Security Service building with signs saying "Free Gal" and "Down with Misdemeanor Courts." They nabbed me, didn't charge me with anything new, but put me away for a month. That was in January 1989—preparations were underway for the Round Table, so it's possible that I was the last political prisoner [of communism] . . . The WiP old guard was tired, for years they have been put through the wringer—they drifted away, started having kids. On 7 January 1990, my daughter Ariadna was born. I had around

> a million złoty of outstanding fines, total. And the average salary at the time was around ten thousand a month.

At this stage of the protest cycle, according to Tarrow, two mechanisms come into play: radicalization and institutionalization. Some activists advocate for more radical forms of protest or are forced to go in that direction by governmental resistance (as we saw in the events in Poznań), while others look for ways to achieve their goals from within the system instead of from the outside. The example of WiP showcases this quite well. In 1988, some of the "old" activists retreated into their private lives or started careers in politics (facilitated by the wholesale systemic changes then underway), in business (following the beginnings of a transition towards market capitalism under Mieczysław Rakowski), and later also in the special services of postcommunist Poland (several WiP activists became active in the Office for State Protection, the successor of the Security Service).

On the other hand, the movement was injected with fresh blood that treated the slogans of freedom, peace, and environmentalism seriously, and not just instrumentally as a pretext to fight communism or build political capital. That is also when both "I Prefer to Be" and WiP received a massive influx of representatives of youth subcultures. As the movement was cleared of those who saw environmental protection merely as a tool for mobilizing against the regime, the new activists were genuinely into the issues that they put on their banners—and were more determined to protest for the sake of nature itself.

This new generation of activists—"Generation 1989" as they are called by historian Padraic Kenney—had points of reference different from their older oppositionist friends (Kenney 2014). The 1970 protests on the coast were ancient times to them, and the strikes in the shipyard and legal Solidarity with its "self-restraining revolution" were just a vague memory from their childhood. Politically influenced by the long crisis of the 1980s, the period of the gradual collapse of the communist economy and the erosion of governmental institutions, they were not satisfied with concessions from the communist authorities and demanded more revolutionary solutions. This put them on a collision course with both the government and the emerging new political elite, as the older generation of Solidarity trade union leaders began to turn away from its civil society base.

Notes

1. Maciej Hojak in email communication with Janusz Waluszko, 15 August 2014.
2. The authors' communication with Mariusz Maszkiewicz, 20 April 2015.
3. Material filmed for the Gdańsk Catholic Magazine by Video Studio Gdańsk in February 1989. Available at: https://www.youtube.com/watch?v=E-gHKBGVjbo

References

Hicks, Barbara E. 1996. *Environmental Politics in Poland: A Social Movement between Regime and Opposition*. New York: Columbia University Press.

Kenney, Padraic. 2002. *A Carnival of Revolution*. Princeton: Princeton University Press.

———. 2014. "Rewolucja Bezideowa, Czyli Skąd Mamy Viktora Orbana." *Kultura Liberalna* 293 (33). https://kulturaliberalna.pl/2014/08/19/mysli-rewolucja-bezideowa-skad-mamy-viktora-orbana/.

Kiełbasa, Władysław. 2021. "Elektrownia Jądrowa Warta." Nuclear.pl. https://nuclear.pl/polska,ejw,elektrownia-jadrowa-warta,0,0.html.

Piotrowski, Grzegorz. 2015. "The 'Other' Democratization in Poland: The Case of Environmental Protection Movement." In *Democratization Through Social Activism: Gender and Environmental Issues in Post-Communist Societies*, 235–64. Bucharest: Tritonic.

Szulecka, Julia, and Kacper Szulecki. 2017. "Polish Environmental Movement 1980–2017: (De)Legitimization, Politics & Ecological Crises." *ESPRi Working Papers* 6. https://doi.org/10.2139/ssrn.3075126.

———. 2019. "Between Domestic Politics and Ecological Crises: (De)Legitimization of Polish Environmentalism." *Environmental Politics* 0(0): 1–30. https://doi.org/10.1080/09644016.2019.1674541.

Szulecki, Kacper. 2013. "'Freedom and Peace Are Indivisible': On the Czechoslovak and Polish Dissident Input to the European Peace Movement 1985–89." In *Entangled Protest: Transnational Perspectives on the History of Dissent in Eastern Europe and the Soviet Union*, 199–229. Osnabrück: Fibre.

Tarrow, Sidney. 1998. *Power in Movement: Social Movements and Contentious Politics*. 2nd ed. Cambridge Studies in Comparative Politics. Cambridge: Cambridge University Press. https://doi.org/10.1017/CBO9780511813245.

Chapter 6

Communism Might Be Over—Nuclear Is Not

The Round Table Talks and the Escalation of Anti-Żarnowiec Protests

The summer of 1988 had something new in the air, something reminiscent of 1980, the summer before the August Agreements and the legalization of Solidarity. Though hardly anyone could expect that a year later the union would be legal again and Poland would have (partly) free elections, something was visibly changing. In those days in late July 1988, several hundred punks and hippies from all around Poland gathered in Białogóra, a coastal fishing village just several kilometers from Żarnowiec, for a Peace Festival called "Hyde Park." Many WiP and RSA activists attended, and they organized a colorful and flamboyant protest against the Żarnowiec NPP, marching through the village and on the beach with flags and banners. Nuclear energy was becoming a hot topic in politics—its importance for the failing regime is symbolized by the fact that a new PLN 20,000 bank note, issued in 1989, featured an illustration of the "Ewa" reactor on the reverse side. Poles would see it often, as the galloping inflation that ensued turned this once considerable sum of money into small change within a matter of months.

At the time when the antinuclear campaign was at its peak in terms of breadth and levels of national mobilization, Polish politics was undergoing very serious changes that would soon lead to the collapse of the monopoly of the communist Polish United Workers' Party (PZPR). Following the wave of strikes in 1988, the political leadership of the Solidarity opposition met with representatives of the government and of the Catholic Church in Magdalenka. This meeting began the gradual process of dismantling the monopoly.

That was what all the struggle in the 1980s was about, wasn't it? In late 1988 this was not at all clear. Back in 1980–1981, Solidarity had "sought dialogue with the regime in order to solve Poland's problems; now they had that dialogue. Was this what Poles had been fighting for over the intervening years? Perhaps inevitably, a profound sense of disappointment set in. From now on, the actors in the gradual victory of the opposition would be the veterans of 1980. The key moments would occur indoors" (Kenney 2002, 250).

As historian Andrzej Paczkowski underscores, this sort of "negotiated transformation" requires an agreement between a moderate oppositionist elite and the reformist wing of the ruling party. It also leads to the marginalization of all forces that might sink the accord, in this case the party hardliners and oppositionist radicals.[1] Towards the end of 1988, one of the main veins of oppositionist radicalism was the ecology and antinuclear protests. Even though they were eventually successful, it is difficult to understand the road to stopping the construction of Żarnowiec NPP without acknowledging the fact that radical environmentalists became problematic for both the communist government and the Solidarity elites.

And so, the paths of oppositionists began to diverge. Wojciech "Jacob" Jankowski recalls:

> In 1988, the Tricity WiP got involved in strikes. The two of us, me and Jarek Cieszyński, sat in the shipyard, working at the printer, among other places. During the August strike, I was sad to see our idealistic stance turn into a stampede for individual benefits and careers. This was fueled by secret conversations between the government "elite" and the Solidarity opposition, the content of which wasn't being consulted with anyone. [In January 1989] Jacek Taylor visited me in prison and invited me to the "youth subtable" in Wałęsa's name. I got out in early February 1989. After consulting within our circle, I declined to participate in the Round Table, even though opinion was split on this issue.

The Round Table negotiations took place between February and April 1989. The so-called environmental subtable was one of merely two (out of fourteen) subtables to which the younger opposition had been invited. From as many as twenty-eight issues that the environmental discussions covered, only one remained unresolved—nuclear energy. Radosław Gawlik participated in the negotiations as a representative of the Solidarity side and became an MP after the June elections. He recalls that nuclear was the only issue on which the two sides were divided from the start, and there was no way they could reach an agreement: "The governmental side advocated for continuing the project, while we had consistently stated that we must shut it down and stop sinking money into it." The opponents pointed out that Żarnowiec was only 10 percent complete, and it was not clear what enormous sums the NPP was yet to devour.

The environmental subtable sessions took place on 22–24 February and 2–3 March 1989. The discussion ended with a discrepancy report, which stated that the government was for continuing the project, and that the opposition was pushing for its immediate abandonment. The government pointed to the demands of the economy and used ecological arguments to justify building nuclear power plants, comparing them to "dirty" coal-based energy. The party experts emphasized that the technology was safe and that Poland needed the energy. Later it turned out, in the second half of 1989 when the radical economic transition plan designed by neoliberal Leszek Balcerowicz was introduced, that demand for energy plummeted, as inefficient heavy industry collapsed. In the so-called Wierusz Report,[2] it was stated that "in February 1990, out of the 28 GW of total capacity of Polish power plants, only 19.5 GW were being used due to the recession." This constituted around 70 percent of capacity, so better results could be achieved by rationing energy use. This was the opinion of not just environmentalists, but also Minister of Industry Tadeusz Syryjczyk. The fact that the government did not really have Poland's energy needs in mind is evidenced by the subsequent plan to have the construction completed by the German company Siemens in return for electricity from the Żarnowiec NPP, which under this scheme was supposed to be diverted back to Poland only during the last few years of the power plant's lifetime.

The opposition's arguments were that nuclear energy carried a certain margin of error and risk, and then there was the waste, the economics, and the lack of demand. "We figured it was Soviet technology—we didn't trust it, and we had good reason not to, as it had failed in Chernobyl," Gawlik explains. The Solidarity side also noted the lack of a waste disposal site or a clear framework for decommissioning the plant after its life cycle was over. At the same time, it lobbied to devote the funds assigned for the construction to other projects.

At the last session of the subtable, Gawlik presented the democratic opposition's standpoint:

> Cutting funding to nuclear energy would allow us to hasten the restructuring of our industry and thus reduce its energy consumption, as well as modernize our conventional energy production capacity, rationalize fuel and energy use, and equip conventional power plants with devices necessary for environmental protection. . . . It is also crucial that we resolve social conflicts which arose because of the arbitrarily enforced program of constructing nuclear power plants. In this situation, the oppositionist side demands a halt to the construction of nuclear power plants (Żarnowiec, Klempicz, and the third planned power plant) until thorough economic analyses have been made [and submitted] for social consultation. . . . We're all agreed here that nuclear power plants just won't fly in this country.[3]

Figure 6.1. Radosław Gawlik speaks at an antinuclear protest organized by the Green Federation, Wrocław Old Town Square, 24 April 1989. Photograph: NAF Dementi, Archive Pamięć i Przyszłość.

Due to a difference of opinion, the future of the Żarnowiec NPP was not decided. A growing role in this debate would be played by increasingly drastic social protests, especially when the Solidarity government of Tadeusz Mazowiecki, created after the June contract elections, initially did not revise its predecessor's energy policy. As the discrepancy report on the issue of nuclear energy was being compiled in Warsaw, in Gdańsk a full-blown anti-Żarnowiec campaign was gearing up. The road towards shutting down the construction of the power plant would be long and bumpy, and as Jarosław Cieszyński[4] noted in February 1989, "Żarnowiec is an issue that is divisive not along the government-opposition line, but along an altogether different one." In the remainder of this chapter we will trace the evolution of this campaign, focusing on the development in the streets—while Polish oppositionist politics increasingly moved into the corridors of power.

The Beginnings of the Campaign Against the Completion of the Żarnowiec NPP

Gdańsk—the birthplace of Solidarity—was the main hotbed of strikes in 1988. It was also quite exceptional in terms of the diversity of local oppositionist groups. Aside from the circle of Free Labor Unions (an organization that preceded Solidarity and later tried to return to the union's "true" workers' spirit) and the Independent Self-Governing Trade Union "Solidarity," there were also moderate and elite groups such as the so-called Gdańsk Liberals (one of them was the later Prime Minister Donald Tusk). But toward the end of the 1980s the political landscape was shaped above all by young and radical activists. These included anarchists from RSA and WiP as well as right-wing patriotic fighters from the Federation of Fighting Youth (Federacja Młodzieży Walczącej, or FMW), the Engaged Society Movement (Ruch Społeczeństwa Zaangażowanego), Fighting Solidarity, and even the fascist-leaning football fans of "Lechia" Gdańsk. The meeting place for the opposition, as well as a source of support and the venue for occasional brawls, was the St. Bridget Church in the parish of Father Henryk Jankowski, the Solidarity chaplain.

Until 1989, the actions taken against the construction of nuclear power plants in Poland were ad hoc in nature, and they only gradually coalesced into a continuous campaign (cf. the radioactive waste disposal site in Międzyrzecz described in chapter 4). Andrzej Szulc, a WiP activist in Gdańsk, participated in church-based meetings for the student community, and he suggested organizing an antinuclear protest in front of a local parish. However, none of the priests agreed to the idea.

Szulc figured that since the Round Table talks were already starting and signaled a much more "relaxed" regime, they could try testing the boundaries of what was possible, if not at the church, then perhaps in a regular street protest, handing out fliers and calling on people to demonstrate. He and his colleagues prepared the text of a statement, Szulc printed the materials, and they plastered them all over the city. At that point they were already in contact with people from the Anarchist Federation, so their ideas spread into other circles. The anarchists had a very different theory of action. They looked suspiciously at "elite" actions such as the Wrzeszcz *daching* in animal costumes described in chapter 4. In their view, all such one-sided forms of protests alienated the broader society, casting it in the role of passive audience instead of inviting it to actively engage. According to the Alternative Society Movement activists, elite actions such as sit-ins would not yield any results, which is why it was necessary to move on to mass events.[5] Janusz Waluszko recalls:

> People, especially young people, were eager to protest or even fight "the reds," but this was about avoiding all that. How do you organize a mass demonstration with people who reach for stones and bottles every Sunday and national holiday in a way that stops them from doing it? And how do you prevent the police from attacking

> the people who gathered in protest and [from] provoking them to retaliate? There was an idea to start the whole thing with a [Catholic] Mass for the victims of Chernobyl, which would allow people to gather in a safe way, and then to form a march after church—police officers were less eager to attack people walking en masse, you don't mess with a crowd. That idea fell through because the priest got cold feet, so we had to start in the street. (Waluszko 2011b)

The Friday Demonstrations on Długi Market

The place and time were selected very consciously. They would meet at Długa Street and Długi Market ("Long" Street and "Long" Market—Gdańsk's characteristic medieval extended rectangular marketplace) because many people used it to go to work or to school, and it was pedestrian only, which would make it difficult for ZOMO vans to get there. The time was Friday at 4 PM so that regular people could come to the demonstration after work, instead of it being just the professional WiP revolutionaries. The other reason for this time was unique to the Polish revolutionary realities. If you were detained for forty-eight hours, which was the usual form of harassment—and also the maximum amount of time for detaining someone for an illegal demonstration (at this point the authorities could no longer pass out arbitrary sentences, though they rarely did so before in any case)—the protester would be out on Sunday evening and avoid missing school or work.

"What if the stone throwers come and start something?" asked a concerned "Jarema" Dubiel, the WiP activist from Warsaw. "They won't," Waluszko replied, hoping that the young radicals would recognize him as one of the few older activists who regularly fought at their side instead of condemning them. Both veteran protesters showed up at the right time and the right place. There was a considerable number of people, but they were just milling around on the periphery. Dubiel said they should start, but Waluszko wanted to wait for more people to come. Suddenly policemen came up to them asking for IDs, to which Dubiel exclaimed, "I told you we should've started already." Waluszko just shouted "No IDs for you!" He then threw the fliers up in the air and yelled "Down with Żarnowiec!" People immediately gathered around and the policemen fled, afraid of the usual course of protests in the city, which would mean getting beaten up by the rioters.

The first demonstration in Gdańsk took place on 24 February 1989. According to Security Service documents, around 70 activists and around 200 pedestrians took part in it. At its highest point, it gathered around 1,000 people. Just before the demonstration began, the IDs of around 90 people were taken down—some of them had fliers and banners, yet there is no record of them being arrested. The banners carried during the demonstration were emblazoned with slogans such as "Down with Żarnowiec—we want to live," "Atomic goo will be the death of you," "Żarnobyl sucks ass," "Even death caps are better than mushroom clouds" (Jarosław Cieszyński was dressed as a death cap mushroom), and "WiP shits on Żarnowiec." The demonstrators walked down Długa Street and Długi Market (the adjacent streets were blocked by ZOMO) and returned to city hall, on the steps of which Wojciech Jankowski gave a speech. He read from the balcony a faux medieval scroll with a proclamation from the noble burghers demanding a referendum. The police took some IDs and tried to nab Jankowski, but in the face of his refusal to "join them at the precinct," they capitulated. After the demonstration, he went to the police station to reclaim his ID, and he recalls that "the cops were terrified. 'Just please do not feel like you're being detained!' the commander begged me." Apparently, the police had orders not to provoke the protesters and not to create any unnecessary conflicts.

The organizers decided that the demonstration would be repeated weekly—until it succeeded. Szulc did not expect this when he prepared the initial fliers. His intention was to test the authorities once, not to have a

Figure 6.2. Leaflets thrown in the air at the first of the regular Friday protests at Długi Market in Gdańsk, 24 February 1989. Photograph provided by Janusz Waluszko.

Figure 6.3. "We want to live!"—protesters pass by the iconic Neptune fountain on Gdańsk's Długi Market, 24 February 1989. Photograph provided by Tomasz Borewicz.

regular event. Would the police crack down on the protesters, as they did during the Sunday riots in front of St. Bridget church? Here it was different. "Maybe they didn't get the order, or they didn't know what to do, maybe that's why we weren't dispersed and arrested right away," Szulc wonders. The point is that until then, in most WiP protests, it was "four guys or so starting the whole thing, and then a crowd of random people joining in. This demonstration was preceded by a flier campaign directed at various circles, so we had people showing up from all sorts of organizations." There were activists from the Independent Students' Associarion, the FMW, the Twe-Twa movement, and other smaller opposition organizations. Twe-Twa was a semiformal group of high school pupils, inspired by their teacher, Tomasz "Belfer" Burek—who would soon become the driving force of the campaign.

Elżbieta Łuczkiewicz was a history student at Gdańsk University at the time and her boyfriend knew Burek. She wanted to get involved in opposition activities, but the violent riots of the "stone throwers" from St. Bridget's parish were not what she had in mind. The peaceful and colorful protest against Żarnowiec—that was something different. She got involved and became a protest regular. There were many like her, people without a history of earlier engagement, who felt the urge to join that particular movement and protest that particular issue at that particular moment in time.

The marches on Długi Market would take place every week until the summer holidays. According to Security Service documents, the next demonstration, which took place on 3 March 1989, gathered around 500 people, 274 of whom were identified. The "protection" force consisted of 225 ZOMO officers whose goal was to not let the demonstration leave the Długi Market area, and 21 undercover officers who were tasked with identifying known RSA and WiP activists—their names and ID numbers appeared in subsequent reports—and with filming the demonstrators.

Soon it turned out that on the one hand WiP was not always interested in continuing the demonstrations, and on the other that the demonstrations gained a life of their own, as they attracted heretofore unknown activists. In order not to tire people out and to attract new participants, elements of artistic "happenings" were introduced into the proceedings. For example, on 10 March 1989, people dressed as animals or in white coats appeared at the demonstration; on 17 March, a cardboard "nuclear reactor" was to be constructed outside the city hall on Długa Street, and then destroyed (this particular plan was carried out on 12 May), and on 7 April, in reaction to repeated calls for the demonstration to disperse, several vinyl LP records were rolled at the ZOMO officers and protesters started yelling "Play something new!"

Figure. 6.4. Protesters on the stairs of the city hall in Gdańsk. In the middle (wearing a hat) is Janusz Waluszko, 17 March 1989. Photograph provided by Janusz Waluszko.

Arkadiusz Bach, then a barely fourteen-year-old high school student affiliated with the Twe-Twa movement, offers a "regular" participant's point of view.

> Like many other Tricity residents of that period, I went to the St. Bridget church every Sunday. It was a meeting place for football fans and various rabble-rousers. In the spring of 1989, I picked up some fliers that were scattered there. It turned out that aside from the Solidarity materials, there were also some that concerned Żarnowiec. I found one saying that every Friday at 4 PM on Długa Street there are protests against the construction of the Żarnowiec Nuclear Power Plant. The following Friday, I hurried to that demonstration. Although I had attended demonstrations at St. Bridget before, this was the first time I felt real kinship with the other protesters. First, the way they protested was important: it was peaceful, which stood in contrast to what was happening outside St. Bridget, where things would get really violent. I also really liked how they expressed themselves through art, for example by way of events which were a frequent sight at anti-Żarnowiec demonstrations. Maybe a hundred people would come to these demonstrations regularly. Of course, at some points there were also a lot of locals, but the core of these demonstrations was around thirty people who would meet up on a constant basis. I remember that the leader of these demonstrations was Tomasz Burek, who was 100 percent involved in all the preparations. I was actually given information about meetings at which all the materials, fliers, banners, and also stencils—i.e., other forms of artistic expression—were being made. That was the first time I saw stencils. . . . I really fell in love with them, and started doing them myself. The meetings took place in Tomasz Burek's home. That's where we would prepare the fliers, make banners and props for the events.

On 14 April, by the Golden Gate at the end of Długa Street, which was blocked by ZOMO, some protesters sat down on the ground, and several elegantly dressed people started reciting poems about the "peaceful atom," parodying the language of socialist-realist poetry of the Stalinist era. During this demonstration, "Jarema" Dubiel and Tomasz Burek proclaimed the creation of the Antinuclear Federation. After the demonstration was over, sixty people signed the contact sheet, most of them young people associated with FMW and the Engaged Society. Prior to that, in spite of a ZOMO blockade, the protesters formed a "train" and left the Długa Street/Długi Market area, heading towards the Central Train Station. It was not the first time this had happened—the previous instance was on 31 March. The size of the demonstrations did not change for quite some time. According to Security Service estimates, they were attended by around 300 people, though dropping over time to 200 and then to 150 people, because the "stone throwers," who were looking for a bigger thrill, stopped attending peaceful marches. Still, the demonstrations continued, starting every Friday at 4 PM.

Attempts at Dialogue with the Government and a "Visit" to Żarnowiec

These demonstrations would regularly pass by the building of the Voivodeship Committee of the Polish United Workers' Party (Komitet Wojewódzki Polskiej Zjednoczonej Partii Robotniczej, or KW PZPR). On 21 April 1989, the Secretary of KW PZPR in Gdańsk, Piotr Rajca, noted: "Today at 4:30 PM, a group of young people, 150 to 200 strong, protesting against the construction of the nuclear power plant in Żarnowiec, passed outside the KW PZPR building in Gdańsk. It is a weekly demonstration of local ecological groups that takes place every Friday."[6] Eventually a representative of KW PZPR, Secretary Mieczysław Kochanowski, invited a delegation of the protesters to the Voivodeship Committee. A group of twenty people attended the talk, while others waited outside the building. Rajca wrote: "Because both sides of this meeting seemed to be a bit surprised at this turn of events, and were obviously willing to continue the talks, another meeting was scheduled, this time with nuclear energy experts."[7]

The next meeting with secretary Kochanowski at KW PZPR took place on 5 May. It was agreed that on 19 May, at the International Press and Book Club on Długi Market, there would be a meeting of experts from both sides, with an audience. And indeed it took place as planned. There were around eighty people at the club with another forty outside, where loudspeakers had been mounted. The main issues under discussion were the safety, costs, and environmental impact of nuclear energy. Both sides stuck to their guns.

Jerzy Hołownia, the deputy director of the nuclear power plant, proposed that the next meeting be held in Żarnowiec, but WiP activists were not interested, citing logistical issues: though the construction site was not far from Gdańsk, traveling there required quite some time and would not be possible for most activists. However, the real reason might have been that they saw this sort of trip as futile since they had already visited Żarnowiec several days before, on 13 May. As Burek recalls, "Trying to liven up the anti-Żarnowiec campaign and develop various new avenues, a dozen of us went to Żarnowiec—because you can't really talk about Żarnowiec [as an initiative] without Żarnowiec [the power plant]." Someone in the organizational core of the protests learned of a train that was taking workers from Gdańsk to Żarnowiec every morning—a regular local train that continued all the way to the plant.

Twenty or so activists, dressed in workers' overalls, showed up on the platform, boarded the train, and rode it past all the security checks and gates. As the train rolled onto the platform at the destination stop near Żarnowiec, the car was festooned with banners saying "Żarnowiec sucks ass," and the activists put on Lenin masks known from the Długi Market demonstrations. "It was this sort of political, ecological, and artistic event," Burek boasted. When they arrived, the train was empty, as was the platform. Suddenly, when they disembarked in complete silence, they heard a voice through the loudspeakers—it was one of the plant's managers inviting them inside for a visit. "That was spooky," says Elżbieta Łuczkiewicz, "but I felt kind of relieved." They did not know what to expect and whether the authorities would treat them as illegal intruders, trespassing on strategic infrastructure, or worse. Instead, they were following the voice from the loudspeakers telling them where to go for a guided tour of the construction site.

Before they went, however, they lay down and sprinkled themselves with powdered paint, so that, when they got up, there were "these beautiful outlines of vaporized people [like the ones known from Hiroshima]."[8] Arkadiusz Bach also attended, with a banner saying "Down with Żarnowiec" and in smaller letters "I want to live." He used a bedsheet from the dresser, for which his mom later gave him a stern talking-to.

> She knew what I was doing because there were anti-Żarnowiec fliers and posters all over my room. She didn't support it because she was very apolitical. She was taught that it's best to just keep your head down and avoid any sort of confrontation. As we rolled into the power plant, I felt like we were entering some sort of a penitentiary: there was a lot of barbed wire. It all looked quite dark and dangerous. A representative of the power plant came out to meet us. I don't know who made this meeting possible. [They received us] quite hospitably in my opinion. They supplied a bus that took us around the construction site and they were really trying. I actually don't remember if there was any dialogue between us. I remember it as more of a guided tour.

Wojciech Jankowski also took part in the meeting with the Żarnowiec NPP director, Kochanowski, but left in disgust after the stone-faced official denied that the construction site used convict labor:

> I had done time in Wejherowo prison, for example, where many convicts were sent to the Żarnowiec construction site. After I left, I visited my friend Krzysiek Gotowicki, who was a conscientious objector prisoner and who worked at the Żarnowiec site. We talked at the canteen for hours. No one even checked my ID or searched me. At this "super secure," as the management claimed, construction site. So that's the sort of liars we were dealing with.

Despite decreasing attendance and the impasse in the dialogue with the authorities, the demonstrations kept taking place until the campaign was suspended for the holidays on 16 June 1989. On 17 June, a delegation from the Twe-Twa movement and FMW from Gdańsk demonstrated in Warsaw at the Sejm (against Żarnowiec) and under the Ministry of National Education (against civilian defense classes in schools and military training at university). Bach was in the small group that took a petition regarding Żarnowiec to the authorities. They transported a load of signatures to Warsaw: a total of around one hundred fifty thousand signatures were collected, from all over Poland. He also brought his graffiti stencils, a new passion he discovered thanks to the recurring demonstrations, and spray-painted walls around Warsaw on the occasion.

Meanwhile, more organizations, both legal and illegal, were joining the protest, including the "I Prefer to Be" movement, the Franciscan Ecological Movement, the Federation of Fighting Youth, Twe-Twa, the League for Nature Protection, the Polish Ecological Club, and the Young Poland Movement, and last but not least the Green Federation. Meanwhile, WiP as such was gradually disappearing, at least in Gdańsk and Gdynia. There were also WiP demonstrations in Warsaw, but they were different people by now, no longer the elitist WiP of the *Future Tense* (*Czas Przyszły*) magazine circle, represented by Jacek Czaputowicz, but rather a more anarchist generation, led among others by Ireneusz Ziółkowski.

Associate professor Jerzy Grzywacz and Professor Gotfryd Kupryszewski also cite the negative opinions on the construction of the Żarnowiec NPP issued by the Gdańsk Division of the Polish Physics Society, the faculty council of the Department of Biology of Adam Mickiewicz University in Poznań, and the Academic Board of the Institute of Oceanology of the Polish Academy of Sciences.[9] Those organizations, including the League for Nature Protection (LOP) and the Polish Ecological Club (PKE), organized a legal demonstration in Gdańsk on the anniversary of Chernobyl, 22 April 1989.

Figure 6.5. The only legal demonstration against the Żarnowiec power plant, Gdańsk, 22 April 1989. Photograph provided by Janusz Waluszko.

Although many protesters were opposed to the Round Table negotiations and called the contract elections of 4 June 1989 nondemocratic and illegitimate, several ecology activists and opponents of Żarnowiec were elected to the Sejm: Stanisław Bożek from the Międzyrzecz district, Radosław Gawlik from Wrocław, and the PKE expert Stefan Kozłowski.

The most important election result was the direct victory in Wejherowo (a town near the Żarnowiec site) of Antoni Furtak, a veteran Solidarity unionist and later an organizer of the Individual Farmers Solidarity, who was actively involved in the anti-Żarnowiec campaign and ran against Henryk Torbicki, the deputy director of the constructed Żarnowiec NPP. A historian of the Kashubian minority, Cezary Obracht-Prondzyński writes that it was the protest against Żarnowiec that united the opposition in Wejherowo after it had been scattered during martial law (2002).

On 26 April 1989, a demonstration took place in the city, gathering six thousand people. Furtak remembers that when information appeared that a nuclear power plant would be built there, resistance started mounting in the town.

> Maybe it wasn't being articulated that loudly, but when you talked to your friends or neighbors, they were all against it. When the time came to reactivate Solidarity in 1989, the leadership proposed that I run for Sejm on the Citizens' Committees ballot. I agreed, but

> my main platform was objection to the construction of the NPP. My opponent was Director Torbicki, who was building that power plant. So it's no surprise that the subject would come up during all of my meetings with constituents. Then we also met at rallies two or three times, where each of us presented their point of view. The result was that I got eighty-six thousand votes, and he got a little over six thousand.

This result was seen as a barometer of people's attitude towards the issue, and MP Furtak subsequently actively campaigned to stop the construction of the power plant.

There was also an additional regional twist. The power plant was being built on land belonging to the Kashubian ethnic community, indigenous to the Gdańsk area and the central part of the Polish Baltic coast, and their attitudes toward the project became quite important in 1989–1990. MPs from the Wejherowo district—particularly Antoni Furtak and Piotr Lenz—would try to "out-Kashubian" each other, with the former underscoring the fact that the construction in Żarnowiec was initiated "without the slightest attempt to get the approval of the rightful owners of this land," and that the degree of interference with the local landscape and their small homeland "was seen as an attempt to destroy the Kashubian community."[10] Jankowski, whose mother was Kashubian, describes it this way:

> As a kid, I often spent my summer holidays in the Nadole village on the Żarnowiec Lake, where my mom was born and grew up. My mom's family home is the only Kashubian homestead left in the area, and is now a museum. The construction of the power plant completely demolished this paradise I remembered from my childhood. The Kashubian houses were replaced by concrete boxes, everyone knew that this construction site was one huge swindle where you could earn some cash on the side and "procure" some building materials that were otherwise unavailable to mere mortals.[11]

On 6 May 1989, a legal demonstration of Kashubian organizations not related to ecological issues, such as the Kashubian and Pomeranian Association (Zrzeszenie Kaszubsko-Pomorskie), took place in Gdynia. Even though the actions taken during the demonstration were limited to reading proclamations, they had a big impact due to their social heft, as an expression of public opinion in a burgeoning democracy. One commentator from the community suggested that the issue of Żarnowiec was one of the most important phenomena for modern Kashubians (Obracht-Prondzyński 2007,

334). Meanwhile, another insider took a very critical view of the association's attitude,[12] pointing out that declaring the Żarnowiec NPP to be a priority issue did not translate into any actual actions, e.g., participation in the legal demonstrations, even though the plant was a threat to the Kashubians' existence as an ethnic group. Archival documents stored in the Gdynia state archive suggest that, indeed, Kashubian minority organizations were receiving financial support from the authorities to influence their support for the NPP, or at least to dissuade them from joining the protest movement.[13]

New Government, Old Problem: Demonstrations Resumed, Rally in Warsaw

The fact that the government had abandoned the Warta NPP (even though the construction site had already been prepared) and the Kopań NPP (where no construction work had begun) did not mean that it would also abandon Żarnowiec. Things did not change much after the Solidarity government of Tadeusz Mazowiecki came to power on 24 August 1989. A Security Service informer codenamed DEL observed that "[t]he decision of the 'old' government to postpone taking any action on Żarnowiec and 'pass the buck' to the new government turned out to be a good one," because electoral promises are often forgotten after the election.

One of the founders of PKE who participated in the environmental subtable negotiations, Andrzej Kassenberg, estimated that the new government's attitude toward nuclear energy was "mostly that it was an outdated Soviet technology, unsecure and costly, and the state was only just beginning to get its budget in order." But at the same time it was not a top priority issue for the new administration because "there were many things that had to be fixed in Poland, and nuclear energy was not on that list."[14]

An analysis of archival materials clearly shows that Żarnowiec posed quite a problem for the Mazowiecki government. A large group of Solidarity experts and MPs were unequivocally advocating for shutting down construction—if not completely, then at least until all the data had been analyzed properly, or a referendum was held on the issue. At the same time, recent oppositionists who suddenly found themselves heading ministries and departments often did not have in-depth knowledge or the time to familiarize themselves with all the issues. In this situation, the role of public administration and lobbying grew, as officials relied on the advice of ministerial and energy experts, who in this case were opposed to shutting down the project at such an advanced stage and argued that, without Żarnowiec, Poland might have a power deficit. Kassenberg adds:

> I remember when the head of the atomic agency issued the following statement. "Solidarity doesn't want nuclear energy because they want to start riots in the country. No nuclear energy would lead to power shortages, people won't be able to watch the news on TV, they'll get mad and go out into the streets." The response from Solidarity was: that would actually be a good thing, because public TV is lying.

The then deputy minister of environmental protection, Maciej Nowicki, saw the government's position somewhat differently: "As far as I recall, the government's position in 1990 was that the construction of the power plant in Żarnowiec should be continued. I know that the minister of industry, Mr. Syryjczyk, was a great proponent of this project."[15]

The argument about Soviet technology being dangerous, as it was associated with Chernobyl (although the type of reactor to be built at Żarnowiec was in fact different), seemed to be the most resonant for some politicians who did not have an opinion on the nuclear issue. However, it could be countered by obtaining Western capital and technologies—an option offered by French and German companies and governments. From today's perspective, and in the eyes of the protesters of that period, the association of democratically elected politicians with foreign corporations, which were not subject to any type of lobbying regulations at the time, was veering into corruption territory.

It was decided that more in-depth consultations with experts should be undertaken. Several months later, Minister of Industry Tadeusz Syryjczyk described this in his speech to parliament:

> I wanted to inform you about the government's stance on the issue of the construction of the power plant in Żarnowiec—practically since our first day in office . . . firstly it was discussed at the Economic Committee of the Council of Ministers [which] has decided that due to the gravity of the issue, a commission should be created [that will] present arguments to the Economic Committee of the Council of Ministers, and subsequently to the Council of Ministers, in order for it to make an informed decision.[16]

Due to the lack of any unequivocal action from the government, protests resumed after the summer holidays, in an expanded and more radicalized form. Already on 29 September 1989, the anti-Żarnowiec demonstrations had resumed in Gdańsk: several rallies took place, as well as a march from the traditional meeting spot on Długa Street to the Solidarity offices near the shipyard. On 27 October 1989, during another protest, the participants were informed about the demonstration in Warsaw planned for 31 October, and about supporting events in Szczecin, Poznań, Kraków, Łódź, Wrocław, and Gdańsk.

At the start of November, MP Antoni Furtak submitted a parliamentary question to the minister of industry regarding immediately shutting down construction of Żarnowiec NPP. He also brought the first thirty-five thousand signatures on a petition on that issue to the Sejm, then handed them over to the ministry. However, he had to wait until 20 January 1990 for the minister's response.

Seeing the indifference of the new government toward the actions organized in Gdańsk, the protest leaders decided that the focus should be shifted to Warsaw. Tomasz Burek as well as Marek Sacharczuk from the Twe-Twa movement went to Warsaw to picket the Council of Ministers building. Burek explains:

> Decisions are made mainly in Warsaw, not on Długi Market in Gdańsk, so that's where you have to show up and be a pain in the ass for them to notice you. . . . That's why we held the rally outside the Council of Ministers [currently the Presidential Palace]. . . . There were six to eight people there, twelve at most. We kept getting new people from local youth and environmental groups. We were like a living information point.

They set up a small tent village on the lawn in front of the building around the entrance. The late autumn weather was not an ally of this kind of activity. Apart from simply reminding the government officials of the issue, they were gathering signatures for a referendum. Sacharczuk adds some further details: "I don't want to brag, but I think I managed to create one of the biggest graffiti, at a roundabout crossing in Warsaw: 'Żarnobyl sucks ass.' Big as f***, on a wall by this huge roundabout, near the Central Station."

On 3 November they also organized a small march from the Ministry of Industry, with some sixty to one hundred people taking part, walking down one of the main streets of Warsaw toward the Council of Ministers building. One of the reasons for picking this date was the visit of the West German Chancellor Helmut Kohl. Apparently Siemens was interested in getting into Żarnowiec and resuming the construction work, so the activists wanted Kohl to know there were social protests in play. But the main reason was the session of the Economic Committee of the Council of Ministers, which was supposed to announce its advisory decision on the NPP.

Figure 6.6. Demonstration in front of the Ministry of Industry, the Warsaw-based activist Ireneusz Ziółkowski holding a can of spray paint. Photograph provided by Ireneusz Ziółkowski.

Figure 6.7. "Mutants" line up in front of the ministry building. Photograph provided by Ireneusz Ziółkowski.

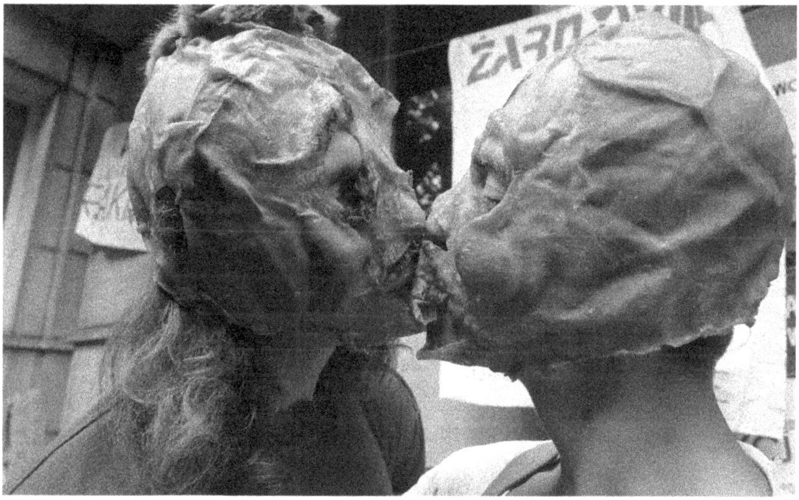

Figure 6.8. Two "mutants" kiss in front of the ministry. Photograph provided by Tomasz Borewicz.

Figure 6.9. Tomasz Burek interviewed during the protest. Photograph: Marcin Poletyło.

Figure 6.10. The legendary hippie drummer Jerzy "Słoma" Słomiński plays in front of the Ministry of Industry, 3 November 1989. Photograph: Marcin Poletyło.

The crowd was diverse, including people from "I Prefer to Be" and the Green Federation, as well as some individuals formerly or loosely associated with WiP. There were also Jerzy "Słoma" Słomiński, a well-known hippie with his drummers, and some of Warsaw's environmentalists, e.g., from the Polish Ecological Club. On the second day of the deliberations, a group of protesters barged into the room despite the guards trying to stop them. The vote on the Economic Committee's recommendation was about to be made.

Although the Security Service had the view that the opponents of the construction outnumbered the proponents four to one, Burek claims the contrary:[17]

> It seemed like we were doomed to fail, because there were fewer opponents of Żarnowiec. A dozen or so [out of eighteen experts] had ties to Żarnowiec, the Atomic Institute, the reactor in Świerk, the Polish Academy of Sciences. But it turned out that people from the State Atomic Agency, including Andrzej Wierusz (the chief designer of Żarnowiec) and Mirosław Dakowski spoke against it (having seen how it was being built, having observed the questionable reliability of the structure, the poor craftsmanship). We barged in and showed the petitions—I had them in my hand, collected from all over Poland. We had 150,000 signatures with us and were waiting on another 100,000 that had already been collected but were still in transit. I told them, "You are taking into account various technical, economic, and security issues, but please also acknowledge the social aspect. Our society rejects this project, or at least this way of making decisions, which inflames social conflicts." . . . A decision should have been made to shut down construction, but the commission's opinion stated that the vote was inconclusive.

The number of participants in the vote, as well as its outcome, remain unclear in light of various media reports and people's recollections. When Minister Syryjczyk was listing the members of the commission created by KERM in the Sejm, he included 22 names and described the result of the vote this way: "9 people were against, 7 were for, 3 were for conditionally. The commission decided that the result was inconclusive and both concepts should be presented [to the Economic Committee]."[18] Similarly, a Fighting Solidarity flier from the end of December 1989 states that out of 21 experts, only 19 voted, with 10 being "for" the continuation of the construction (of whom 3 had reservations), and 9 "against." According to *Przegląd Tygo-*

dniowy (Weekly review), there were 19 experts: 9 voted for, 9 against, and the president abstained. Meanwhile, Joanna Radecka reported in the *Poza Układem* (Out of the system) magazine a vote of 9 to 9, with MP Jacek Merkel casting the deciding vote for the construction to continue. The *Wybrzeże* (Coast) weekly also wrote about a split vote, mentioning Merkel's negative role during the proceedings. *Rzeczpospolita* (Republic) cited 21 experts and a split vote.

Jacek Merkel was an MP from Gdańsk, a former Solidarity unionist linked to Lech Wałęsa. He explained his support for Żarnowiec.

> Once I became an MP, my role was completely different from that of a union activist. I was an MP, a member of parliament from Gdańsk. Żarnowiec was being built there, so that problem was much more important to people from Gdańsk than it was to people from, say, Białystok. . . . The fact that there are protests against the nuclear power plant in Żarnowiec does not mean that 100 percent of local residents agree with this opinion. In a democratic country, everyone has the right to demonstrate for any views they want. So these attitudes were made clear, but there were also people who thought it was cool that we would have this power plant. The problem is we had to adopt this decision under uncomfortable circumstances. . . . The public has its opinion, and I have the right to have mine. Since I'm an MP, I have my own view, which is that there isn't a way to generate energy that does not impact the environment. No one will tell you: this way of producing energy is definitely good, and that one is bad. At every technical university they teach you that there are no good solutions. There are only degrees of deviation from the optimum, and the optimum depends on the criteria you use. What are your criteria for evaluating this power plant?

However, he asked that they put the debate in the context of 1990, with the construction of the Żarnowiec NPP at a fairly advanced stage: "It's not like we're still debating whether to do it with cows grazing on the future construction site. The power plant is there, we put time and money into it. If we waste that, we have wasted energy, which is not ecological."

The growing involvement of foreign companies hoping to take over the Żarnowiec investment—not just the abovementioned Siemens, but also the Belgian Tractebel—is an important thread at this juncture. Asked about MP Merkel's position, his colleague from the Solidarity related Civic Parliamentary Club (Obywatelski Klub Parlamentarny, or OKP), Antoni Furtak, responded:

> From the point of view of Tractebel, Merkel was responsible for getting Wałęsa to calm people down and contain the social protest. They'd go in once the conflict was defused. It's possible that they wanted to exert pressure and picked the right man to do it. At one point, Jacek Merkel had quite a bit of influence on Wałęsa, so Tractebel might have used a man who they knew had this influence for their own gain.

The accusations of lobbying for foreign companies would return, and Furtak claims he had documents showing Merkel's and future prime minister Jan Krzysztof Bielecki's non-transparent ommunication with Tractebel, which Furtak wanted to present to the second Solidarity convention in 1990, having organized an antinuclear demonstration outside Olivia Hall where the convention took place. However, Olga Krzyżanowska, another supporter of nuclear energy within Solidarity who was responsible for the agenda, did not allow a vote of no confidence for the two MPs. This internal division within the Solidarity camp would only prove to become more visible and more troublesome for the antinuclear protesters.

Notes

1. Andrzej Paczkowski in conversation with Kacper Szulecki, Warsaw, 13 October 2008.
2. Team for the Żarnowiec NPP called up by the president of the State Atomic Agency, "Report on the Consequences of the Chernobyl Catastrophe," Warsaw, 31 August 1991, available at: http://www.paa.gov.pl/sites/default/files/archiwalne/arch32.pdf
3. Stenogram of the eight seating of the Subcommittee for Ecology, 10 March 1989, pp. 28–33.
4. Material filmed for the Gdańsk Catholic Magazine by Video Studio Gdańsk in February 1989, available at: https://www.youtube.com/watch?v=E-gHKBGVjbo
5. In a polemic with Jarosław "Jarema" Dubiel of the Freedom and Peace movement in the pages of the samizdat journal *A'cappella*, RSA activists, as anarchists, pointed out that nonviolent struggle in the form of elite sit ins and hunger strikes is not much different from terrorism, as it eliminates society from action. See Polemic, *A'cappella*, No. 16, 1989, p. 17.
6. State Archive in Gdańsk, 2384/19584, To the Central Committee "Informacje o aktualnej sytuacji w województwie," I-VI 1989, P. Rajca, dalekopis nr 593, Gdańsk, 21 IV 1989, p. 3 [in the files p. 109]. It is interesting that, in the eyes of P. Rajca, the dispersing demonstration was almost twice as numerous as the actual demonstration at Długi Market and Długa Street, which was estimated by an officer of the Security Service at one hundred people. See IPN Gd 0027/3842, vol. 13, p. 26. Also telegrams no. 2705 of 24 February 1989 and no. 3377 of 10 March 1989 show larger numbers of participants than the analogous Supplementary Report (pp. 100, 102).

7. State Archive in Gdańsk, 2384/19584, To the Central Committee "Informacje o aktualnej sytuacji w województwie," I-VI 1989, P. Rajca, dalekopis nr 593, Gdańsk, 21 IV 1989, p. 1 [in the files p. 103].
8. T. Burek in Waluszko 2011a.
9. J. Grzywacz i G. Kupryszewski, Żarnowiec—ryzykowna inwestycja [a poster published by the Poligraphy Division of the Gdańsk University in Sopot].
10. Summary of MP A. Furtak's interpellation by Vice-Marshal Teresa Dobielińska-Eliszewska, Stenographic Report of the 18th sitting of the Sejm on 20 January 1990, p. 321.
11. W. Jankowski in communication with K. Szulecki, 9 October 2018.
12. Wojciech Kiedrowski, Kurhan żarnowiecki; idem, EJ w Żarnowcu. W oczekiwaniu na ostateczną decyzję, "Pomerania" 1989, nr 6; idem, EJ w Żarnowcu. Wiadomości dobre i złe, "Pomerania" 1989, nr 9.
13. State Archive in Gdańsk Branch in Gdynia, 265, *Elektrownia Jądrowa Żarnowiec w budowie, 1982-1996* [Żarnowiec Nuclear Power Plant under Construction, 1982–1996], bag 7, list of documents no. 61, items 180–185, Bulletin. Materials from the printing house; contracts for work: ibid., item 188, Contracts for the Bulletin; regulations for the "*Biuletyn budowy EJ Żarnowiec* [Żarnowiec NPP Construction Bulletin]": ibid., bag 11, document list no. 92, item 340, Regulations for the operation of the NPP Construction Bulletin.
14. A. Kassenberg in an e-mail to K. Szulecki, 15 October 2018.
15. M. Nowicki in an e-mail to K. Szulecki, 22 October 2018.
16. Stenographic report of the 18th sitting of the Sejm on 20 January 1990, pp. 321–22.
17. The Security Service and its informants from the pronuclear lobby were of an opposite opinion, estimating the advantage of Żarnowiec's opponents at 4:1, cf. BU IPN 1419/475, vol. 4, pp. 147, 152.
18. Stenographic report of the 18th sitting of the Sejm on 20 January 1990, p. 323.

References

Kenney, Padraic. 2002. *A Carnival of Revolution*. Princeton: Princeton University Press.

Obracht-Prondzyński, Cezary. 2002. *Kaszubi: między dyskryminacją a regionalną podmiotowością*. Gdańsk: Instytut Kaszubski w Gdańsku: Uniwersytet Gdański.

———. 2007. "Między kulturą a polityką. Przypadek Zrzeszenia Kaszubsko-Pomorskiego." In *Lokalne Wzory Kultury Politycznej: Szkice Ogolne i Opracowania Monograficzne*, ed. Jacek Kurczewski, 325–44. Warszawa: Trio.

Waluszko, Janusz. 2011a. "Wspomnienia Tomasza Burka, Współorganizatora Kampanii Przeciw Budowie Elektrowni Jądrowej Żarnowiec: Spisane i Opracowane Przez Janusza Waluszko." https://www.siemysli.info.ke/kampania-przeciwko-elektrowni-atomowej-w-zarnowcu-wspomnienia-tomasza-belfra-burka/.

———. 2011b. "Żarnowiec—Wczoraj i Dziś Protestu Przeciw Budowie Elektrowni Jądrowej w Polsce." *Przegld Anarchistyczny* 12.

Chapter 7

When the Government Won't Listen

Four Acts of Desperation (1989–1990)

Due to the split vote over Żarnowiec described in chapter 6, Economic Committee KERM experts were not able to present the government with a single position on the issue; instead, they decided that two representatives of the commission, along with its head, would present two scenarios at a Council of Ministers session in December. In the meantime, construction work continued, often without the necessary permits, which was soon to be used by the power plant's proponents to exert pressure on the government by presenting it with a fait accompli. On the other hand, the protests continued as well. The conflict was headed towards an unavoidable clash. In this chapter, we describe the most dramatic phase of the antinuclear protests. As the new Solidarity government chose to ignore or downplay the protests, protesters felt they reached a wall and saw no other option but to ram through it somehow.

After a series of rallies held outside ministerial buildings, and the inconclusive KERM vote, the group protesting in Warsaw moved to the headquarters of the Polish Socialist Party–Democratic Revolution (Polska Partia Socjalistyczna–Rewolucja Demokratyczna, or PPS–RD). Tired after two weeks on the street, with some of the protesters already leaving for home, they were about to depart for Warsaw Central Station to board their respective trains when suddenly the PPS–RD headquarters was attacked—a group of masked people with football scarves broke into the building with metal pipes and knives. After a short fight, the activists managed to defend themselves and the attackers backed out. Tomasz Burek went to the police to report the attack, and as he was returning to the party offices, he was arrested—apparently because he matched the profile of a potential suspect in the case he himself filed just minutes earlier. After he showed them a document he received from the police station, he was let go, but the police did not seem too eager to look any further, and after two days they were still not able to identify anyone. "We tracked those guys down ourselves," Burek explains. "[It] turned out they were skinheads, hooligans with ties to the National Rebirth of Poland (Narodowe Odrodzenie Polski), kids of [the] Security Service and police officers."

Act 1: The Blockade of the Cargo Terminal in Gdynia

The Warsaw escapade was hardly a success. Picketing the Council of Ministers did not help the activists break through the perceived media blockade, the possibility of mobilizing local support was limited, and government officials did not see the need to dialogue with the protesters, who from their perspective were merely one among dozens of discontented constituencies at the time of political and economic transition.

After Burek finally returned to Gdańsk, there was no time to rest. The next day he received the information that some reactor parts were to be shipped to Gdynia by sea, and that they would arrive at the cargo terminal within days. He decided to call for all the help he could get. Locally, he mobilized the participants of the regular Friday demonstrations, both the protest veterans and the youth from Twe-Twa and FMW, along with various unaffiliated people, in order to have enough boots on the ground to set up a blockade of the terminal. He also called Eryk Mistewicz, now a political public relations specialist, who was at the time affiliated with "I Prefer to Be" and worked at the Scout Radio in Elbląg, not far from Gdańsk. Mistewicz was a very prolific journalist for the movement's magazine *Na przełaj* (Cross country), where he described the nuclear energy issue. He wrote about the shoddy craftsmanship at the Żarnowiec construction site and about how people from the area were building themselves houses using materials from the power plant. It all contributed to this image of slapdash communist craftsmanship.

In Elbląg, Mistewicz managed to initiate one of the most vibrant centers of the "I Prefer to Be" movement. In the words of Adam Fotek, who worked with him:

> I was creating the Elbląg branch of our movement at the time. We didn't have a place to meet. The Scout Radio and *Na przełaj* announced that we could meet at their premises. A lot of people came to that meeting, around fifty from Elbląg alone, but also people from all over Poland. That meeting was interesting and fun. There was good vegetarian food, a lot of underground publications, there were people who were involved in all sorts of actions and movements: animal rights activists, vegetarians, some pacifist movements, conscientious objectors, some musicians. I remember

> there were drummers, we played together, there was this Indian vibe, sitars.

At one such meeting, Mistewicz took Fotek to the side. Fotek remembered that

> he loved this cloak and dagger, clandestine part of it. You can't really call it conspiracy theories, because the Security Service [was] a real thing, always wondering who the agent at this meeting is, trying to identify those people, running parallel meetings for the people you could really trust that was our daily bread. That evening, he [Mistewicz] told me that on the next day, first thing in the morning, parts for the Żarnowiec nuclear reactor were to arrive at the Gdynia terminal. It was our only chance to block that terminal, so they wouldn't be transported to the power plant, because once they reached Żarnowiec it would be over. Eryk said, "Listen, if you know any people here, then maybe we could try to scout things out, just be careful so the police don't grab us—only trusted people. Try to put a team together, pass this on."

After Burek contacted him, Mistewicz sent out an appeal via radio but also went door-to-door in Elbląg with Fotek, talking to people, assembling the team. Fotek continues: "We reached Tricity by train in the night. People from the Tricity 'I Prefer to Be,' mobilized by Eryk, awaited us at the Gdynia train station—quite a sizable group. So there were several dozen of us when we arrived at the terminal." Largely thanks to the efforts of Mistewicz, a total of one to two hundred people showed up, few of them were "professional protesters." "A lot of cool young people, weird ones, impulsive ones, but very few veterans," he summed up. They were people from the Green Federation, the "I Prefer to Be" movement, and several people from WiP, mostly from southern Poland, including two people from Katowice and Warsaw.

With some bitterness, Burek noted that hardly anyone from the local WiP old guard appeared, apart from Andrzej "Theologian" Szulc. That was the moment when Burek stopped identifying with the Freedom and Peace movement. "I preferred to say I was there as a private person," he would say. When WiP was not able or willing to provide a broader structural backing to the protest, "I Prefer to Be" assumed the role of the network. Somewhat paradoxically, the semiofficial movement, which many political activists despised, took over as the leading protest network in late 1989 and continued in that role in 1990–1992, becoming a backbone for the remnants of Poland's environmental protest movement (Szulecka and Szulecki 2017).

But back at the terminal, they had around a hundred people; most just came on trains with what they had or managed to pack. No food, no proper clothes, and it was the end of November and early December, while their goal was to block a massive industrial area. Fotek recalls:

> The idea for a blockade came up. Though we didn't have any specifics. We only knew that it could influence things, so why not just try to block that terminal and stop those components from leaving? But how? What does this terminal look like? What are the access points? We didn't know squat. We were completely unprepared. We didn't know that we were going to be there for a month. We went for a day, maybe two or three.

That's how the month-long blockade of the Gdynia harbor began. At 5 AM on 16 November 1989, activists from WiP, "I Prefer to Be," the Twe-Twa movement, the Engaged Society Movement, the Federation of Fighting Youth, the Green Federation, and one of the radical splinter groups known as Solidarity "Brawl" entered the terminal building. We have to bear in mind that the organizers of the protests had close ties with the local Solidarity group, and the union was of course strong in all workplaces in the Tricity harbor, the cargo terminal included. The protesters declared that they were going to block the transport of reactor components. The harbor Solidarity group called on its members to boycott the transloading and appealed to the government for a referendum on stopping the construction of the Żarnowiec NPP. According to some reports, Solidarity unionists used heavy equipment to block the wharf at which the ship containing reactor components was moored.

However, the leaders of the Gdańsk region Solidarity called on workers to proceed with the transloading, and only two days later, on 18 November 1989, the protest was abandoned. Already on 17 November 1989, *Tygodnik Gdański* (Gdańsk weekly) wrote about a symbolic blockade of the wharf by Solidarity being dropped. Simultaneously, the MP Jarosław Merkel was agitating among the environmentalists to stop their blockade.

It is worth remembering that no decision regarding the fate of Żarnowiec NPP had been made at that point, so the transport of another batch of components for the reactor would give a strong argument to its proponents, who were using a fait accompli to force the government to go ahead with the project. The blockade not only prevented that from happening, but—together with the subsequent hunger strike—became a difficult to ignore "pang of conscience" for the public, particularly for some Solidarity politicians with ties to the Tricity.

Zbigniew Stefański, a shipyard worker and participant in the 1980 and 1988 strikes at the Lenin Shipyard, was at the time affiliated with the radical "Brawl" group:

> I learned that we had to block the terminal. So I went there. Except I was working then, so I had to choose: work or the blockade. We didn't know when that blockade would be over, but we had to do it. We had to, because we got a heads-up that the reactor dome was arriving (on a Czech ship, interestingly enough). So I went on unpaid leave, even though that really hits you hard, financially, and I went there. Went with our group to that terminal. From what I remember, it was a bit chilly. And then things got crazy, because it wasn't about blockading the terminal, but about [trying to stay] in that terminal, inside, when you weren't allowed to.

The protesters put up banners and said that they would not let those reactor casings through. They posted guards at all gates and kept watch at all times so that the cargo would not get shipped out somehow. Aleksander Kłosiewicz paints a picture of that desperate action: "There were several dozens of us. Several people were hunched around a brazier, warming up, because it was winter. Others stood guard in the night—taking shifts, in freezing temperatures, wrapped in blankets and duvets and what have you. Looking like human tents. We watched and waited. Tired, sleep deprived." What the participants found surprising was that the police did not intervene, even though they would have broken the blockade within minutes.

The locals helped to gather information; they spoke to the terminal authorities, guards, and dockers to let the protesters know what was actually going on inside. The local residents also showed protesters the best lookout spots, from which they could effectively observe the entire terminal without the need to guard every gate. They only set up watch at the unloading gates and in various strategic points. "There was a train platform next to the cargo terminal—a perfect place to keep an eye on the reactor casing, which was stored there. We set up these shifts of 'lookouts.' It was usually three to four people who'd keep watch during the night. That reactor casing was quite far away, but you could see it clearly through binoculars and would know if anything was up," Arkadiusz Bach recounts.

First, they used a disused bus stop to hide in when it was raining. Then the frost and snow came. They were invited to use a nearby church as a dormitory, but due to the group's diversity and haphazard nature, they were soon thrown out. "This guy showed up and started a row with the priest from that church. . . . We had to leave that church after a day or two," Fotek explains. Tomasz Burek took the lead and managed to come to an agreement with the terminal authorities and establish the terms of the activists' presence there: where they could go, where they could not, and so on, rules that allowed them to blockade the terminal but also control the situation, so the dockers would have no reason to remove them from the premises. In any case, as Bach says, "we had this large tent that we pitched just outside the entrance to show the harbor authorities that even if they threw us out of that hallway, we'd just pitch tents outside and keep protesting."

Hygiene was an issue. The residents of nearby apartment blocks in the Oksywie district allowed the protesters to use bathrooms at their homes, which proved to be incredibly helpful, not only because of dirt, but also for the opportunity to warm up. One of the residents was Beata Zajkowska. Every day, a dozen or so people would go to her bathroom to wash up and get dressed. She started recruiting other friends, some new young people showed up and invited the protesters to their homes. Fotek recalls: "We were able to sleep in a normal bed, in a normal apartment, from time to time. To get washed up, in some complete stranger's bathroom. After that whole anti-Żarnowiec campaign, 'I Prefer to Be' in the Tricity got a big influx of fresh blood. It was young people from Oksywie."

The locals would bring them something to drink—hot tea, coffee—and better food, clothes, blankets, some mattresses. But resources were limited, and they needed to publicize the blockade. Eryk Mistewicz left for Warsaw to gather support for the protest. The antinuclear protest networks were activated, mobilizing people in Warsaw, and in the Tricity.

People kept arriving, more and more of them, from all over Poland, from various organizations. Fotek remembers:

> Some drank, others smoked weed. It was a ragtag group. Disorganized, because whoever wanted to come—did. Most of them didn't know each other. We didn't know who was who. Someone would get stoned, another guy would get wasted, someone would puke all over the terminal. There were problems all the time. We started imposing some sort of order through self-control and organizing shifts, to get a handle on this strange crowd and suss out who's helping, who's hindering us, who's with us and who needs to get the f*** out.

They killed time with long conversations, playing and listening to music. Bach recalls:

> I remember this sailor who could play the guitar really well, and who entertained us all night long. He came to the terminal to sit

> with us, and also brought a lot of food. I remember when we got a whole load of wieners, the thin ones, in plastic wrapping. I don't know who gave them to us. I remember those wieners best, because at one point we got a ridiculous amount, a dozen boxes. We were really happy, had them done all sorts of ways, until we couldn't even look at them.

Another man brought a large jar of caviar and said, "Once this here protest is over, have yourselves a party and eat this caviar." Fotek adds:

> It was incredible, actually, because we were suddenly receiving things that we wouldn't usually get to eat in communist times. Most of that food was from abroad. It was weird stuff: with some of it we didn't know what was inside until we opened the can—and in some cases, we didn't know even then. Caviar? When people don't have anything to eat, they don't have hot tea, or warm clothes, this jar of caviar is just completely mindboggling.

Figure 7.1. A transport of reactor parts blocked by the environmentalists at the Gdynia terminal, 14 December 1989. Photograph provided by Tomasz Borewicz.

Act 2: The Limited Hunger Strike

But before they could eat caviar, they decided to stop eating altogether. On 19 November, facing an impasse, a decision was made to initiate a hunger strike of limited duration (fourteen days) in order to underscore the importance of the protest and draw attention to it. Initially they began the protest outside, but the terminal authorities immediately let them into the main building corridors, possibly afraid of the martyr-like imagery of desperate activists holding a hunger strike in the snow and freezing in the process.

Twenty protesters participated, while the blockade and the information campaign in the Tricity continued. The group taking part in the hunger strike had to be large enough to make an impression, but at the same time, since the weakened strikers would not be useful for lookout duties and, if the blockade was broken, could not put up a fight, the number had to be realistic, given the limited human resources of the protesters. They also wanted each organization to be represented in the hunger strike. However, affiliations proved fluid. One activist from Kraków was affiliated with the Green Federation but had initially been involved in "I Prefer to Be." Since Fotek signed up for the hunger strike as someone from "I Prefer to Be," the other activist signed up as the Green Federation. "Not to mention the fact that some punks and anarchists showed up and also went on hunger strike, coming up with some organization name on the spot," remarks Fotek.

According to Stefański the primary goal of the hunger strike was "to get rid of this shit, to get rid of the nuclear power plant in Żarnowiec," and another was "to have a referendum in which people could democratically decide what would happen and what wouldn't." The idea of a referendum, which was already put forth during the protests in Warsaw, gradually became the key demand of the hunger strike. "The authorities wouldn't talk to us—we were just a bunch of punks, easily ignored, we didn't know anything, couldn't do anything. But we were the nation, we elected that government," Stefański continues. If after fourteen days the government did not enter in negotiations for a referendum, they planned to move to an open-ended hunger strike. Kłosiewicz explains the technical side.

> Some people ate, others would just lie down, drink something warm [or fruit juice]. Sharing information and working each other up so that we wouldn't give up. [We'd sleep] on foam mattresses set up on cold tile floors. The people who participated in the hunger strike didn't stand [watch] because that cost too much energy, so you'd grow weak much more quickly. We'd sit around, someone played the guitar, someone else had a tape recorder, so we'd listen to music,

write petitions, sort letters, prepare fliers, paint banners, we'd collect and sort information about different protest actions taking place independently around town.

Simultaneously with the blockade and the hunger strike at the harbor there were still demonstrations happening in the city. On 30 November, another demonstration took place at Długi Market in Gdańsk. Among the speakers were Grzegorz Czarnecki from Gdańsk University's Independent Students' Union, who informed people about the blockade of Gdynia, and Anna Walentynowicz, a legendary trade unionist in whose defense the initial 1980 strike had begun, who called for a refusal of the unloading of the reactor components.

After the rally, people marched from Długa Street to the Press House at Targ Drzewny (Wood Market), where the protesters barged into the building, demanding that the media inform the public about the position of the opponents of nuclear energy. The occupation of the Press House was a reaction to the information blackout regarding the protest and issues of nuclear energy, both in governmental media and in outlets that had until recently been considered oppositionist. This blackout is confirmed by an analysis of Solidarity publications from that period—including the nationwide *Tygodnik Solidarność* (Solidarity weekly), where the subject never even came up, and the Gdańsk region Solidarity newspaper, where information was scarce. It even extended to media that seemed to represent public opinion (in contrast with partisan publications): the liberal-Catholic *Tygodnik Powszechny* (Universal weekly) from Kraków only mentioned the issue once, in a letter to the editor written by proponents of the Żarnowiec NPP. Next to that letter, the magazine published an article by then MP Józefa Hennelowa that condemned the protesting "kids" who were being used by the cynical "apostles" of ecology.[1]

Following the demonstration at the Press House, a statement from the demonstrators was published in *Głos Wybrzeża* (Voice of the coast).[2] On that same day, also in Warsaw, a protest against the construction of the Żarnowiec NPP took place at the Sejm: a banner saying "Żarnowiec is a ticket to the kingdom come" was hung from the observers' gallery.

During that period, the disconnection or even animosity of many older Solidarity activists towards pacifists, ecologists, and other new social movements was beginning to show. The younger activists continued demonstrating and organizing actions in the streets not only after the Round Table, but also after the June elections and the forming of the Mazowiecki government, but formal political support for their cause was rare. The Ministry of Environmental Protection remained in postcommunist hands—Bronisław

Kamiński from the satellite United People's Party, whose representatives had headed the ministry since 1987, became the new minister. He had twenty years of experience but was not an antinuclear ally.

Nuclear energy soon became an uncomfortable subject. However, just because many Solidarity politicians distanced themselves from the protests did not mean that they endorsed nuclear energy or were averse to environmentalists. Tomasz Bedyński, a historian and then activist in the Independent Students' Association, explained:

> I think they feared that the opposition would be split along the line of scientific and civilizational progress, which was symbolized for many elites and Warsaw professors by nuclear energy. The opposition feared that it would be accused of obscurantism, of acting against Poland's economic interest, endangering the future of the country, which is why they did not dare touch the subject. We had great sympathy for this young, new generation that tackled the issue, but we kept our mouths shut, because we were afraid of divisions. We feared that we would disagree on another important issue—one that could cause further fractures within the opposition. I suspect that the Mazowiecki government didn't have a definite

Figure 7.2. Tomasz Burek is painting a banner during the hunger strike. Photograph provided by Tomasz Borewicz.

position on nuclear energy, they simply didn't have one. And since they didn't, how could they have negotiated with anyone? My other suspicion is that they did have a position—they were for nuclear energy as a sign of civilizational progress—but were afraid to make it known because of the social context. They were afraid of a confrontation. They were anxious about confronting the people with whom they had been in opposition just a while ago, those young people who generated so much sympathy for their cause. I'm sure that Warsaw's business and intellectual elite was for nuclear energy, and the government has to take the interests of its core support groups into account.

Act 3: The Indefinite Hunger Strike

In the face of the government's continued ambiguity towards the future of Żarnowiec, some twelve to fifteen of the protesters began an indefinite hunger strike on 8 December 1989. It started in student dorms, then moved to the Gdańsk University's student hotel on Polanka Street, in the Oliwa district. The striking protesters were first examined by doctors and nurses, and they remained supervised by Jerzy Jaśkowski and nurse Magda Pleskot, who were both linked to the antinuclear protest movement. Not everyone was fit for this demanding form of protest, and others were already exhausted by over two weeks of fasting and had to stop.

Despite pressure from the government and from various notable individuals, such as Lech Wałęsa and Archbishop Tadeusz Gocłowski, the protesters were determined to refuse food until they achieved victory. The archbishop paid the protesters a visit already during the initial hunger strike. He wanted to convince them to drop the protest. He said that a hunger strike was not the solution, that they could die. Stefański agreed, and boasted that they had a plan, that if one of them died, another one would come and take their place. "He said that it was murder, that you can't treat your body like that, that it's the temple of the spirit, etc." Another participant recalls: "Bishop Gocłowski said that there were certain things at play that meant the construction of Żarnowiec had to go on, but wouldn't say what they were exactly." Fotek, who was very well read in the Bible, used the time before the visit to prepare for the discussion looking up passages in the Scripture that would support their cause. The archbishop "left royally pissed off. . . . It turned out that not only did the protesters not listen to this titan of authority, but they also knew the Scripture better than him. Though it was literally just a handful of quotes from the Bible that we had dug up."

The resentment against Lech Wałęsa was also building. He was not a very popular figure among the Gdańsk radicals to start with. In a mocking samizdat article, the young anarchists linked with the WiP movement reportedly stood outside Wałęsa's flat in Gdańsk one night, singing the nursery rhyme "the old bear is fast asleep" while others referred to the "old Solidarity" figures as "relics" of "prehistory" (Szulecki 2019, 197).

Stefański complained that while he had to go on unpaid leave and risk his health in a hunger strike, Wałęsa would later bask in the glory of the successful campaign, claiming that he "had stopped Żarnowiec," when in fact he had no opinion on the NPP or was moderately supportive. "People like Wałęsa now give each other medals, congratulate each other, gather to brag about what they've done for Poland. Gentlemen, it wasn't you, for f***'s sake, it was us. Us, the faceless ones, we risked our asses so that this shit wouldn't get built right under our noses, because you apparently did not realize the danger." During the limited hunger strike, Stefański left the terminal with posters and leaflets and, together with some other protesters, ended up near Wałęsa's home:

> We had that petition regarding Żarnowiec, it was about holding a referendum. Wałęsa lived several hundred meters away, so someone said: "Stefan, he's your friend from the Shipyard, go to him." He did know me, and quite well, I was with him on the strike committee at the Gdańsk shipyard in August 1988. So ok. I went up to his place. Guys were holding me up so I wouldn't collapse. I grabbed the fence and pressed the buzzer. The officers on guard duty first thought we were drunk or something, but eventually Wałęsa said through the intercom: "Yes?" So I went: "Listen, Lech, here's the thing. My name is Zbyszek Stefański." "Yes, I know you." "I'm very happy that you do, but this is about your signature. We have this petition against Żarnowiec. Would you sign it?" [To which Wałęsa replied,] "With a cherry on top? You'd prefer a candle factory! I'm not signing anything here. If you have official business, you know where to find me. During office hours. Goodbye." And now this man claims that he was the one who stopped Żarnowiec from being built. And he's not the only one—there are many more schmucks like him.

The atmosphere was getting tense. The protesters were not sure if their desperation was leading anywhere, or if their protest actually stood a chance. According to Kłosiewicz:

> We kept cheering each other up and thinking about what would happen next. How would it all play out? Who would help us? How

would they help us? Was there even a chance? We were idealists. We wanted to stop this power plant that everyone was scared of and that we didn't like, at all costs. I suspect that we didn't even fully realize the extent of the consequences of a potential malfunction, we just knew we didn't want it to be constructed in that particular spot, right next to a population center as big as the Tricity, we just didn't want that to happen.

Local politicians and parliamentarians visited too. They tried to talk the protesters out of the desperate hunger strike, saying that it didn't make sense, that these things needed to be dealt with at the top, that this was high politics. Kłosiewicz adds:

And we stubbornly explained to them that high politics is for politicians, and we want to show everyone what real people think about this. Real people, not the establishment, because the establishment, as we knew very well, is not easy to talk to. "We will look into this," they'd say. "Someone will look into this." Not one person said: "I'm with you, I think you're right." . . . We were being dismissed—they saw us as some delusional punks.

As a matter of fact, a number of sympathetic activists and politicians visited. There was Jacek Czaputowicz from the Warsaw WiP, and Antoni Furtak, who was one of the starkest opponents of the NPP in parliament. Bach recalls:

At first, there was a lot of enthusiasm, but then came moments of doubt, especially at the Student House. But then again, we also had people coming over and lifting our spirits, bringing in this new energy, showing us that there's a point. That also affected us. I'm sure we were also affected by the presence of foreign press—obviously the things we were doing were attracting attention and the coverage wouldn't be limited to our country, which still had censorship. It would spread around the world. We had only one goal: a referendum. It was all about informing the people honestly about things, which hadn't been done for years in Poland.

Klaudiusz Wesołek, a long-time student activist affiliated with WiP as well as the Federation of Fighting Youth and the Independent Students' Association, was taking part in the strike and received a phone call from minister Syryjczyk, whom he had known from earlier activities. Syryjczyk offered what was perhaps the most honest and true explanation of the government's stance, something that in fact had nothing to do with officials' perspective on nuclear energy. If the government buckled now, then people would start going on hunger strikes in various factories once they tried to implement reforms and close some of them down. In late 1989 and early 1990 that was not just a plausible scenario. The economic transition was beginning to hit all sectors of industry, and the rank-and-file workers that only a year before were the firm base for Solidarity elites, allowing them to negotiate with the PZPR, were now often left to themselves in closed down factories.

Act 4: Breaking the Blockade

On 13 December 1989, the eighth anniversary of the introduction of martial law, Solidarity organized a large concert in support for South African activists called "Solidarity Anti-Apartheid." Several participants in the terminal blockade were the guests of honor. Grzegorz Piotrowski called this a "new chapter" in the relations between the labor union and the young protesting activists, because until that moment, the union leadership had been distancing itself from the issue, and even the Gdańsk Ecological Forum did not support the blockade (Piotrowski 2017).

Even though the hunger strike was now publicized, the managers of the construction project decided to break the blockade and transport reactor components to the construction site of the Żarnowiec NPP. Alerted by the media, a handful of activists rushed to Gdynia the next day, where they tried to stop the transport. Even though the blockaders had developed an "alarm" system—in case of an emergency, specific people were to phone everyone from their assigned contact sheet—only about fifteen people were on hand to block the transport. Parts of the reactor were shipped out of the harbor and the blockaders were beaten up, most likely by employees of the Żarnowiec power plant. Stefański recalls passionately:

> We were on the hunger strike and . . . I remember like it was yesterday, someone yelled: "F***, they're shipping them out!" What do we do? First, we had to actually get there, because by that time we were at the student hotel. We went to the terminal, to the gate through which they were supposed to ship them out. . . . I noticed those f******, hulking mountains of flesh, like guards of honor. In brand new work clothes. Where have you ever seen a construction worker in brand new clothes? Unless they've just started their day. It's possible that they were riot police units, or construction workers

> from Żarnowiec. We waited. . . . The cargo was about to be shipped out. What do we do? The gate opened and the truck rolled out, wheels big as f***, all soiled in that mush, that mud mixed with snow. We couldn't let the bastard through. No other choice—we had to lie down on the road. So we did. And those pseudoworkers! A worker wouldn't grab you by your arms and legs, then kick you if you tried to break free. A worker wouldn't do that. I'm a worker myself. When they threw me to the side, I got up and went back, but it was utter desperation. At some point we had to push our way through, because they brought in several busloads of those people to protect the transport. . . . I remember thinking that we had to stop the truck at all costs. I remember vividly how I fought them. In all that commotion, I didn't even realize when and how they agreed to transport the thing to Babie Doły [a military airfield].

According to one account, the power plant employees were drunk, but the police did not intervene. Piotr Książek, Chief Specialist on Technology and Construction Coordination, presented the Żarnowiec NPP side of the story.[3] Even based on his explanation—in which he mentions the "delicate" conduct of the power plant employees, but still describes people being pulled off the street, choked, and even held upside down by their legs—it is obvious that a crime had been committed, because violence was used, and not in self-defense. He also mentions a video recording that—according to Burek—"shocked" the director of the power plant and the prosecutor.

This bout of violence did not achieve much. Time was on the side of the protesters. It started getting dark. The vehicle could not go any further. More and more people were showing up. The two sides agreed to a compromise. The third reactor components would go to the air base in Babie Doły to join the other two that were already stored there. The protesters allowed it to be shipped out unmolested but signed an agreement with the Żarnowiec management that until a clear and final decision was made on Żarnowiec, those reactor components would not leave the air base. A committee was formed consisting of one representative from Żarnowiec, one MP, and Tomasz Burek, acting as leader of the protest. This committee had the right to check at any time if the terms of the agreement were being upheld, i.e., if the reactor components were still stored in those hangars, whether no work or manipulation was being done, and so forth. After that the blockade was over.

The significance of the blockade, and how differently the story of Żarnowiec could have ended if construction work was continued in December 1989, was underscored by deputy director of the NPP, Henryk Torbicki.

> If we had six more months, and had put roofs over those reactors, constructed a tiny part of that facility, then the construction wouldn't have been abandoned, but merely paused for a few years, and then continued. . . . But because there were protests, a decision was made not to fight them, because that could lead to an accident, and instead to hide the reactors and the steam generators at an airport. That lasted about half a year. We were running out of time to perform certain technical adjustments to those components. We couldn't do it at the airport, the conditions there would not allow it. If we didn't bring the objects to us, their warranty would be void. We got permission from the government to transport the components to Żarnowiec. We promised to do it in a way that would not cause any social unrest. We received support from law enforcement, with officers posted nearby. We knew that if there were any complications, they'd come to our aid and try to contain the situation so that it wouldn't get out of control, but there was no need to do that. We did, however, spread false information about a set date for the transport. Protest groups mobilized several times, waiting for us. When they finally lost faith in the validity of this information, we once again put it out that we would have the components transported on a particular date. . . . When someone throws themselves under a car, it's obviously a drastic sight. I know that no law enforcement agencies intervened. As for the transfer between Gdynia and Babie Doły, yes, our people did indeed pull the blockaders away from the road, but they weren't excessive about it.

The reactor components shipped out to a military facility on the night of 14 December 1989. However, the indefinite hunger strike continued, as its aim was to force the government to agree to a referendum on Żarnowiec.

Construction Put on Hold, Further Protests in the Tricity and throughout Poland

Finally, on 22–23 December 1989, the long-awaited Council of Ministers session took place. A commission of experts created by the Economic Committee of the Council of Ministers was to present two different options: continuing the construction work or immediate shutdown. The opponents prevailed, though not decisively, and the government decided to halt construction for the year 1990 in order to gather more data and opinions regarding the fate of the Żarnowiec NPP. The official statement read:

> The Council of Ministers, having heard from experts invited to attend the session—Professor Włodzimierz Bojarski, Professor Jacek Karecki, and the president of the State Atomic Agency and governmental plenipotentiary for the development of nuclear energy—[and] having noted a divergence of positions regarding the future development of the Polish energy sector, have deemed it appropriate to *halt the construction of the power plant for the entire year of 1990.*

The Council also tasked the minister of industry with overseeing the construction site and preparing, by the end of 1990, a program for developing the Polish energy sector. It likewise tasked the press secretary with initiating "rational social consultations."[4] But there was neither an unequivocal decision to shut down the construction site nor one about the future of the Polish nuclear program or a possible referendum on that issue. Antoni Furtak was critical, saying that this decision was "merely a sidestep meant to distract the public and shift the responsibility to the Sejm."[5] The end of the protest at the harbor did not mean the hunger strike was over, and it certainly did not stop other groups from getting involved in the issue.

In case the blockade of the terminal was broken, another protest was organized. Marek Czachor, a scientist at Gdańsk University of Technology and a member of Fighting Solidarity, recalls:

> When the reactor components were to be taken to Żarnowiec, there was a blockade. We blocked the road at the spot where it turns towards Władysławowo, branching out from the main Gdynia-Wejherowo route. We blocked the road before that fork for a good couple of hours . . . I don't remember if we stopped any vehicle carrying reactor components. I suspect that it was more of a symbolic blockade.

Similar protests were organized by the Solidarity of Individual Farmers. In Gdynia alone, on 20 December 1989, 120 people demonstrated. Another anti-Żarnowiec protest took place on 8 January 1990, this time in downtown Gdańsk. The march moved down the main transit route through Gdańsk, blocking traffic. It reached the former Gedania Cinema, where a Solidarity convention was taking place. The protesters entered the conference room with banners and demanded to speak to the delegates. This resulted in 110 Solidarity workplace commissions signing a petition to the government, demanding a referendum on the fate of the NPP.

These actions were redundant in light of the efforts of the group that organized the terminal blockade, but it was more important to point out that

Figure 7.3. Protesters break into the Gedania Cinema during a Solidarity Gdańsk region meeting, asking the union to support anti-Żarnowiec protests, 8 January 1990. Photograph provided by Janusz Waluszko.

the Solidarity leadership, including Wałęsa, was either passive (despite their earlier declarations) or, in case of Merkel and Bielecki, supported the nuclear lobby. The redundancy was the result of a lack of an interface between the radical and moderate groups. During the Round Table, WiP served as that interface, but it subsequently all but ceased operations, at least in the Tricity. That is why the Żarnowiec rallies of Fighting Solidarity in Gdynia towards the end of 1989 had not been coordinated with the actions of the group blockading the terminal.

Even though Fighting Solidarity did not have an official position on nuclear energy, Czachor underlines the group's involvement in the protests.

> Our apartment, which was ten minutes away from the Gdynia train station, served as the headquarters for the rally we organized at that train station. We were very much involved in it, which in practice meant that we lost our apartment. There were twenty people from all over Poland camped at our place at any given moment: from very distinguished personages, to girls who ran away from home, to undercover agents and provocateurs. We'd sleep three hours a day. After

> some time, it became unbearable, physically and mentally. We'd be at that train station from 6 AM to 10 PM, every day, in shifts. There was a table where we collected signatures under petitions against the power plant. We also had this big poster board. That table attracted a whole lot of people. At one point we absolutely lost control over what was happening. It was madness.

Another demonstration took place in Gdańsk on 12 January 1990, near the train station. Approximately one thousand people gathered there around 3 PM, though Solidarity's *Informator* (Informant) magazine, which was hostile towards the idea of further protests, reported that only sixty people showed up. A rally was held, and the Wały Jagiellońskie Street—the city's main artery—was blockaded for around twenty minutes. Posters for RSA and the "Liberty" Federative Labor Union (Zawodowy Związek Federacyjny "Wolność") were put up, and one of the activists appealed to everyone to show solidarity with the hunger strikers, stressing that nuclear energy is a matter that affects everyone. Activists from the reactivated Free Labor Unions and Polish Socialist Party–Democratic Revolution joined the rally. Protesters marched to city hall where councilmen were called on to issue a decision in line with the public's demands. ZOMO brought in water cannons, fearing a riot in the nearby jail on Kurkowa Street, because the prisoners started chanting "Down with Żarnowiec." These fears were not completely unfounded: after Mazowiecki's Solidarity government took over, Poland experienced the biggest wave of prison riots in its postwar history when it was revealed that the anticipated amnesty did not cover some of the convicts, particularly repeat offenders. The riots were violently pacified.[6]

Fotek, who left the hunger strike and returned to Elbląg, also co-organized a protest performance there.

> We started this protest performance by giving out anti-Żarnowiec fliers and informational leaflets. I remember we had toilet paper, which was a luxury item at the time. We had rolls of it, people were very intrigued by that, and we'd unroll it, write slogans like "Żarnowiec is shit," "Stop Żarnowiec," then roll it up again, and give out these toilet paper rolls to people saying, "Here, wipe your asses with Żarnowiec." I only remember that one, because it was so humorous.

Meanwhile, demonstrations of solidarity for the hunger strike were also taking place in Warsaw. Ireneusz Ziółkowski, an artist and philosopher from Kraków who moved to Warsaw where he became a key figure in the "second generation" of the local WiP recalls:

Warsaw had this advantage that if you started a brawl here, you had a chance to get through to the media. [The] topic was touchy enough for the previous government, and before long for the new one as well, that it kept being swept under the carpet to avoid riling people up. The quieter you were on the issue, the farther you'd go. [When] the hunger strike happened, we were doing our own thing, not necessarily related to Żarnowiec, but we got a call that we need to get through to the media, that if we start stirring shit up in Warsaw, there's a chance we'll get some coverage at last and break this news embargo. It was the thirtieth day of the hunger strike, the situation was really serious, and yet everyone was ignoring it, there was nothing in the national news on the subject. So we got some guys together. . . . There was this group of people we could count on, not more than ten. Plus, we had always worked with the anarchists. We organized the first thing on 11 January in the shopping arcade behind the Centrum Department Stores, in downtown Warsaw, on the roof of that arcade, with a speaking tube, throwing fliers. And we also had people on the ground level giving out fliers, for several hours. That was our first event.

Then, on the fortieth day of the hunger strike, on 16 January, we organized a solidarity event on the Rotunda roof [a modernist bank building at Warsaw's busiest intersection], because [the] situation was getting dire—people were still starving. . . . Two or three people climbed up on the roof. Another two or three were on the ground level, gathering signatures, giving out fliers, and we unrolled an information banner saying that it was the fortieth day of the hunger strike in Gdańsk regarding Żarnowiec, etc. We had a folding ladder that we set up, got up on the roof, and then stashed the ladder somewhere so that no one could follow us there, and sat on that roof with our speaking tube for several hours.

The police, well, they tried telling us to come down, but we simply refused and that was that. We also invited the media, so that there would be TV coverage, some press agencies, newspapers. They showed a short piece about it in the afternoon and then also on the evening news. Finally, the information got through. There was interest in the issue, but most people just walked past us—their workday was over, and they were going home. But a lot of people passed through that area, and most at least got some sort of impression on the issue. It was also important that on the next day a local government session was to be held that would decide if there would be a referendum. It was important for us to do this on the day before, so that they'd feel the pressure from the public, not just in Gdańsk, but all over Poland, to show that this thing had reach.

In 1990, the issue increasingly found traction within official structures. On 13 January, a local "Solidarity" Association of Citizens' Committees (Porozumienie Komitetów Obywatelskich "Solidarność") demanded a referendum on the future of the Żarnowiec power plant. On 15 January, in Reda, Solidarity of Individual Farmers, Fighting Solidarity, and the Gdańsk Antinuclear Committee organized a blockade of exit routes from the city. On 15–16 January, more anti-Żarnowiec rallies occurred in Gdańsk. The second one—fifty people strong—took place outside the headquarters of the Voivodeship National Council (Wojewódzka Rada Narodowa, or WRN) due to a special session planned for that day, to which a representative of the hunger strikers, Tomasz Burek, was invited.

The WRN was still Communist in composition—the democratic local government elections were yet to be held. This meant that it was stacked with people from the old regime who were vulnerable to pressure from the central government representative, Minister Syryjczyk, who argued that a referendum would undermine democracy and lead to a conflict between the central government and local governments. Suddenly, after months of intensive protests, dramatic scenes at the terminal, and Poland-wide campaigning on nuclear energy, it became evident that what was at stake was something broader. Not only the question of energy sources, but also the shape of Poland's young democracy.

Notes

1. A. Hrynkiewicz, Z. Kolenda, "Żarnowiec—porażka rozsądku" [Żarnowiec—the defeat of reason], *Tygodnik Powszechny*, nr 3, 1990; J. Hennelowa, "Uwaga: dzieci" [Watch out: kids!]. ibid.
2. "Przeciw Żarnowcowi" [Against Żarnowiec], *Głos Wybrzeża*, 1 XII 1989.
3. Książek, Report on the operation to transport large-size reactor elements from MPH Gdynia to JW 3851, 20 December 1989; same, [explanation in letter to the District Prosecutor's Office in Gdynia], 15 I 1990.
4. Quoted after the Stenographic Report of the 18th sitting of the Sejm on 20 January 1990, p. 323.
5. Ibid., p. 328.
6. J. Fedor, "Bunt" [Rebellion], *Tygodnik Gdański*, nr 16, 1989, s. 7; A. Zadworny, "Za pięć minut spalimy ten kryminał" [In five minutes we are going to burn down this jailhouse], *Gazeta Wyborcza*. http://wyborcza.pl/alehistoria/1,139245,16278960,Za_piec_minut_spalimy_ten_kryminal.html.

References

Piotrowski, Grzegorz. 2017. "Żarnowiec-Grobowiec. Opozycja Ekologiczna w Polsce i Kampania Antynuklearna." *HistMag*. https://histmag.org/Zarnowiec-grobowiec-Opozycja-ekologiczna-w-Polsce-i-kampania-antynuklearna-15099/3.

Szulecka, Julia, and Kacper Szulecki. 2017. "Polish Environmental Movement 1980–2017: (De)Legitimization, Politics & Ecological Crises." *ESPRi Working Papers* 6. https://doi.org/10.2139/ssrn.3075126.

Szulecki, Kacper. 2019. *Dissidents in Communist Central Europe: Human Rights and the Emergence of New Transnational Actors*. Palgrave Studies in the History of Social Movements. Palgrave Macmillan. https://doi.org/10.1007/978-3-030-22613-8.

Chapter 8

The Boundaries of a New Democracy

Experiments with Participatory Governance and a Grassroots Referendum (1990)

The political transition in Poland is usually associated with the semidemocratic elections on 4 June 1989, or with the Round Table negotiations that preceded them and allowed for a peaceful handover of power. As we have seen in previous chapters, however, this process was more complex and has to be viewed in the context of longer-term state-society relationships as well as political struggles within the democratic opposition. The 1980–1981 period, when the Independent Self-Governing Trade Union "Solidarity" was a mass social movement aimed at changing sociopolitical relations at many levels, was already a historical reference point. By 1988, as Kenney notes, the union "no longer had ten million members but perhaps tens of thousands of active participants" (2002, 253) and had to fill an enormous political void. The new protest movements that emerged in the mid-1980s covered a different set of issues, constituencies, and approaches to regime change. The strikes in 1988 resembled on the surface those of the summer of 1980, but the expectation of this new generation of workers and activists was noticeably different.

The Solidarity elite chose to negotiate with the government, something that only a year earlier would have been seen as nearly impossible and welcomed as a major achievement. Lech Wałęsa, no longer treated as a "private individual" by the purposefully uninterested governmental media, was invited to a one-on-one live TV debate with the head of the official trade unions (Szulecki 2019, 197). The renowned dissidents and veterans of the Worker Defense Committee (KOR)—Jacek Kuroń and Adam Michnik, seen as dangerous "antisocialist elements" and radicals—were invited to the negotiation table. This new "constructive opposition" could use the more radical political currents as contrast but also as a source of empowerment because ultimately the diversity of the opposition made the moderate Solidarity elite stronger (Kenney 2002, 250).

However, that context affected the relationship of the now post-Solidarity elite with the rank-and-file unionists, and with more radical and independent movements. They had to be kept at bay so as not to rock the boat too much, so as not to derail the process, and so as not to enrage the Soviets—which was the ultimate threat. A split emerged between those that sat at the Round Table or endorsed it and those that contested the very idea. Similarly, the June elections—which were open to up to 30 percent of opposition candidates in the lower chamber (*Sejm*) and 100 percent in the upper chamber (*Senat*)—were contested by radicals, left and right.

And so throughout 1989 we saw an open-ended political transition, where different visions of what is democratic and how best to achieve a more democratic political sphere grappled. On the one hand, the Mazowiecki government was under severe pressure. The fact that the Communists gave a green light to a government formed by the former democratic opposition had strings attached. The PZPR leadership was perfectly aware of the depth of the economic crisis in which the state found itself, and by sharing power, it also shared or even pushed responsibility onto the post-Solidarity camp.

The 4 June elections resulted in a certain path dependency within the transforming system. The People's Republic of Poland had a parliament, held elections, the MPs met regularly, all the practices known from Western democracies were observed—all but open political competition, pluralism, freedom of speech, and independent oversight of political institutions. That said, after the elections the opposition MPs found themselves in a fully developed and well-entrenched institutional context. Parliamentary practices had a long pedigree, civil servants who worked in ministries, the parliament chancery, and the president's office were still doing what they had done for years. The entire revolutionary and democratic momentum of the 1980s "carnival of revolution" was immediately diminished.

Not everyone accepted this. Many MPs saw themselves as direct representatives of their constituencies and wanted to act as bridges between the people and the state, searching for a more direct democratic language and forms of expression. However, the levels of social unrest and anger, as well as the looming conflicts over economic transformation, tied the government's hands. In that way, Poland adopted and normalized a very insulated, representative form of liberal democracy, where bottom-up impulses were toned down and civil society groups were marginalized.

However, until well into 1990 debates over the shape of Poland's democracy and concrete cases of citizen involvement were visible. These involved experiments with a democracy that would be closer to the people, more engaging, and more grassroots. Two of these experiments with "democracy of proximity" (Rosanvallon 2011) were linked to the antinuclear protest, and we will look at them in the remainder of this chapter. The first aimed at an expansion of local participatory governance, the other at the possibility of introducing elements of direct democracy into a representative system.

Różan: Participatory Governance Practices at a Waste Disposal Site

Różan is a town in the Mazovian Voivodeship, located ninety kilometers from Warsaw, in the Lower Narew Valley. Under Russian administration during Poland's Partitions, a Tsarist army fortification was constructed in 1905–1907. The fortifications have housed, since 1961, the National Radioactive Waste Disposal Site (Krajowe Składowisko Odpadów Promieniotwórczych, or KSOP). Its surface area is just over three hectares. Several hundred meters away stand residential buildings, and around eight hundred meters to the northeast of the compound is the Narew River. The International Atomic Energy Agency classifies Różan as a surface waste disposal site. It receives around three hundred cubic meters of processed (condensed) low- and mid-active waste a year. This waste is mostly the byproduct of research at the National Nuclear Research Center in Otwock-Świerk, but the center's radioactive waste management facility also buys waste from other entities. Fire sensors and diagnostic and therapeutic medical equipment containing radioactive elements are stored here, among other things. Aside from constant oversight performed by the proper services in Świerk, the site is also systematically monitored by the Różan City Council's Commission on Radiological Protection, whose members—local residents—have gone through a special training in Świerk and participate in background radiation readings.

This generally harmonious cooperation with representatives of the nuclear industry was established through a series of protests at the turn of the 1990s, when barrels filled with radioactive material started appearing in Różan, even though its inhabitants had not been informed about the actual purpose of the facility. Additionally, no effort was made to properly store the waste—the barrels were dumped chaotically without proper safety measures. Sometimes, even though the barrels were marked as containing radioactive material, the locals used them for their own needs. It was only after articles appeared in the national press, especially reports by Eryk Mistewicz in the *Na przełaj* magazine, that the local population realized what danger this "troublesome neighbor" might pose.

In October 1987, the Różan Communal National Council issued a protest to the PRON National Council and the Ministry of Environmental Protection regarding the planned expansion of the waste disposal site—but it went unanswered. The direct reason for the protests was the discovery of an empty container near an elementary school. At the start of 1990, people blocked the road to the KSOP using tractors and excavators, threatening to dig a ditch across the road if their demands were not met.

It was only then that talks began between the local population and the State Atomic Agency and the Nuclear Research Institute in Świerk. Based on the agreement they reached, the site was cleaned up, the barrels were moved to enclosed spaces and the commune started receiving a small compensation for hosting the site on its land. Most importantly perhaps, the local residents were finally officially acknowledged as *stakeholders* and the Różan City Council's Commission on Radiological Protection was created. The commission is one of several self-governing bodies on the communal level, but it is unique for Różan, and its members have the right to oversee the waste storage site's activity and monitor levels of radioactivity in the area.

The Commission has not detected any serious radiological hazards aside from a relatively high concentration of tritium in the Narew River. This suggests that there might be a connection between the lower levels of the fortifications and the riverbed—which was what the opponents of the site's expansion had feared. In the early 1990s, there was a debate in the press between those who thought the site might pose a radiological danger to the local population and their opponents, who claimed that the area has one of the lowest cancer incidence rates in the country. One of the members of the Commission (who asked to remain anonymous) explains:

> I often walk around that area and the dosimeter doesn't show heightened radiation—honestly, it's higher in the city center. The fortifications themselves are safe as well. With one exception: there's this one corridor. When I went in, the counter immediately started buzzing, and the reading went off the scale. I ran away as quickly as I could. My friends say that supposedly in the 1960s the Russians used to dump something into a well located down that corridor.

The first funds obtained from the financial compensation were used to renovate the school next to which the empty barrel was found. The initially small compensation from the early 1990s, thanks to the introduction of precise legal regulations, is currently one of the main sources of income for the commune. Pursuant to the Atomic Law Act, a commune on whose territory a KSOP is located is entitled to an annual payment from the national budget in the amount of 400 percent of the real estate tax income in the commune in the previous year. These funds are meant as a compensation for any losses suffered by the commune due to hosting a waste disposal site. In case of

Różan, this amounts to around PLN 8 million a year, plus PLN 1–2 million from an additional allotment. Even though the local government uses this money to protect the social interest of local people by ensuring low taxation, access to water, children's holidays, and care for the elderly, the site itself still causes issues and disturbs the functioning of the local community.

In a 4 March 2013 letter addressed to the secretary of state in the Ministry of Economy, the mayor of Różan stated:

> KSOP . . . effectively restricts the development of the entire Różan Commune. I'm referring here to both the restrictions on residential construction, and the fears of potential investors interested in doing business in Różan. These fears are not assuaged by the commune's reasonable tax policy, incentives for investors, or our excellent technical infrastructure (above all our roads) and our location on National Routes 60 and 61.

The limited expansion of participatory governance—within the framework of existing self-governance institutions (first the National Council, now the City Council on the communal level)—helped diffuse the conflict and achieve social acceptance at a minimal level by toning down safety concerns. However, the process has also created an economic dependence of the local community on the nuclear waste storage, while the more fundamental question of the future of the waste disposal site and its relationship with the community remains unaddressed.

Let the People Have a Say—A Grassroots Referendum on Żarnowiec

In January 1990, the Gdańsk protesters, Tomasz Burek among them, were exhausted from the hunger strike and the demonstrations in Warsaw. The governmental side stood by its position, not interested in any kind of negotiation. The deputy prime minister told Burek that the reason was simple: talking to them and meeting their demands, even just some of them, would encourage other protesters, who would assume that since the Żarnowiec people got concessions this way, they could follow suit. So the people's demands were not heard on principle. This was evident also at that session of the Voivodeship National Council (WRN), whose aim was to make a formal and legal decision on a referendum organized by the local government.

Burek was invited to that session as a representative of the protesters. He presented his position, said why the protesters wanted the people to speak out in a referendum, instead of limiting the discussion to technocratic circles involving "some expert whose only claim was that he knew better because he had a master's degree in nuclear studies." He also underlined the economic aspect: could Poland afford to build a nuclear power plant when there were better, cheaper, and faster ways to produce electricity?

The minister of industry, Tadeusz Syryjczyk, also came to the meeting in Gdańsk and issued a statement that the locals interpreted as a detailed set of instructions from the central government to the remnants of the old local government. (The local authorities were still untouched by the political shifts in Poland over the last year, while Syryjczyk represented the Solidarity-linked cabinet of Tadeusz Mazowiecki). In a nutshell, according to Burek's account,

> Mazowiecki's government, a democratic Polish government, proclaimed that a referendum undermines democracy. . . . We were in this absurd situation where a newly elected Polish government, which hailed from the democratic opposition, rejected something essentially democratic and claimed that a direct vote—instead of voting through some representatives—is dangerous to democracy and will lead to political chaos. That it will cause a rift between the central government and local governments. So he was against a referendum. The moment he voiced this opinion, the comrades from the Voivodeship National Council knew that if they didn't want conflict with the new government, they didn't have a choice [but to decide against the referendum].

Indeed, the decision to organize a local referendum on the voivodeship level was defeated by four votes. The main thrust of the opposition came from people related to citizens' committees, but it was the Communist politicians, with links to the Żarnowiec construction, who tipped the scales.

Several days later, minister Syryjczyk fended off accusations of trying to influence the WRN in the Sejm, justifying his presence at the session and his lack of support for a local referendum differently.

> The government thinks . . . that the debate on the subject should be brought to the public first, that all arguments for and against the project should be presented, and then the issue should be brought before the Sejm. Due to continued protests and pressure mounted by numerous people on the government to take a position on this issue, I have asked the prime minister to authorize me to appeal to the protesters who have initiated a hunger strike. My appeal would once again outline the government's position, while underscoring

> the fact that *making such decisions is the task of the Sejm*, which *may potentially also call a referendum.*
>
> As for the Voivodeship National Council session on a local referendum, which took place in Gdańsk recently, I was authorized to state that we think it would be a bad idea for a local referendum to decide an issue that extends beyond the region, and is in fact a national issue. [WRN] rejected the motion to organize a referendum . . . but did, in my presence, petition the Sejm to organize a national referendum on this issue. . . . If this referendum were to be organized, from a financial point of view, it would be prudent to tie it to local government elections. . . . We realize that we can't implement a nuclear energy program against public opinion.[1]

These last sentences caused a protest from the president of the State Atomic Agency (Państwowa Agencja Atomistyki, or PAA), Roman Żelazny, who emphasized that "it would be a regrettable situation if the local election campaign became dominated through mere coincidence by issues of nuclear energy."[2]

The Agreement on a Grassroots Referendum and the End of the Hunger Strike

When a minister from the Mazowiecki government opposed holding a local referendum on Żarnowiec, and the Voivodeship National Council did not allow it to be held, the situation seemed hopeless. The hunger strike had gone on for over forty days by then—a time after which starvation starts producing irrevocable changes within the human body—and some people "exhibited martyr tendencies, i.e., planned to continue the hunger strike until the very end" (Piotrowski 2017). Even though the government froze construction for a year to analyze the situation and make a decision on the future of Żarnowiec, the entire nuclear program, and Poland's overall energy policy, the issue was far from settled. A strong nuclear energy lobby continuously pressured the government to go on with the project, especially since foreign investors were offering their help.

In Warsaw, WiP's Irek Ziółkowski was waiting for the WRN's vote results. The day after, he and his team blockaded the roundabout next to the Rotunda building in the heart of Warsaw. The blockade lasted for only twenty minutes but was held during rush hour, creating a huge traffic jam. "We were dressed up as some sort of mutants, etc., with banners about Żarnowiec and the hunger strike. We also passed out fliers," he recalls. They treated the decision against a referendum "as a provocation," and so blocking traffic was not enough. The Warsaw activists called in colleagues from other cities and held a three-day anti-Żarnowiec protest outside the Sejm—from 18 to 20 January. "There were several dozen people there, for sure. It was a series of events that supported the main thrust of the protest in Gdańsk," Ziółkowski explains.

The referendum became a bone of contention, as it would constitute a precedent—were the government and the Sejm to agree to a direct popular vote on this issue, dozens more were waiting in the wings, because in the early stages of the systemic and economic transformation of Poland, the grocery list of pending changes was very long. Meanwhile, the hunger strikers were waiting and did not intend to drop their demands. That was when Tomasz Bedyński and Paweł Siedlecki—assistant to MP Antoni Furtak—figured that since a state-mandated referendum was off the table, a *grassroots* one could be held instead.[3]

On 18 January 1990, a debate was held in the Sejm regarding the parliamentary question of MP Antoni Furtak on the abandonment of the Żarnowiec NPP project, which he had submitted to the prime minister back in November. In his question, MP Furtak suggested that the protests would not stop, and that eventually "even with the construction having been completed, the fully operational power plant will have to be shut down, as was the case in other countries."[4]

Two visions of democracy clashed during the debate, and the role of the nuclear lobby proved to be quite controversial. In response to Minister Syryjczyk's explanations, MP Furtak asked whether

> the fact of such extensive social mobilization against this project is not a sort of referendum? I find it strange that a government elected by the will of the people does not take the will of that people into account, that a Solidarity government doesn't take into account the arguments of the Solidarity side of the ecological subtable from the Round Table negotiations. That among the "for" and "against" arguments the voice of people materially interested in continuing the construction seems to hold sway.[5]

Minister Syryjczyk admitted that the voice of nuclear energy advocates was very loud and that "it is a fact that the majority of people who work at the construction site or see for themselves a future in Polish atomic energy are interested in its development."[6] But he asked whether this was wrong by definition. PZPR MP Piotr Lenz, on the other hand, accused Furtak of needlessly riling people up: "You are saying that the protests will not stop. You are also saying that you will lead those protests. Esteemed Member of

Parliament! I think that as a public figure . . . you have no right to assume the moral responsibility for leading any movement that aims to enforce any kind of solution." He also appealed for "a moratorium on strikes [hunger or otherwise] and street demonstrations."[7] MP Furtak was very vocal about defending the hunger strikers.

> I'd like to take this opportunity to protest the fact that for nearly three weeks, twenty days in total, there has been an information blackout regarding the hunger strike. This has led some determined young people who participate in this strike to announce that they will continue this fight until the construction is scrapped. Today, some call these young people blackmailers, while others call them crazy. Meanwhile, it was their determination that finally broke the information embargo on this issue. The same sort of information embargo as the one we have experienced during those darkest, most horrible years. It's those young people, on the forty-third day of their hunger strike, that remind us that it is our duty to represent tens of thousands of people who signed those petitions, obligating us to act. After all, they are our constituents. . . . I hope that the opinions of these people will be acknowledged when decisions are made. Decisions that should take the will of the people into account.[8]

The deputy of the Civic Parliamentary Committee (i.e., the Solidarity parliamentary club), Krzysztof Dowgiałło, moved to expand the day's agenda to include the issue of a national referendum, but his petition was rejected. Questioning Minister Syryjczyk's statement that a local referendum would constitute a precedent, he informed the Sejm that "in this situation, the Gdańsk Voivodeship Association of Citizens' Committees is considering holding a grassroots local referendum."[9]

The people behind the grassroots referendum proposed to organize it in May, during the local government elections. Jacek Starościak, who was working together with the strikers and others in the local office of the Gdańsk parliamentarians from the Civic Parliamentary Committee, was desperately looking for a way out of the situation, one that would be accepted by the protesters and allow them to maintain their dignity, and at the same time advance their cause. The protesters were filled with doubt regarding the politicians' promises, asking what actual influence this ephemeral thing, this citizens' agreement, has over local and municipal governments. Doubts kept mounting; there were some who wanted to continue to protest. Together with Tomasz Bedyński they convinced the protesters that the Civic Parliamentary Club (OKP) office would take it upon itself to organize the grassroots referendum. They agreed to the plan. Starościak and Bedyński drafted a joint appeal to stop the hunger strike, and below it they included a statement from the strikers: "Should a grassroots referendum be called by the Gdańsk Voivodeship Association of Citizens' Committees, we are ready to stop our protest on the same day and actively participate in organizing a grassroots referendum. Gdańsk, January 19." The statement included six signatures of the hunger strike participants.

When Tomasz Bedyński first went to visit the striking activists, he saw "a group of young people who were absolutely exhausted—both physically and mentally." They had been pushed to the brink, emotionally, so every word, every facial expression, every redundant gesture could lead to an explosion. "That's how tightly wound up they were. Therefore, we decided to mainly listen to them. I realized that above all they needed to vent—air out all their resentment towards everybody." He found their posture absolutely honest and listened to their grievances—towards Wałęsa, Solidarity, Mazowiecki, and the rest of the world. They claimed that no one understood them and that they were also the voice of public opinion. They knew that public opinion would be on their side in a referendum, and yet no one in power was listening to them, no one was taking them seriously. Bedyński recalls: "I understood that the only argument that could work in this situation was declaring that we would be the ones to organize this referendum, which is a huge social initiative—we would step in to pick up the government's slack. We'd show the politicians that we didn't need them."

The following day, Starościak informed the mayor of Gdańsk that they urgently needed to use the conference room at city hall to organize a meeting to create the Citizens' Referendum Committee, and that the mayor needed to be in attendance. He agreed.

They decided that the organizational committee could not be headed by one of the protesters, nor should it be steered by a politician or someone from an MP's office. Instead, they asked Doctor Piotr Krzyżanowski, a chemist who also worked for the Helsinki Committee. Starościak recalls: "He was very tall and very knowledgeable . . . so he wouldn't be easily pushed around, and I also knew that he wouldn't become a slave to a narrative he didn't entirely support." Together with his father, Maciej Krzyżanowski, an economist from the Maritime Institute, he headed the group until the referendum itself. The logistical support and rooms were provided by the MPs' offices, while the trustworthy and impartial network was largely driven by the members of the liberal Christian Catholic Intelligentsia Club.

On 20 January 1990, after it was promised that a grassroots referendum would be organized, the protesters yielded and stopped their hunger strike after forty-four days. Zbigniew Stefański, who was one of the remaining strikers, recalls how a noisy TV crew barged into the student hotel where they were holding the strike:

> We were so confused, and I didn't know what was going on—I was running from the cameras so no one would bother me, because you know, during a hunger strike you just don't have the energy to deal with things. Everything annoys you. You don't want to see anyone. You just want to lie down and that's it. Suddenly someone comes saying that there will be a referendum. I proclaimed that I was ending my hunger strike, in front of the cameras, at the student home. I was happy. We were all happy. We won. We got what we were fighting for. I felt faint—all that tension had left me, and my legs went soft.

Rallies of campaigners took place on 25 and 26 January 1990, at the behest of the hunger strike participants, with twelve people with banners and a black RSA flag blocking a main Gdańsk arterial road. Fliers were disseminated by a large number of smaller independent organizations that were involved in the campaign in Gdańsk over the preceding months. A crew from the Gdańsk branch of national TV was present. According to other sources, around five hundred people participated in the protest, one of the hunger strikers—Zbigniew Stefański—gave a speech.

Between Representative and Direct Democracy: The Parliament Debates Żarnowiec and the Referendum

Meanwhile, on 26 January 1990, in Warsaw, a heated debate took place in the Sejm regarding the Żarnowiec Nuclear Power Plant, sparked by 170 MPs from the Citizens' Parliamentary Club (related to Solidarity), who submitted a resolution to abandon the construction of the power plant. The president of PAA, Roman Żelazny, lamented the government's decision to stop the construction and underscored that Western partners from industrialized countries "that know how to spend money efficiently and rationally" want to "provide far-reaching aid" to Poland's nuclear program.[10] His arguments were met with strong resistance from a group of OKP MPs, although the debate showed that the battle lines were not drawn clearly between the Solidarity and PZPR camps. OKP MP Henryk Sienkiewicz expressed his surprise that the "all-knowing MPs" were to make the decisions "instead of the [energy experts] who had been dealing with this issue for over ten years,"[11] and he claimed that public opinion was "overly interested in this topic." Meanwhile, PZPR MP Joanna Proszowska supported the resolution to abandon the construction of the power plant.[12]

Several potent narratives emerged from the debate, along with already established ones. Żarnowiec proponents brought up forecasts of energy consumption, the "ecological" dimension of nuclear energy as an alternative to coal, and the funds already spent on the construction, accusing their opponents of shortsightedness, wastefulness, and irrational phobias. The opponents of nuclear energy countered those arguments. OKP MP and PKE expert Stefan Kozłowski stated pointedly that "we are questioning all the energy consumption assessments made so far, which were based on the assumption of 4 percent economic growth, and therefore also a different rate of growth in energy consumption."[13] It was pointed out that the funds needed for the construction of the NPP could be used to drastically improve the state of the environment in Poland, particularly the quality of air and water in Silesia. The question of negligence at the NPP construction site—including reports of corruption, theft of materials, and shoddy craftsmanship—was also particularly resonant.

An important line of division was drawn between technocrats and democrats in terms of managing the energy sector. PZPR MP Stefan Wanot attacked opponents of the Żarnowiec Nuclear Power Plant and the protesting ecologists:

> Emotional displays, hunger strikes, populist slogans, and sometimes even demagoguery are not conductive to an objective assessment of the problems of nuclear energy in Poland. We have managed . . . to turn a technical and economic issue into a political one, stoking public anger. This paradox is deepened by the fact that we are trying to solve the problem with a political decision, namely foregoing the construction of Żarnowiec or holding a referendum on the future of nuclear energy in our country.[14]

The agrarian MP from the Polish People's Party "Revival" (Polskie Stronnictwo Ludowe "Odrodzenie"), Stanisław Wiąckowski, defended the protesters in his over ten-minute-long speech against the power plant: "Can we, in a country in which we have achieved the current level of democratization, ignore the will of the people? Did we talk about pluralism and democracy all this time only to stop listening to the nation now, to disrespect the voice of the people who have repeatedly exhibited wisdom superior to that of its leaders?"[15]

PZPR MP from the Wejherowo district Piotr Lenz referenced the 120,000 signatures collected on a petition against the continuation of the construction, presented in the Sejm by MP Antoni Furtak, but questioned their meaning: "But is this a voice against the power plant? No, it's a voice that is saying: I am afraid, and I have the right to be afraid . . . because we weren't able to present our argument to the people honestly, thoroughly, and objectively."[16] Furtak, elected in the same district, spoke sharply: "Fellow Members of Parliament! We have been elected by the will of the people. Today thousands of these people demand that we stop this construction and expect us, MPs, to take an unequivocal stand on this issue. I hope this stand will be one against the continuation of this project."[17]

Proponents of nuclear energy also tried to present the opinion of the president of PAA as the position of the government and therefore prove that the Sejm resolution against Żarnowiec would be tantamount to a vote of no confidence against the government of Tadeusz Mazowiecki. OKP MP Krzysztof Dowgiałło, however, sharply questioned this interpretation:

> The will of the residents of our coast, evidenced by these signatures and protests, is a decisive argument that no government should take lightly. These people are not manifesting their lack of faith in the government, but rather their lack of faith in the technocrats who do not want to or are unable to see these problems in all their complexity. . . . The issue of nuclear energy in Poland can and should be decided by way of a national referendum.[18]

Minister Syryjczyk explained the decision to freeze the construction of the power plant for the year 1990 in order to make a comprehensive decision about the direction and viability of the Polish nuclear program, pointing out that there was no way the construction could be continued using Soviet technology, and that if the Żarnowiec NPP was to be the only nuclear power plant in Poland, then the appropriateness of devoting funds to this end seemed questionable. However, his words and those of other MPs betrayed the extent of the pressure from the nuclear lobby and foreign investors. At this early stage of systemic transformation, the practice of lobbying was still nebulous, and it was unclear how to treat attempts made by various interest groups to influence politicians. MP Wiąckowski noted sneeringly that "Director Torbicki from Żarnowiec has all but moved into the Sejm,"[19] which was countered by PZPR MPs who pointed out that Torbicki was an expert who was there at their invitation.

The situation was not resolved due to the lack of a quorum. According to observers, this was intentional. The issue was not reexamined during the next three Sejm sessions, or during the budget debate, despite MP Radosław Gawlik's attempts. This was due to pressure exerted to finish the construction with the help of Western companies, mainly French and Belgian investors interested in taking over Żarnowiec.

The president of the State Atomic Agency did indeed create a team of experts under the leadership of Andrzej Wierusz, which was tasked to present additional, independent analyses of the project and help decide the future of nuclear energy in Poland. The team was created in June 1990, and it issued a negative opinion, proposing an unconditional abandonment of the project (this is the so-called Wierusz Report). The Agency's president, Żelazny, unhappy with the team's efforts, created another group, composed of—among others—the deputy director of the Żarnowiec power plant, Torbicki. That team produced the "correct" answer, i.e., it supported continued work on the project. However, the construction site was eventually shut down, even though it took further pressure from the public for that to happen—from local, national, and international sources.[20]

A Week of Direct Democracy: The Miracle and Disappointment of the Referendum

In Gdańsk, preparations were underway for the grassroots referendum. However, it turned out that organizing it might be difficult: the central election commissioner, Solidarity lawyer Jerzy Stępień, had at the behest of the Żarnowiec NPP workers' self-governing council decreed that the referendum was unlawful, and that it couldn't take place in the same room as local government elections.[21] Tomasz Burek, Tomasz Bedyński, and Anna Jędrzejewska started pondering what they could do in this situation. Burek recalls the feeling of uncertainty:

> Why did Stępień in his letter space out the letters in the word *room*? None of the other words, regardless of their importance, were underscored in any way. We started wondering if Stępień wasn't trying to suggest a solution—yes, the referendum couldn't take place in the same *room* as local elections, but there was nothing preventing it from taking place in the same *building*. So if there was a school with numerous classrooms, just don't put both ballot boxes in the same classroom. Have the elections in one room, and a second commission with a second ballot box for the Żarnowiec referendum in a different one.

Time was limited—they had one week to organize the referendum from scratch, which meant choosing a question, printing the ballots, assembling commissions and electing their presidents, verifying personal data, creating protocols for counting votes, organizing the people to supervise the whole process, and completing all the necessary paperwork. Burek joked:

"It was typical Solidarity. We're master improvisers." They called people up. Bedyński organized a group of lawyers who went over the election statute, the commission president election process, ballot templates, and protocols, all within one day. All the formal documents were adjusted to comply with the election statute. All those documents were being printed by the Solidarity printing house day and night, possibly without the knowledge of the union's leadership, even though hundreds of thousands of ballots consumed tons of paper. The documents had to be put in separate packages that contained everything needed for each local commission—templates for electing commissions and their presidents, protocols for the referendum—and had to be delivered to every polling station. The forms were sorted and packaged by young people from the League of Nature Protection and by scouts from Gdynia and Wejherowo, working day and night.

Then they encountered a huge problem that almost derailed the whole process. How do you get these documents to all the polling stations? How do you make sure they get them in time to sort through them all, to assemble the commissions, to elect their presidents, to fill out the forms, and even to construct ballot boxes according to specifics, making them white and red, in Poland's national colors, as official ballot boxes had to be?

Burek came up with an out-of-the-box idea. They could use the transportation network of the Społem grocery cooperative—a chain predating Polish Communism, rooted in the prewar cooperative movement, that had a shop in practically every village. But Społem refused. And Burek had another epiphany—he went to the Gdańsk brewery, talked to the Solidarity unionists there, and in the morning, whenever a truck headed out to deliver beer to a town in the Gdańsk region, the driver would also bring the documents and a request to have them handed over to a local figure of authority. Burek recalls:

> Of course, we also called those people, or sometimes reached them through some other channels, but mostly it was the brewery trucks. And it worked like a charm—within half a day, all nine hundred packages had reached their destination. Even if a truck wasn't going to a particular village, the driver would leave the package at a gas station, and the guy from the station, or some store, felt obligated to deliver it to the destination. Everybody helped.

Since they knew they could not hold a referendum in the same room as the elections, and in some villages there would often be only one room, for example at the fire station, in several cases the referendum was held right outside the polling station. Usually someone would organize a bus, and the referendum commission would sit on the bus, with all the proper credentials and paperwork. There was a ballot box, and people heading to the elections would step into the bus and vote in the referendum. In one case it was a regular car. The ballot box was inside, and the commission stood next to the car.

While the governmental officials and Citizens' Committees were complaining for two months that they could not find volunteers for the local election commissions, the grassroots referendum committee—despite the government's statements that there would not be a referendum, and despite having only one week to organize it—managed to staff all the polling stations. In some locations entire families signed up, but Małgorzata Tarasiewicz, a WiP activist who organized the referendum in Sopot, recalls that it was not equally rosy in all districts. "A lot of people voted, and they voted eagerly. I am sure that it was a representative vote, but the organization was far from perfect."

Their process was accompanied by a campaign of (mis)information in the media, with the proponents of the Żarnowiec NPP undermining the legitimacy of the referendum and, until the electoral silence that preceded the vote, claiming that the plebiscite would not take place. The antinuclear network refuted these claims, and on the last day before the vote, Burek sent out information to the Polish Press Agency and all newspapers and radio stations that there would be a referendum, but as he recalls: "Some media didn't broadcast this message, and some people only learned about the referendum after the fact, they had no idea." This probably influenced the turnout, as less than half of eligible voters participated. However, we have to recall that turnout was also low in the local elections and in most consecutive parliamentary elections in Poland. Burek wondered, "Who knows, maybe if it wasn't for the misinformation, the turnout would have been much higher, especially seeing how involved people got."

Despite the problems with reaching the voters with correct information, out of nine hundred polling stations, the referendum did not take place in only six. Four of these were in Tczew, where the Citizens' Committee was headed by Olga Krzyżanowska, whose husband worked in a company with ties to Żarnowiec (she was also the person who refused to put the issue of Żarnowiec on the Solidarity meeting agenda).

The referendum took place, and it was a record in many ways, not merely because of the short time it took to organize. Nearly a million people were eligible to vote. Burek boasted that the only bigger initiative of this kind was in France, in Normandy, on the Le Hague peninsula, where a uranium reenrichment plant was to be built, but that was a smaller area, not an entire province. "Going back to those WiP stories about several people showing up somewhere in toadstool costumes, climbing onto some roof, and standing there for an hour—there's just no comparison in terms of quality and degree of involvement," he stressed.

On 27 May 1990, in a grassroots referendum in the Gdańsk Voivodeship, with 44.3 percent of all those eligible to vote having cast their ballots, 86.2 percent voted against the construction of the nuclear power plant, and 13.8 percent for it. In Gdańsk itself, 88 percent of voters were against the project. The turnout in the local elections was comparable to that of the referendum (45.8 percent). Proponents of the NPP questioned the accuracy of the referendum, and even the validity of using the term "referendum." Meanwhile, the credibility of the result of the referendum is supported by earlier polls by the Gdańsk branch of the Polish Sociologist Society, according to which over 80 percent of the region's residents were against the project.

The media—especially media outside of Gdańsk—were reluctant to inform the public about the referendum and its results. Burek, who at the time worked for the largest pro-Solidarity daily, *Gazeta Wyborcza* (Electoral gazette), had his article on the referendum shelved. Similar articles written for *Przekrój* (Cross section) and other national publications were also rejected. Local newspapers wrote about the referendum, but no national outlet provided information, aside from a press release from the Polish Press Agency about the results, the low turnout, and the "no" vote on Żarnowiec. The

Figure 8.1. Protest in front of the Olivia arena where a Solidarity conference was held, 22 April 1990. Photograph provided by Tomasz Borewicz.

details of the grassroots referendum and its broader significance for the antinuclear campaigners remained untold.

At the Gdynia branch of the National Archive in Gdańsk, there is a collection of materials on the referendum, including protocols made by representatives of the Żarnowiec NPP who tried to point out all the shortcomings they could identify. Even they conceded that the government lost in this instance, although they questioned the magnitude of this defeat. The term "poll" was also being used interchangeably to describe the vote. One representative wrote that "due to the turnout being too low, the referendum was not considered to be legally binding, and the construction of the power plant continued apace."[22] This is not entirely correct—the referendum was not legally binding because it was a social referendum, which only has an advisory role. A total of 387,843 people voted in it, but even if many more had, it would still not be legally binding. It is, however, a fact that the government ignored the results.

Epilogue: International Pressures and the Final Moratorium on Nuclear Energy

Alongside organizing further protests against nuclear energy—like the ones in Bielsk, Gdańsk, Gorzów, Kalisz, Katowice, Kraków, Lublin, Łódź, and Wrocław on 12 June 1990—the environmental movement was also, in the spirit of the constructive opposition of that era, looking for an alternative to nuclear energy in the form of renewable energy. To this end, on 2–3 June 1990, the Agreement for Alternative Energy was formed, which included nearly all ecological movements: the Green Federation, the Workshop for All Beings, the Gdańsk Ecological Forum, the Silesian Ecological Movement, the "I Prefer to Be" movement, the Scouts' Movement for Environmental Protection, the Freedom and Peace movement, the Freedom and Peace Community, the "Ryby Piły" (Saw Fish) movement, and starting 2 August 1990, also the Polish Ecological Club. Finding energy alternatives was, however, a long-term goal, and the main focus was obtaining an immediate decision that would permanently halt the construction of the power plant.

In August 1990, the Ministry of Industry prepared the long-awaited document titled *The Energy Policy of the Republic of Poland for the Years 1990–2010*. Although it did not include nuclear energy in the national energy balance until 2000, it left the door open for its potential development after 2000 (up to 2,000 megawatts of total installed capacity in 2005 and 6,000 megawatts in 2010). This document would later be approved by the Sejm, but the future of the Żarnowiec NPP remained unclear. Burek explains: "The petitions, the protests, the referendum—all that had rocked Poland a bit, made Żarnowiec a public issue. But this did not cause a qualitative change. The relationship was still 'us' and 'them'—the government, be it red or Mazowiecki's."

That is when the Polish antinuclear activists threw the metaphorical boomerang and decided to call upon the international environmental community to pressure the government from the outside. Looking for foreign support, Burek contacted a Green Federation activist from Kraków, who provided him with a reference letter and some links to Western environmental groups. And so, in July 1990 he hitchhiked all the way from Gdańsk to Vienna, "speaking no foreign language, having no other contacts and only five dollars in my pocket." Once there, he knocked on the door of the Austrian Green Party. He brought two backpacks—one with bootleg rock music he intended to sell to gather some funds, and the other with materials on Żarnowiec. He got the materials translated into English, emphasizing the case of the referendum, as its scale and grassroots organization were unprecedented, and not only in Eastern Europe. He underlined the nexus of nuclear energy and undemocratic governmental practices.

With the Greens' aid, Polish antinuclear activists were able to launch an international campaign. "These guys were professionals, they organized many campaigns," Burek admitted. Through their transnational network, the Austrian Greens approached other European Green parties as well as Greenpeace and agreed that a coordinated action would be held on the same day against Żarnowiec.

In August and September 1990, this resulted in protests organized by union members and environmentalists. There were miscellaneous initiatives—for example, a group of members of the European Parliament issued a protest in Brussels regarding Żarnowiec. Protests were held both outside Polish diplomatic missions and outside the offices of companies that wanted to work with Warsaw on the construction of Żarnowiec. One such protest ended with the occupation of the Polish embassy in Stockholm, which prevented the ambassador from attending a conference (held on 2–3 September 1990, in Ronneby, Sweden) regarding the protection of the Baltic Sea. As a result, Poland was represented only by Prime Minister Mazowiecki. He was not prepared, unfortunately, as the ambassador had all the relevant data. When asked about Poland's plans for dealing with the ecological danger of building Soviet reactors, the prime minister responded on the spot that he would shut down the Polish nuclear program for fifteen years. Having uttered these words in the presence of a neighboring head of state, not to mention the media, he could not back out. The sequence of events is important here, as the incident took place just before the—long delayed—decision to shut down the Żarnowiec Nuclear Power Plant construction site was adopted (which happened on the next day). Maciej Nowicki remembers the road to that decision:

> The matter . . . was discussed by the Environmental Protection Commission. Minister Kamiński should have been present at that session, but he sent me in his stead. I was the deputy minister of Environmental Protection, Natural Resources, and Forestry, and was also in charge of matters related to the protection of the atmosphere, seeing as I had specialized in it for twenty-five years as a scientist. . . . As an expert in modeling the spread of air pollution I knew that a malfunction would cause the emission of ionizing radiation in a radius of a dozen or maybe even several dozen kilometers, which would include the Gdańsk agglomeration. . . . I also received information about the poor quality of the concrete that had already been used for the foundations. In communist times, the theft of cement was very common, which meant that the concrete was less durable than anticipated. The third argument was the matter of utilization of radioactive waste. The Soviet Union pledged to retrieve it, but in 1990 this didn't seem as certain as it did in communist times, and should the foreign policy of our eastern neighbor change at any point, there was no place to store that waste in Poland.
>
> I presented these arguments at the session of the commission, going against the position of the representative of the Ministry of Industry. The commission voted against continuing the construction of the power plant in Żarnowiec and later, during the plenary session of the Sejm, the halting of that construction was finally sealed. I know that my performance at the Sejm commission was the subject of a conversation between Prime Minister Mazowiecki and Minister Kamiński and almost led to my dismissal because I presented a position that went against that of the government. It was considered to be a punishable display of disloyalty. However, I was not dismissed.[23]

As proponents of nuclear energy point out, there was also the matter of the sudden change in the approach of the potential foreign investor, the Belgian company Belgatom. In February 1990, Belgatom prepared a report on the possible continuation of the construction of Żarnowiec, and on September 3, they sent a short but devastating expert opinion to the Polish Ministry of Industry. The documents stated that "in its current shape, 'Żarnowiec' NPP would not be granted a license in a Western country" and that "the technical analysis has led us to the conclusion that improvements can be made to the current design, but definite conclusions cannot be made without a deeper and more thorough analysis" (Kiełbasa, Hryszko, and Kuźniarski 2021).

The Council of Ministers adopted a decision to abandon the construction of the Żarnowiec NPP on 4 September 1990. Minister Tadeusz Syryjczyk underscored the fact that there were no grounds for continuing or even freezing the project, which did not rule out developing nuclear energy in the future, as long as it met certain requirements. According to Antoni Furtak,

> [Minister] Syryjczyk presented the following opinion to his party colleagues: "We can't afford to complete the construction at this time, because our budget can't handle it." However, I think that if it weren't for the protests, there would have been a different option: the investment would be spread out over a longer period of time but continued. I know one thing: the letters, the initiative, the organization of environmentalists, all those people who gathered signatures—that played a huge part. The signatures made their way to the Sejm. Over three hundred thousand signatures. I formally delivered a petition to the deputy prime minister in the name of those thousands of people. My friends helped me bring the boxes up to the podium. To this day, I remember the camera flashes and reporters immortalizing this unusual cargo in the Sejm's plenary hall.

This might not have been the only reason, but without the public protests, the construction might have gone on for a long time, despite the negative opinions of experts, e.g., the PAA's Wierusz Report, and the lack of funds for completing the project. The government's decision to scrap the NPP project was ratified by a Sejm resolution on 9 November 1990, which still allowed for the possibility of constructing new generation nuclear power plants in the future if economic efficiency and radiological safety could be ensured.

What could be seen as a triumph for Poland's environmental protest movement would turn out to be its death knell. The long and desperate protest depleted resources. In the new era of economic and political transition, activism became a costly thing. New institutionalized structures were not yet in place, while those who wanted to protest faced the stifling reactions of the police and the state administration (Szulecka and Szulecki 2017; 2019). While the Żarnowiec campaign gradually came to a close, another one began—against the construction of a hydropower plant and dam in Czorsztyn, on the opposite end of the country, near the border with Czechoslovakia. The campaign lasted several years but failed to mobilize enough support, and its failure marked the end of spectacular and successful protest actions. The next one would only take place fifteen years later (Szulecka and Szulecki 2013).

Notes

1. Stenographic report of the 18th sitting of the Sejm on 20 January 1990, pp. 324–25. See also p. 337. Italics added.
2. Stenographic report of the 19th sitting of the Sejm on 26 January 1990, p. 208.
3. The very idea of a social referendum appeared earlier and was mentioned by a member of the WiP movement, Jacek Fedor, in the collective interview for *Gdański Magazyn Katolicki* realized by Video Studio Gdańsk in February 1989. The recording is available at: https://www.youtube.com/watch?v=E-gHKBGVjbo.
4. Stenographic report of the 18th sitting of the Sejm on 20 January 1990, p. 321.
5. Ibid., 328.
6. Ibid., 336–37.
7. Ibid., 330–31.
8. Ibid., 328–29.
9. Ibid., 332.
10. Stenographic report of the 19th sitting of the Sejm on 26 January 1990, p. 208.
11. Ibid., 217.
12. Ibid., 244.
13. Ibid., 224.
14. Ibid., 228–29.
15. Ibid., 211.
16. Ibid., 216.
17. Ibid., 239.
18. Ibid., 240.
19. Ibid., 214.
20. *Opinia o budowie Elektrowni Jądrowej Żarnowiec*, Warsaw 1990; State Archive in Gdańsk, Gdynia branch, 265, *Elektrowni Jądrowej Żarnowiec w budowie*, item 370, *Odpowiedzi PAA na Raport Wierusza*, file 99.
21. Letter from the general election commissioner J. Stępień to the Workers' Self-Government of the Żarnowiec NPP under construction, Warsaw, 16 May 1990, GKW/VII/282/90.
22. B. Kozłowski, "Decyzja o likwidacji Elektrowni Jądrowej Żarnowiec," *Polska.pl*, 2012.
23. M. Nowicki in an email to K. Szulecki, 22 October 2018.

References

Kenney, Padraic. 2002. *A Carnival of Revolution. Central Europe 1989*. Princeton: Princeton University Press.

Kiełbasa, Władysław, Jarosław Hryszko, and Łukasz Kuźniarski. 2021. "EJ Żarnowiec 1982–1990." http://atom.edu.pl/index.php/component/content/article.html?id=116:marnowiec-1982-1990&catid=85.

Piotrowski, Grzegorz. 2017. "Żarnowiec-Grobowiec. Opozycja Ekologiczna w Polsce i Kampania Antynuklearna." *HistMag*. https://histmag.org/Zarnowiec-grobowiec-Opozycja-ekologiczna-w-Polsce-i-kampania-antynuklearna-15099/3.
Rosanvallon, Pierre. 2011. *Democratic Legitimacy: Impartiality, Reflexivity, Proximity*. Princeton: Princeton University Press.
Szulecka, Julia, and Kacper Szulecki. 2013. "Analysing the Rospuda River Controversy in Poland: Rhetoric, Environmental Activism, and the Influence of the European Union." *East European Politics* 29 (4): 397–419. https://doi.org/10.1080/21599165.2013.836701.
———. 2017. "Polish Environmental Movement 1980–2017: (De)Legitimization, Politics & Ecological Crises." *ESPRi Working Papers* 6. https://doi.org/10.2139/ssrn.3075126.
———. 2019. "Between Domestic Politics and Ecological Crises: (De)Legitimization of Polish Environmentalism." *Environmental Politics* 0(0): 1–30. https://doi.org/10.1080/09644016.2019.1674541.
Szulecki, Kacper. 2019. *Dissidents in Communist Central Europe: Human Rights and the Emergence of New Transnational Actors*. Palgrave Studies in the History of Social Movements. Palgrave Macmillan. https://doi.org/10.1007/978-3-030-22613-8.

Conclusion

Two years after the Żarnowiec project was scrapped in 1990, the number of employees at the Institute of Atomic Energy fell from 1,100 to a mere 280. The final decision on the construction site itself was taken by the new government of Jan Krzysztof Bielecki—the same person who strongly lobbied for continuing the construction of the power plant. This time, on 17 December 1990, the Council of Ministers in Resolution no. 204 declared that the Żarnowiec NPP was to be liquidated by 31 December 1992. The liquidation itself did not go entirely smoothly, as was pointed out by both sides of the conflict. Deputy director of the plant, Henryk Torbicki, recalls:

> The government made the decision to liquidate. A staggering amount of assets was involved. We feared that they would be squandered or fall into the wrong hands. When the liquidator first arrived, he made a terrible impression. The fate of the liquidated power plant came to rest in the hands of the Gdańsk Voivode,[1] who oversaw this process. There was a strike. After around thirty days, an agreement was signed.

The compromise was worked out, after several hours of negotiations, by a resourceful young MP from Gdańsk, one Donald Tusk, who twenty years later would reopen the nuclear power issue in Poland. Meanwhile Jerzy Jaśkowski notes that the construction of the NPP was profitable for the nuclear lobby and the government even—or perhaps particularly—if the complex was never finished. "There was but one reason: it was easy to siphon funds out of it."

Likewise, the construction site of the Żarnowiec NPP—despite assurances by the government—was never utilized in any way. It was neither used for industrial nor tourist purposes, despite the already constructed hotel buildings and their proximity to a forest, a lake, and the sea. The facilities were allowed to fall into disrepair and get looted by scrap hunters. Billions of zloty invested into the construction site were wasted. In 1994, the Supreme Audit Office revealed numerous irregularities in the NPP liquidation process, but no one was held liable.

For many who participated in these events, the closing down of that construction site was a turning point. For most proponents and workers involved in the project, it spelled the end of their dreams of a future career. Jerzy Bijak, the director of the power sector planning company Energoprojekt, recalls, "When the resolution was passed in the Sejm, I said: never again, I won't ever again get involved in nuclear energy in this country." Director Torbicki got into the food industry, while others retired. But even for the opponents of Żarnowiec, the success of protests did not necessarily translate into a bright future—some of them struggled to find their footing in Poland's new political and economic reality, while the environmental movement had to wait a long time for another equally spectacular success. The words of the hunger strike's veteran, Zbigniew Stefański, capture much of the bitterness of the "victors": "One thing pisses me off—that often people like us, the actual fighters, are forgotten, pushed to the sidelines. We sacrificed practically everything."

Money, Wind of Change, or a "Chernobyl Effect": What Explains the Success of the Żarnowiec Campaign?

The struggle over nuclear energy—particularly the protests against Żarnowiec Nuclear Power Plant—became the biggest ecological conflict between the government and public opinion. Adam Ostolski, a sociologist and leader of the Green Party in the 2000s, called the campaign a "founding act" of the Polish environmental movement, describing the shutting down of the "nearly completed" NPP as "a success that served as a springboard for further activity" (Ostolski 2009). Other researchers too acknowledged the importance of the campaign as "the most well known in the 1980s" (Żuk 2001) and "one of the biggest protests in Poland" next to those against the construction of the Czorsztyn dam, against holding a Spanish *corrida* bull fight in Gliwice, against logging in the Białowieża Forest, against the culling of wolves in the Bieszczady Mountains, and against the highway on St. Anna Mountain (Kula 1999).

But for the environmental movement and especially for the proponents of radical actions in defense of the natural environment, it was not so much a foundation for further successes as a crowning achievement, after which came a long slump. The protests against the dam in Czorsztyn, which are often compared to the Żarnowiec affair—both campaigns began in communist times and were concluded after the transformation—were not successful. What is more, their participants, who hailed from similar circles (WiP, RSA, Green Federation), were being repressed and harassed even in 1992 (Szulecka and Szulecki 2017). Of the three logics of protest (Della Porta and Diani 2006, 176–77)—that based on *numbers* (how many people can be mobilized?), on *damage* (how much havoc can protesters cause?), and on *bearing witness* (standing up for your values even against all odds)—only the latter was available to the environmental protest movement in the 1990s, making it more niche and sensitive to alternative values and culture.

How can we account for the success of the campaign against the Żarnowiec NPP? There might be several explanations. For many, the main reasons for shutting down the nuclear power project were "techno-economic." The Minister of Industry at the time, Tadeusz Syryjczyk, although not favorably disposed toward environmentalists or toward allowing public opinion to influence important decisions, wrote the following.

> 1) Redundancy in terms of the national energy balance, 2) questionable profitability compared to conventional power plants, and 3) ambiguity in terms of security—regardless of the negative attitude of public opinion toward the project—moved me to recommend to the Council of Ministers that the [Żarnowiec] NPP project be liquidated. (Melańczuk 2020)

Żarnowiec was a typical socialist construction site, where neither real needs nor human, social, cultural, or financial costs were taken into account. This should be contrasted with the self-awareness of the activists who participated in the campaign against nuclear facilities—in their statements, they frequently mention the lack of public money and the fear of a nuclear facility's malfunction (after Chernobyl), sometimes reinforced with distrust toward Soviet technology and the party's indifference toward the issue.

Others place the emphasis on social resistance and its various forms. This can be linked to a change in values. Environmental awareness is often linked, following Inglehart's theory, with the rise of postmaterialist values (Inglehart 1994). However, there was nothing particularly "postmaterial" in protesting for a healthy and safe environment for humans. Neither were the Polish antinuclear protests about self-expression and quality of life.

It is interesting to observe the course of all the actions in this long campaign. Despite the participation of anarchists from RSA and the "stone throwers" (mostly hailing from the Federation of Fighting Youth), who every Sunday and on important national holidays took part in street clashes, the Friday demonstrations in Gdańsk and subsequent protests were always peaceful in nature. Piotr Gliński notes that the political culture of the environmental movement in Poland features at least four pacifist elements—its countercultural, post-hippie pedigree; its intelligentsia pedigree; its resultant rationalism; and, finally, its oppositionist pedigree. Each of these groups rejected violence as a means of achieving their goals.

This explains the methods, but not their effectiveness. The effectiveness of peaceful and nonviolent resistance is mainly affected by historical circumstances. According to Modzelewski, depending on the circumstances, one can divide resistance into heroic moralism (ascetic self-denial in the face of repressions; the goal of the resistance is to demonstrate one's rejection of wrongdoing), autotelic or reformist resistance (systemic conditions and moderate levels of repression make resistance somewhat easier, but it becomes a goal in itself), and revolutionary resistance where dissent is clearly a means to achieve social change (Modzelewski 1987). The last type, since it renounces violence, is quite rare in practice: for example, it is difficult to take power in a country without confronting the state's army, although the Czechoslovak "Velvet Revolution" is an example of this type of revolution. Using this typology, we might say that the protests organized in the second half of the 1980s by WiP were autotelic (expressing defiance, defense of repressed activists), until the antinuclear campaign was transformed by the mass protests in Międzyrzecz in 1987, Poznań in 1989, and Gdańsk-Gdynia in 1989–1990, which led to the blockade of the construction of a radioactive waste disposal site and the Warta and Żarnowiec power plants.

However, it is difficult to unequivocally determine whether historical circumstances were indeed favorable to environmental protests in that period—or at least favorable enough to explain their success. This theory seems to be undermined by the example of Czorsztyn, which was also a site of protests at the time. Despite the abolishment of censorship, the democratic transformation of 1989–1990, and the loss of the Communist Party's monopoly on power in Poland, the Solidarity government (starting from 24 August 1989) and some of the labor union's leading activists (Bielecki, Merkel) were as favorably disposed towards the construction of the Żarnowiec NPP as their predecessors. It was during Mazowiecki's tenure as prime minister that the protest entered its harshest stage, and the decisions on the referendum and the shutting down of the power plant had to be all but forced through grassroots mobilization. Zbigniew Wierzbicki, the doyen of the Polish ecological movement, went as far as to write that following Solidarity's ascension to power, despite the hopes of many, the ecological crisis only got worse.

The cause was, however, helped by the awakening of society, which often actively supported the protests. An independent public opinion that was not easily manipulated by official media was also a contributing factor. This political awakening gradually subsided after 1989 with the "betrayal" or, as David Ost would have it, the "defeat of Solidarity" (Ost 2006). Some post-Solidarity elites thought that social mobilization and open protests posed a danger to the stability of political and economic transition and suppressed them using police forces, while also using their personal authority and new media to delegitimize them. In the case of Żarnowiec, this antidemocratic shift—pitting indirect, parliamentary democracy against more directly democratic and populist alternatives—appeared in full force. That is why independent activists write about insufficient means of expressing public opinion in a parliamentary system (meaning political parties or elections, or even lobbying), and the need for direct action. The term "populist" is meant in an analytical rather than a derogatory sense. Much of the antinuclear movement's rhetoric juxtaposed a self-interested and detached "elite" (technocratic, industrial, communist) with a "people" who needed to be heard, building on the assumption that the protesters indeed represent a popular will.

The public's skepticism towards the elitist, insulated approach to politics was confirmed by Mazowiecki's defeat in the presidential election in October 1990, followed by the parliamentary victory of the postcommunist Democratic Left Alliance (Sojusz Lewicy Demokratycznej, or SLD) in 1993, and then Lech Wałęsa's loss to the former Communist Party minister Aleksander Kwaśniewski in the subsequent presidential race. However, the later stabilization of the political landscape came at the expense of civic activity. Gliński underscores that the "us" vs. "them" mentality between the environmental movement and the new government survived, analogous to the division between government and society during communist times. For the government, this meant missing out on an opportunity to accelerate the development of civil society, and it arguably pushed the environmental movement towards more populist positions and methods bordering on soft terrorism, using individual martyrdom to hold the public opinion ransom on moral grounds. This led to further radicalization and growing disenchantment among many ecological activists, particularly those hailing from protest movements. Piotr Rymarowicz, in a 1990 issue of *Zielone Brygady* (Green brigades), a magazine that would consolidate the environmental movement throughout the 1990s, called Żarnowiec the "first big victory of ecologists since Solidarity's takeover,"[2] claiming that the government's agreement to the protesters' demands came in reaction to its dip in popularity, as was the case with the Communists towards the end of their tenure (e.g., the Rakowski government's abandonment in 1989 of the construction of the Warta Nuclear Plant in Klempicz).

After the Solidarity camp took power, and the Citizens' Committee was dissolved, its Commission on Environmental Protection and Natural Resources ceased to exist. It should, however, be underscored that during the tenure of the three posttransformation ministers of environment (Bronisław Kamiński, Maciej Nowicki, and Stefan Kozłowski), significant changes were made to the Polish environmental policy. These changes included the transfer of national forests to the Ministry of Enviroment (and away from the production-oriented Ministry of Agriculture), the creation of a list of Poland's biggest polluters, and the establishment of the National Fund of Environmental Protection and Water Management, which had a significant—for postcommunist times—budget funded with fines and payments for improperly using natural resources. This last solution was unique in Europe and gave institutions that dealt with environmental protection very substantial funds for exercising their mandate, which significantly improved the state of the environment in Poland in the 1990s and at the start of the 21st century. Both reforms were called for by the opposition during the Round Table negotiations.

Rymanowicz's categorical opinion (shared by numerous other activists) owes much to the growing rift between, on the one side, technocrats at the ministry and at research institutes, and, on the other, radical environmentalists working in the field. The latter's disillusionment stemmed from the "abandonment" of the cause of Czorsztyn by many eco-experts, progressing professionalization of the environmental protection sector, and a wider divergence of perceptions on the success or failure of postcommunist transformation in Poland between big city centers and the provinces (Szulecka and Szulecki 2017; 2019).

Therefore, we have to conclude that the success of this protest was not based on favorable political circumstances: the Solidarity government remained unfavorably disposed towards demands from the public, refusing to meet them on principle, and fearing that the success of one protest would lead to many others, which would in turn endanger the "protective umbrella" set up over political and economic transformation. In this situation, even the fact that continuing the construction of the power plant was impossible due to economic and technical reasons did not matter much—since the protest had already started, the government could not yield, and once it did, it could not admit that it did so due to the protest or because it acknowledged public opinion.

If we reject the "techno-economic" explanations (cost, faulty technology, etc.) and the broader "structural" ones (the protest was successful because it happened under favorable historical and political circumstances) as unpersuasive, the secret of its success must lie in the protest itself—its organization, methods, and range. In earlier chapters, we identified several characteristic features of this campaign, which later turned out to be unique in terms of Polish environmental protests:

- the systematic nature and regularity of the campaign despite a changing of the guard among its participants
- a broad and actively expanded social base
- the involvement of public opinion and various opinion leaders

- varied argumentation fit for different forums
- providing alternatives instead of resorting solely to the "ecology of fear"
- and particularly the protesters' determination, which was brought up in some interviews.

During other environmental campaigns, these factors often pop up individually and are sometimes mutually exclusive. Our interviewees pointed out the lack of the abovementioned elements—both external and internal—in other campaigns: a disconnect between the activists and society, the fact that no issue since nuclear energy involved such scale of wasteful public spending, the lack of a Chernobyl-scale symbol as a negative benchmark, or "a negative, rabble-rousing campaign based on emotions and weak arguments."[3]

The exceptional success of the anti-Żarnowiec campaign owes much to a skillful combination of radical actions (which are elite by definition) and public outreach (including cross-border appeals and mobilization aimed at the international community, which was possible due to the social mobilization of that era and the resulting interest in Polish affairs around the world). An important feature that allowed for mass participation and increased visibility even in a context of limited information circulation (i.e., censorship under communism and then a media blockade by the Solidarity government) was the idea of organizing protests in big cities (Gdańsk, Gdynia, Warsaw) instead of at the construction site where the protest would go unnoticed and could be dispersed without consequences, or with violence. That was the case with the Czorsztyn dam protests and the campaign against a motorway crossing St. Anna Mountain (in 1998), where protests at remote sites were difficult to maintain over a longer period of time, and where police and private security companies were able to force the protesters off the premises (Szulecka and Szulecki 2017). The lack of witnesses motivated the authorities, construction site workers, and security companies to use violence, as was the case during the recent logging in the Białowieża Forest (Szulecka and Szulecki 2019). This was not the case in Gdańsk, despite the presence of significant riot police forces and the fact that most of the demonstrations took place in times when street clashes were very common. The only act of overt violence was the breaking of the blockade at the Gdynia harbor—far away from prying eyes—which the authorities subsequently tried to cover up by giving significant concessions to the protesters.

This strategy allowed for different people to join the protests. The marches in Gdańsk were very democratic, as the organizers quickly became merely faces in a crowd—sometimes passive or even absent. This increased the involvement of citizens who had a sense of ownership of the protests, which proved crucial during the organization of the referendum. The campaign's reception was thus better than if it had been headed by radicals from various subcultures, which could lead to conflicts with local communities, even those favorably disposed towards the environmentalists' demands.

Another contributing factor was support from the independent media—despite censorship, the initial phases of the campaign were reported in a wide range of samizdat publications, which in the case of Poland reached considerable circulation levels (Wciślik 2021). This element became less visible in the second half of 1989, when independent media outlets began closing down, while some pro-Solidarity media were hostile toward social protests in general (e.g., *Gazeta Wyborcza*), or the antinuclear campaigners in particular (e.g., *Tygodnik Powszechny*). Finally, pressure from the outside was also important, as it provided additional support for local and national events, creating new opportunities for political activism. In the case of Żarnowiec, the pressure from ecologists and activists from abroad on the home stretch led to Prime Minister Mazowiecki's public declaration, which made the decision to shut down Żarnowiec unavoidable.

The anti-Żarnowiec campaign featured Greenpeace-style elements, although they were not the result of professionalization. On the contrary, they resulted from amateurs' enthusiasm, which yielded better results than many subsequent actions by professional ecological organizations or campaigns modeled after Greenpeace.

The Chernobyl Effect—Political, Not Merely Emotional

There is also one last element that is unique for the antinuclear campaign, and which was not present in the subsequent environmental struggles of the 1990s: the Chernobyl disaster looming large. Many of our interlocutors pointed to the Chernobyl disaster as a watershed and a turning point in their opposition activity. As we have seen in the first half of this book, the environmental catastrophe in Poland was tangible, and environmental awareness was gradually rising, partly with the help of official media and organizations. However, the Chernobyl catastrophe became a catalyst on more than one level. It was a frightening event, which made the question of nuclear safety something for everyone to consider. The fear of nuclear following 1986 was real—and there are good reasons for this. Additionally, Chernobyl's failure was associated with Soviet technology and a communist technical culture, which made it easy to discredit Żarnowiec and the other domestic NPPs—even if the reactors to be built were of a very different type.

The spark of Chernobyl fell on already flammable sociopolitical terrain, which is illustrated by the scale of protests that followed the catastrophe—using preexisting structures of mobilization and tapping into new, previously unreachable resources. After the initial outrage, Chernobyl's role as an easily recognizable symbol proved lasting, as was the engagement of many activists who first took to the streets to protest the government's reaction to the Soviet incident, and who later stayed within the broad antinuclear movement to pursue other more localized goals. It could be argued that without Chernobyl, the growth and expansion of the antinuclear and broader environmental movement would not be so spectacular, although former activists underline that the active core of that movement was never very numerous—counting several hundred to perhaps some one thousand people, whereas the impact of Chernobyl was that of a wakeup call for others to get involved, and a powerful reminder for the broader public.

Furthermore, Chernobyl was also associated with Soviet-style *governance*, based on secrecy, unreliable data, and ignoring public concerns. This symbolic meaning of Chernobyl allowed for a political critique of the Polish authorities, making it the core of the antinuclear movement's message. Although the pronuclear experts and pundits were trying to cast the antinuclear movement as irrational, emotional, and driven by fear, the core of the campaign's message was related to political problems: access to information, participation in decision-making, accountability of technocratic experts, social acceptance and burden sharing of risks associated with nuclear technology and waste, and, finally, democratic governance overall.

Since the nuclear power issue was framed as political, not only environmental or a question of reactor safety, it allowed the antinuclear movement to connect its struggle to the broader cause of the democratic opposition, and to employ a language of democratization as well as a certain democratic imagination that was unique to this strand of social dissent. That imagination had strong populist undertones in its emphasis on participatory governance, democratic proximity (Rosanvallon 2011), and an antitechnocratic attitude, praising broad social involvement. The subversive and radical nature of the antinuclear movement's democratic imagination put it in open conflict with the ruling postdissident elite.

Beyond 1989—Challenging Mainstream Histories of the Opposition

That conflict's long-lasting legacy is visible today in the historiography of Poland's transition, which is written by postdissident elites themselves. If one were to render the course of time in musical language, the opposition symphony's rhythm is beaten out by a few significant dates: 1956, 1968, 1976, etc. The lively *molto vivace* of the Solidarity carnival of 1980–1981 is followed by a long interlude before the happy ending of 1989. Then the symphony ends and there is only time for applause.

The dominant narrative of the "fall of communism" traces the origins of the opposition to the 1960s and sees the emergence of the Workers' Defense Committee as the turning point and a shift in the balance of power between the dissidents and the regime. Since that time, the joint ranks of the liberal intelligentsia and the workers' leaders challenged the communist state's grip over the working class. This was realized in the 1980s general strike and the emergence of Solidarity. For the Solidarity leadership, the 1980s was arguably a prolonged "dark age," and the unexpected fall of communism was presented as the culmination of years of effort. The period between its actual introduction in 1981 and the new wave of strikes in 1988, which supposedly led directly to the Round Table talks, the negotiated transition, and to semi-free elections and the rise of the Third Republic is sometimes depicted as a "long martial law." In the mainstream opposition historiography those eight years are elongated to the size of a geological epoch.

Focusing on 1989 bends the perception of time in our thinking about recent history. What came before it is "history"—a distant past that can be told like a heroic epic. What came after 1989 is "now," even if for many adults alive today the early 1990s is also a distant history, perhaps on par with the First World War, a time they did not experience and know only secondhand.

The history of antinuclear protests in Poland challenges that narrative, both in terms of the chronology and the alleged inevitability of the final outcome. 1989 is a very important date, but the earth did not jump out of orbit then, history did not end, and communism did not disappear overnight. Scholars need to revise their thinking about the past and start treating the 1990s as a period no less historical than the 1980s. Research on the political and social shifts of the 1980s, which was started with Padraic Kenney's (2002) and David Ost's (2006) landmark monographs, and has recently picked up pace, leads to a historiography more sensitive to different threads, perspectives, ideologies. Focusing on social history—not just political history—allows us to tell new stories about Poland. Not about communist and postcommunist Poland, but about a single Poland of "late modernity"—probably beginning somewhere in the 1960s and continuing until today. Instead of describing the experience of the People's Republic of Poland using the word "totalitarianism," which closes all discussions and obliterates the real social memory, that new historiography ought to focus more on the mechanisms of this regime, and makes us better equipped to analyze the conflicts and cleavages of contemporary Poland.

The Round Table and the June 1989 elections, while part of the change, did not bring about the collapse of communism overnight. Many important things had already begun earlier. After 1985, the scale of repression against the opposition clearly diminished. In 1987, the authorities gave in to societal pressure on the Międzyrzecz nuclear waste depot issue. In June 1988 the government caved on the important issue of the military oath: there was no longer any mention of an alliance with the Soviet army, substitute service was introduced, and later that year economic activity was freed, while strikes and numerous environmental protests continued. These strikes and protests show that the rupture dividing the new Third Republic from the old People's Republic of Poland is not easy to locate in time—the harshest police actions against environmentalists and opponents of nuclear energy took place in 1989 (in Poznań) and during the government of Tadeusz Mazowiecki, although the environmental movement originated from the Solidarity camp.

Furthermore, the symbolic date of 4 June 1989, the date of the negotiated elections, is also somewhat problematic when viewed from afar. Andreas Langenohl argues that under the combined pressure of imported economic neoliberalism and the postdissident discourse on "civil society," which radically juxtaposed state and society, there was "virtually no role for elections as a legitimate and reasonable hinge between society and the political system" (2021), and that these no-choice elections (cast as a plebiscite between the communist and anti-communist camps) left a strong mark on the remainder of Polish democratization. This critique is compatible with our analysis in this book. The dispute over the form and content of Polish democracy has continued unabated from the 1970s until today, and the antinuclear protests as well as the broader environmental movement were important contributors to that discussion, for a time. The Round Table was neither the founding moment nor the original sin of the Polish transformation. The people who sat at the table all came from somewhere and in their vast majority they did not disappear into the shadows. Continuity, not rupture, is the stuff of Poland's contemporary history.

There is one more aspect of the antinuclear protest movement, and the broader environmental movement, that challenges an important part of the mainstream history. The narrative of the Polish transition has usually accepted the rationality of the "negotiated transition," which saw the dialogue of the moderate Solidarity elite and the moderate Communist elite, while bracketing off the Communist hardliners, who could derail the process by refusing to give in and hand over power. It also implicitly meant the marginalization of the "radical" opposition. However, the definition of "radical" in this context is very unclear. Initially, Adam Michnik and Jacek Kuroń, dissidents with some thirty years of experience and among the architects of the future agreements, were deemed too radical for the party apparatchiks. The authorities depicted radical protest movements, striking workers, and other independent groups as dangerous and nonconstructive. But it is far-fetched to equate the party, which controlled the armed forces, the police, and the Security Service, with several hundred or at best several thousand mostly young people eager to throw stones at riot police, and to claim that both sides constituted comparable security threats to a peaceful transition. The "moderation" argument is popular in the literature, following the example of the Spanish *ruptura pactada* (negotiated break) and Portugal's 1974 transition. But a closer look at these cases shows that in fact many "cautionary parameters" set out by democratization studies were violated, while democracy, somehow, prevailed (Bermeo 1997).

The Polish case illustrates two different conceptions of the role played by social movements in the process of democratization—a populist approach to democracy, emphasizing participation from below, and an elitist approach, according to which democratization must be a top-down process (Della Porta and Diani 2006, 246). The protesters' visions of democracy were not new; they were in fact the logical consequence of the entire tradition of Polish dissent, whose refrain was always participation, transparency, and self-governance. Ever since the 1965 "Open Letter to the Party" by Kuroń and Modzelewski, the opposition contrasted authoritarian practices of the communist state with the genuinely democratic postulates of "power to the people," initially understood as workers' self-government (Szulecki 2019). This was also visible in KOR and the Free Trade Unions, and it peaked in Solidarity. The Eastern European dissident tradition emphasized the autonomy of civil society, which should be able to deliver more just, fair, and legitimate political outcomes than the state. At the same time, the democratic opposition was to different degrees, and more or less explicitly, critical of *liberal* democracy, and this criticism was a feature of all dissident-led movements across the region. These ideas were largely forgotten and overwritten by the "There Is No Alternative" approach of the post-1989 transition.

The Environmental Movement in Poland since Żarnowiec: A Decline or Mere Evolution?

It seemed that despite the divisions in the former oppositionist camp, environmental protection would become one of the main issues in the youth movement. But it very quickly stalled or simply moved in a different direction. A real Green Party took a long time to coalesce in Poland, and there is no broader social and political vision that an ecological movement could try to bring about. The Green Federation's program could have served as such, but the federation ceased to exist as a national movement—and there is no other popular eco-political organization currently operating in the country.

Several phenomena emerged within the ecological movement that civil society scholars have qualified as weakening or "neutering" factors. The first one was the already mentioned professionalization, which led to further "NGO-ization"—grassroots organizations were replaced by formal "third sector" institutions. Citizens' initiatives that had been developing since the mid-1970s, including the independent labor union movement and subsequently also the countercultural, youth-based opposition, created an expansive "parallel polis" similar to that created by traditional religious structures. However, after 1989, Western European and American governments and institutions made it their goal to bolster "civil society" within the former Eastern Bloc. Their definition of civil society was in large part based on the liberal vision of Alexis de Tocqueville and underscored the role of various organizations and associations in bridging the space between the individual and the state. However, Tocqueville's idealistic vision was in practice translated into multiplying stable and professionalized nongovernmental organizations, which became dependent on outside financing and sometimes detached from their social base. Therefore, the organizations that represented the core of "civil society" in this new understanding became something decidedly different from the spontaneous, grassroots dissident movements that Western observers admired so much when they were operating behind the Iron Curtain (Szulecki 2019).

Sociologists Kerstin Jacobsson and Elżbieta Korolczuk see in this an at least partially conscious action by neoliberal elites, who supported directing prosocial activity toward such organizations while marginalizing other forms of political involvement and mobilization—particularly demonstrations and strikes (Jacobsson and Korolczuk 2017). A more prosaic though no less important factor was the economic transformation in Poland, which forced environmental activists to find secure employment, thus significantly limiting the amount of free time they could devote to various social activities without endangering their livelihoods.

A phenomenon noticed by scholars and practitioners alike is grant dependency. According to critics, nongovernmental organizations are implementing "timid" ecological programs using grants from governments and sponsors, even though using governmental funds puts any "nongovernmental" organization in an ambiguous position. In this model, the role of professional NGOs is to stabilize the system, with their activity visibly depoliticized, while the 1980s protest movements aimed to do the opposite: to politicize issues that were excluded from public debate and considered to be the province of experts and technocrats. This depoliticization process bears a resemblance to the vision espoused by the Italian leftist Antonio Gramsci, who unlike de Tocqueville, did not see civil society as inherently good but rather as a battleground for competing political visions, on which the dominant elites were trying to assert their supremacy and maintain the status quo. We should also mention project-based thinking imposed by the grant system—i.e., planning in terms of short-term and narrowly defined goals that are hard to combine into a broad and cohesive strategy of environmental protection.

Professionalization and dependence on grants also cause many organizations to drift away from their social base. If they do not rely on membership fees and small donations, but instead focus on expert-based activity and lobbying, they might become "uprooted" from local communities. However, this criticism bears the signs of the internal conflict between "experts" and "activists" in the ecological movement, which has been raging since the early 1980s. Józefina Hrynkiewicz traces the rift between ecological experts and radical activists to the beginnings of the Polish Ecological Club (Hrynkiewicz 1990). Even though it was not dissolved, that organization's collapse after martial law prompted many members to leave, and during the 1983 conventions the proponents of a "mass movement" lost to "experts," who avoided confronting the government and focused on presenting alternative courses of action. To advocates of radical actions, whom the "experts" saw as immature, this constituted selling out. PKE and Foundation for Ecological Development (Fundacja na Rzecz Ekorozwoju) activist Andrzej Kassenberg sees the matter differently:

> For PKE, it was reports that mattered: influencing national policy or the policy of individual cities. They didn't feel a need to demonstrate in general, also regarding issues related to nuclear energy. Some in the ecological movement saw PKE as being too expert oriented, and its publications as too obtuse. But a group of people, some of whom were PKE members, including me, joined around Professor Stefan Kozłowski [a member of PKE and opponent of nuclear energy], strongly advocated for abandoning nuclear energy at the ecological subtable.[4]

One of the lessons of Żarnowiec is that both groups need each other, because expert defiance alone is often not enough, and direct protests without a broader organizational umbrella are doomed to fail, as was the case in Czorsztyn and the St. Anna Mountain. Despite the critical opinion of numerous scholars, thanks to the structure of the ecological movement described above, ecologists were not entirely powerless when the Polish government returned to its nuclear program after fifteen years. Today the lack of political organization is obvious, public opinion is less focused on environmental issues than during the 1980s, and the anti-communist aspect of the Żarnowiec protests is no longer valid. Nevertheless, the reactivated Polish nuclear project was met with a long-unseen intensity of grassroots protest.

The Future of Polish Nuclear Energy

Wojciech "Jakob" Jankowski remembers how he was hitchhiking back from his first Zen retreat along the Baltic coast in 1999. A car pulled over, and he immediately recognized the driver—"Oh, Mr. Korwin-Mikke!" he exclaimed, greeting the controversial Polish politician, leader of the ultra-conservative but economically liberal Real Politics Union, who would later acquire international notoriety as a member of the European Parliament. "Yes, yes, yes!" replied Janusz Korwin-Mikke, known for his machine-gun speed of spitting out words. After an extended mutual introduction some miles down the road (he is also known for his speeding habits and his belief that the faster people drive the shorter time they spend on the road, thus decreasing the likelihood of accidents), Korwin-Mikke condemned Jankowski as a "mindless leftist" who has "unfortunately effectively blocked the construction of a nuclear power plant." Jankowski asked, "Do you really think the Commies could have built a safe and solid nuclear power plant?" Korwin-Mikke paused, dumbfounded: "The Commies? No, I guess not."

Fifteen years after the decision to suspend construction of the Żarnowiec NPP and the introduction of a moratorium, the Polish government for the first time officially mentioned a possible return to this energy generation technology. In a document from July 2005, nuclear power was only tentatively hinted at. It was mentioned a total of four times in thirty pages—the first time in a discussion of the future of Poland's energy mix, to which nuclear power would be an important supplement, combining diversification of sources and reduction of greenhouse gas emissions.

A consensus emerged among politicians of the main right-wing parties on nuclear energy, considering it "progressive" and important for Poland's modernization. Before the parliamentary elections in September 2005, the national-conservative Law and Justice Party chairman Jarosław Kaczyński declared: "Poland needs a nuclear power plant, because nuclear energy has a future, and its production today takes place in safe conditions. That is why what the environmentalists are doing can be called hysteria. A modern country that cares about its energy security should have a nuclear power plant" (Dudała 2005). All the key elements of the pronuclear argument can be seen here: NPPs are needed and safe, and at the same time "have a future" and are an attribute of "modernity." Opponents of NPP construction are therefore either hysterics or do not care about the country's energy security. When the liberal-conservative Civic Platform won the 2007 snap elections, ousting Law and Justice, neither the direction nor the justifications changed significantly. Neither strand of the post-Solidarity camp (the nationalists and the liberals) treated the Żarnowiec experience as relevant to Poland's energy policy in the twenty-first century.

The expected date for launching the first NPP was set at 2020–2021. The government selected the goal and even drew plans for a future energy mix with nuclear energy in it, but acquiring social acceptance for the technology was pushed to the background. The order is significant here. The Ministry pointed to objective but imprecisely defined needs (energy security and environmental protection) and presented the NPP as the solution, estimating the fastest possible implementation time. Social issues were a troublesome background: "A separate problem is the need to provide reliable information on nuclear power in connection with the anticipated possibility of introducing this type of electricity generation in Poland."[5] This was to be remedied by a "social campaign for nuclear power acceptance" planned for a five-year period.

This technocratic approach to technology was to prove typical for attempts to reactivate the Polish nuclear project. The democratic political process would be reduced to managing social acceptance for a preconceived option. According to sociologist Piotr Stankiewicz, this technocratic or expert approach, characteristic of twentieth-century industrial reality, is based on several assumptions in a "positivist-scientist" spirit. First and foremost, that deciding on the development of new technological solutions is a task "primarily—if not exclusively"—for engineers (Stankiewicz 2014). In practice, this approach can be seen in the form of the "deficit model of risk communication," which assumes that all social protests are related to the insufficiency (deficit) of scientific knowledge and education of the so-called ordinary people (Szulecki 2018). The second typical element is depoliticization of decision-making processes in the field of technology and its removal from the sphere of public debate. This is accompanied by the instrumental use of economic models, where their role is reduced to 1) tools for producing support for political initiatives, rather than evidence on which policy making could be based (Süsser et al. 2021), and 2) a discourse of inevitability and lack of rational alternatives to nuclear energy, which is emulating earlier examples from the Czech Republic (Osička et al. 2021). Last but not least, the government introduced legislation that made it easier for the Agency for Internal Security (Agencja Bezpieczeństwa Wewnętrznego, or ABW, the democratic heir to the Security Service) to infiltrate, monitor, and potentially detain environmental activists and opponents of the nuclear power plant, while an external consultancy hired by the Ministry of Economy prepared a communication strategy that divided the public into "friends" and "enemies" of the project, and provided instructions on how the "enemies" could be "eliminated" from public debate (Szulecki and Kusznir 2017; Szulecki 2020).

Three localities on the Baltic coast were once again chosen as potential sites, among them Żarnowiec. Residents of the municipalities directly involved were not consulted before the decision was made, and they often learned about the shortlisting of sites from the media. Piotr Laskowski, from the village of Gąski, recalls that he read about the fact that his hometown was being considered for NPP construction from a TV news strip on 25 November 2011. Before that, "there wasn't even any preliminary information."

Excluded from the decision-making process, the residents quickly began to organize. The Civic Committee "Bez Atomu" (Without atom) of Mielno municipality, the "No to nuclear power in Lubiatowo" Civic Committee of Choczewo municipality, and the "No to nuclear power in Krokowa" Civic Committee of Żarnowiec were formed. In July 2012, all three formed an agreement and created a civic coalition called "Nuclear-free Pomerania." The bitterness of the residents of the selected communes was enormous, because of the extent to which the investor and the government ignored the local communities. A resident of Gąski Commune at a meeting in December 2012 said, "You came to us, to our commune, like invaders, occupiers, without any consultations, social consent, you came and declared that a power plant will be built here."[6]

The most important manifestation of grassroots self-organization and acting against the technocratic logic of the authorities was the grassroots local referendum in Gąski (a tourist-dependent commune where one of Poland's best-known seaside resorts, Mielno, is located). Although not legally binding, it was supposed to be an attempt to fill the democratic deficit in the planning process.

On 12 February 2012, 94 percent of the residents of Gąski and Mielno opposed the plans to build a nuclear power plant or any nuclear sector infrastructure in a referendum that saw a 57 percent turnout. The result of the referendum had an indirect impact on the Ministry of Transport, Construction, and Maritime Economy, annulling the location indication made earlier by the West Pomeranian Voivode. However, the voivode once again reinstated the location decision, effectively blocking the property of Gąski residents and investments in the commune for five years (they were not allowed to sell the land that was earmarked for the NPP). The commune's residents lost their case before the Voivodship Administrative Court in Warsaw to have their village removed from the list of locations. The court, however, did not acknowledge the social context and only confirmed the correctness of the procedure. The referendum also did not influence the plans of the utility company, which immediately after the announcement of the results declared that it "accepted the referendum result with understanding. . . . It is worth noting, however, that the decision about the referendum was made on the basis of fragmentary information, both on nuclear power itself, as well as the investor's future plans." The utility company regretted that the local government and community were insufficiently involved in the dialogue with company representatives.

The Law and Justice party's return to power in 2015 initially put the project on halt, but after 2018 nuclear construction plans returned with more force than ever before. Once again, the government used the argument of inevitability and produced models that showed that nuclear power was the only reliable option for Poland's decarbonization. Climate change became an important new rationale for developing nuclear energy, and a new strand of the climate protection movement emerged, focusing specifically on the development of domestic nuclear capacity. Part of a broader global tendency, the pronuclear activists replaced the fear of a nuclear Armageddon—so important for the 1970s and 1980s movements—with the threat of a climate apocalypse (van Munster and Sylvest 2015). They are also eager to use the language of urgency and to attack the majority of environmentalists skeptical of nuclear energy.

The threat of a Chernobyl-like incident has faded over the last three decades. And while anti-communist dissent as well as skepticism toward Soviet technology is no longer present, the Polish government's way of handling energy policy seems to copy the mistakes made in the 1980s. Furthermore, nuclear fallout from the Fukushima disaster "demonstrates how risks from pursuing national security through nuclear will be borne primarily by civilian populations exposed to bio-accumulation of radioisotopes across time" (Nadesan 2013, 29). Levels of risk, costs, the problems of nuclear waste, and the technocratic and antidemocratic political aspects of the nuclear sector are still arguments on which antinuclear protest campaigners can build in the Polish context, putting governmental plans in question.

Notes

1. The head of the voivodship, Poland's regional authority.
2. *Zielone Brygady* 1(7) (January 1990): 7, available at: http://www.zb.eco.pl/zb/rok1990.htm.
3. Grzegorz Peszko in an email to Janusz Waluszko regarding the Czorsztyn campaign, 17 January 2011.
4. Andrzej Kassenberg's email communication with Kacper Szulecki, 15 October 2018.
5. Notice of the minister of economy and labor of 1 July 2005 on the state energy policy until 2025, p. 1454.
6. Quoted in Stankiewicz 2017, 322.

References

Bermeo, Nancy. 1997. "Myths of Moderation: Confrontation and Conflict during Democratic Transitions." *Comparative Politics* 29(3): 305–22. https://doi.org/10.2307/422123.

Della Porta, Donatella, and Mario Diani. 2006. *Social Movements: An Introduction.* 2nd edn. Malden, MA: Blackwell Publishing.

Dudała, Jarosław. 2005. "Jarosław Kaczyński: Trzeba rozbić stary układ—nowy przemysł." wnp.pl. 2005. https://www.wnp.pl/artykuly/jaroslaw-kaczynski-trzeba-rozbic-stary-uklad,-2241.html.

Hrynkiewicz, Józefina. 1990. *Zieloni: Studia Nad Ruchem Ekologicznym w Polsce 1980–1989.* Warszawa: Uniwersytet Warszawski.

Inglehart, Ronald. 1994. "Values, Ideology, and Cognitive Mobilization in New Social Movements." In *Challenging the Political Order: New Social and Political Movements in Western Democracies*, ed. Russell J. Dalton and Manfred Kuechler, Reprint, 43–66. Europe and the International Order. Cambridge: Polity.

Jacobsson, Kerstin, and Elżbieta Korolczuk, eds. 2017. *Civil Society Revisited: Lessons from Poland.* Studies on Civil Society, volume 9. New York: Berghahn.

Kenney, Padraic. 2002. *A Carnival of Revolution. Central Europe 1989.* Princeton: Princeton University Press.

Kula, Marcin. 1999. *Ekologia humanistyczna.* Warszawa: Wydawnictwo Wyższej Szkoły Przedsiębiorczości i Zarządzania.

Langenohl, Andreas. 2021. "Displacing Elections in the 'Jump to the Market': Dispersed Traces of Neoliberalism in Poland's Transition from Socialism." *Topos* 0(1). http://journals.ehu.lt/index.php/topos/article/view/1047.

Melańczuk, Maciej. 2020. "Tadeusz Syryjczyk: Przesłanki decyzji w przedmiocie likwidacji EJ Żarnowiec." EJŻarnowiec.pl, 29 April. https://ejzarnowiec.pl/2020/04/tadeusz-syryjczyk-przeslanki-decyzji-w-przedmiocie-likwidacji-ej-zarnowiec/.

Modzelewski, Wojciech. 1987. "O Skuteczności i Nieskuteczności Metod Walki Bez Użycia Przemocy." In *Studia Nad Ruchami Społecznymi*, ed. E. Lewicka-Banaszak, P. Marciniak, and W. Modzelewski. Warszawa: Uniwersytet Warszawski.

Nadesan, Majia Holmer. 2013. *Fukushima and the Privatization of Risk.* Palgrave Pivot. New York: Palgrave Macmillan.

Osička, Jan, Filip Černoch, Veronika Zapletalová, and Lukáš Lehotský. 2021. "Too Good to Be True: Sugarcoating Nuclear Energy in the Czech National Energy Strategy." *Energy Research & Social Science* 72 (February). https://doi.org/10.1016/j.erss.2020.101865.

Ost, David. 2006. *The Defeat of Solidarity: Anger and Politics in Postcommunist Europe.* Ithaca, NY: Cornell University Press.

Ostolski, Adam. 2009. "Krótki kurs historii ruchu ekologicznego w Polsce." In *Ekologia: przewodnik Krytyki Politycznej*, ed. Michał Sutowski, 401–24. Warszawa: Wydawnictwo "Krytyki Politycznej."

Rosanvallon, Pierre. 2011. *Democratic Legitimacy: Impartiality, Reflexivity, Proximity.* Princeton: Princeton University Press.

Stankiewicz, Piotr. 2014. "Zbudujemy wam elektrownię (atomową!). Praktyka oceny technologii przy rozwoju energetyki jądrowej w Polsce." *Studia Socjologiczne* 212(1): 31.

———. 2017. *Gra w Atom: Społeczne Zarządzanie Technologią w Rozwoju Energetyki Jądrowej w Polsce.* Toruń: Wydawnictwo Naukowe Uniwersytetu Mikołaja Kopernika.

Süsser, Diana, Andrzej Ceglarz, Hannes Gaschnig, Vassilis Stavrakas, Alexandros Flamos, George Giannakidis, and Johan Lilliestam. 2021. "Model-Based Policymaking or Policy-Based Modelling? How Energy Models and Energy Policy Interact." *Energy Research & Social Science* 75 (May). https://doi.org/10.1016/j.erss.2021.101984.

Szulecka, Julia, and Kacper Szulecki. 2017. "Polish Environmental Movement 1980–2017: (De)Legitimization, Politics & Ecological Crises." *ESPRi Working Papers* 6. https://doi.org/10.2139/ssrn.3075126.

———. 2019. "Between Domestic Politics and Ecological Crises: (De)Legitimization of Polish Environmentalism." *Environmental Politics* 0(0): 1–30. https://doi.org/10.1080/09644016.2019.1674541.

Szulecki, Kacper. 2018. "Conceptualizing Energy Democracy." *Environmental Politics* 27(1): 21–41. https://doi.org/10.1080/09644016.2017.1387294.

———. 2019. *Dissidents in Communist Central Europe: Human Rights and the Emergence of New Transnational Actors.* Palgrave Studies in the History of Social Movements. Palgrave Macmillan. https://doi.org/10.1007/978-3-030-22613-8.

———. 2020. "Securitization and State Encroachment on the Energy Sector: Politics of Exception in Poland's Energy Governance." *Energy Policy* 136. https://doi.org/10.1016/j.enpol.2019.111066.

Szulecki, Kacper, and Julia Kusznir. 2017. "Energy Security and Energy Transition: Securitisation in the Electricity Sector." In *Energy Security in Europe: Divergent Perceptions and Policy Challenges*, ed. Kacper Szulecki, 117–48. Energy, Climate and the Environment. London: Palgrave. https://doi.org/10.1007/978-3-319-64964-1_5.

Van Munster, Rens, and Casper Sylvest. 2015. "Pro-Nuclear Environmentalism: Should We Learn to Stop Worrying and Love Nuclear Energy?" *Technology and Culture* 56(4): 789–811. https://doi.org/10.1353/tech.2015.0107.

Wciślik, Piotr. 2021. *Dissident Legacies of Samizdat Social Media Activism: Unlicensed Print Culture in Poland 1976–1990.* London: Routledge.

Żuk, Piotr. 2001. *Społeczeństwo w Działaniu: Ekolodzy, Feministki, Skłotersi: Socjologiczna Analiza Nowych Ruchów Społecznych w Polsce.* Wyd. 1. Warszawa: SCHOLAR.

Index

www.ingramcontent.com/pod-product-compliance
Ingram Content Group UK Ltd.
Pitfield, Milton Keynes, MK11 3LW, UK
UKHW021838100926
8556IPUK00004B/413